BEYOND THE NUMBERS

HOW LEADING COMPANIES MEASURE AND DRIVE SUCCESS

William L. Simon

VAN NOSTRAND REINHOLD
I(T)P® A Division of International Thomson Publishing Inc.

New York • Albany • Bonn • Boston • Detroit • London • Madrid • Melbourne
Mexico City • Paris • San Francisco • Singapore • Tokyo • Toronto

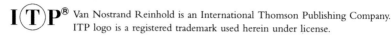 Van Nostrand Reinhold is an International Thomson Publishing Company.
ITP logo is a registered trademark used herein under license.

The ideas presented in this book are generic and strategic. Their specific application to a particular company must be the responsibility of the management of that company, based on management's understanding of their company's procedures, culture, resources, and competitive situation.

Printed in the United States of America

http://www.vnr.com   Visit us on the Web!

For more information contact:

Van Nostrand Reinhold   Chapman & Hall GmbH
115 Fifth Avenue   Pappalallee 3
New York, NY 10003   69469 Weinham
                                      Germany

Chapman & Hall   International Thomson Publishing Asia
2-6 Boundary Row   60 Albert Street #15-01
London SEI 8HN   Albert Complex
United Kingdom   Singapore 189969

Thomas Nelson Australia   International Thomson Publishing Japan
102 Dodds Street   Hirakawa-cho Kyowa Building, 3F
South Melbourne 3205   2-2-1 Hirakawa-cho, Chiyoda-ku
Victoria, Australia   Tokyo 102 Japan

Nelson Canada   International Thomson Editores
1120 Birchmount Road   Seneca, 53
Scarborough, Ontario   Colonia Polanco
MIK 5G4, Canada   11560 Mexico D.F., Mexico

1 2 3 4 5 6 7 8 9 10 QEBFF 01 00 99 98 97 96

Library of Congress Cataloging-in-Publication Data available upon request.

ISBN 0-442-02346-4

CREDITS

Portions of the remarks by Francis Corby, Harnischfeger Industries, are from a benchmarking site visit organized by the American Productivity & Quality Center, 123 N. Post Oak Lane, Houston. The author is indebted to Ms. Carla O'Dell, president of QPQC, for permission to use this material.

To Arynne

CONTENTS

Special Perspectives

Start-ups and the "Virtual Corporation"

Afterword

Glossary

Notes

Index

"The role that the CFO of a business should play [is that he or she should be] a broad business person, and . . . the right-hand of the leader of the business.

"It's a very natural function for the finance leader because of the ability to be able to look all across the functions. We don't expect him to have comments only on financial issues."

Dennis Dammerman, CFO, General Electric

"The finance function is changing from one that's mostly an accountant role, a scorekeeper role, to one that's a partner in the business, that's involved in strategic thinking."

Stan Meresman, CFO, Silicon Graphics

"Finance is losing a lot of its definition, not because it's not bringing value to the company but because we're aligning ourselves with processes. The finance function in the future will have only very few people that are "financial." What we have is people disseminated throughout the organization, in manufacturing, in materials, on the distribution side, that have very good financial skills, that are comfortable with numbers, that are comfortable with doing analysis, that can help the business people, the process leaders, be successful. That's basically how we're deploying our operations.

"Traditionally, we had a transaction orientation and we focused on the past. We need to spend time focusing on the future.

"My view of a finance person is a person who sees needs and helps drive business to meet those needs."

Tom Zusi, CFO, AlliedSignal Aerospace

"In the past, we steered by the wake; in the future, we'll steer by the new metrics."

John Staedke, Former CEO, Hitachi Data Systems

ACKNOWLEDGMENTS

It's my delight to use this opportunity for showering praise on my wife, Arynne, for the exuberance and joy she brings to the world around her. I continue to respect and rely on her valuable insight and opinions, and her exceedingly demanding level of feedback. She amazes all who know her by her ability to live successfully and graciously the equivalent of six simultaneous high-speed lives and yet seems effortlessly to maintain an aura of contentment and good cheer. Members of her huge fan club would agree with me that Arynne has an uncanny ability to increase life's pleasures and somehow make people she meets feel better about themselves.

In addition to her corporate consulting career, she is, at this writing, in the process of starting a software company, BridgeWorks, Inc., that's mentioned in these pages.

Patience and understanding are virtues we often take for granted as qualities we expect in those we love. These qualities in my daughter, Victoria, and my stepson, Sheldon Bermont, are often pushed to the limit when I'm coping with a deadline. I offer copious appreciation for their forbearance. My wife and two children lead my list of my best and most valued friends.

Thanks to a special friend, sometime writing partner, and mentor, Gil Amelio, who is currently hard at work transforming Apple Computer, and who inadvertently transformed my career as an outgrowth of the book we wrote together, *Profit from Experience.*

Acknowledging my editor might seem simply expedient, but John Boyd deserves the mention. He conceived the idea for this book and then had the persistence to convince me to take the project on—I still don't know how he managed that.

If you call my office, the reassuring voice you'll hear belongs to Jessica Dudgeon, who continues to attack the never-shrinking pyramid of papers that Arynne and I need organized. It's Jessica who deals with people, plans, and airline reservations and who manages to keep our schedules in sync.

Any writer would be fortunate to be able to rely on the services of Marianne Steuber, Beth Parks, and Judy Olmstead, who smoothly transcribed the many hours of interviews and entered changes and edits.

I'm indebted to my pragmatic entertainment attorney, Ira Epstein, Esq., of Weissmann Wolff, Los Angeles, for being there with answers and guidance whenever I have needed him and for being, with his wife, Noddy, stimulating dinner companions as well. Other people who come to mind are Peter Abeles, of Conti Financial, New York and Los Angeles, and James Esposito, Esq., of

Dechert, Price & Rhoads, New York, who provided valuable information about the form of representations and warranties used in major corporate loans.

And to the participants, listed below, who generously devoted valuable time for the interviews and for revising and amending the text, I express my sincerest gratitude. That these are all extremely busy people whose efforts create jobs and contribute to the economy makes their efforts on this project all the more laudable. I hope they will feel rewarded by having their valuable ideas and perspectives passed along to readers of this book.

It pleases me that this experience has stirred in some of the interviewees the sense that they have in them a book of their own waiting to be put down on paper. I hope they will succeed in overcoming the inertia that has given rise to the old writer's adage that "no one likes to write; everyone likes to have written."

In the following list, thanks especially to those whose names appear but whose interviews, for reasons of manuscript length or content balance, are not included in these pages.

So, my special thanks to the interviewees:

Chuck Berger, Radius Corp.
Tom Brown, Aetna Insurance
Fran Corby, Harnischfeger
 Industries
Yogen Dalal, Mayfield Fund

Dennis Dammerman, General
 Electric
Geoff Darby, Visioneer
Stephanie Dorris, Exponential
 Technology
Darrell Duffie, Stanford University
Dan Eilers
Cheryl Francis, R.R. Donnelley &
 Sons Co.
Brian Frenzel, Centaur
 Pharmaceuticals
Howard Green, Apple Computer,
 Inc.
Loren Hall, Allstate Insurance Co.
Russ Hughes, Apple Austin
Pat Keating, San Jose State
 University

Randy Komisar, Crystal Dynamics
Steve Kraus, Sears, Roebuck
Arun Kumar, KPMG Peat
 Marwick LLP
Don Macleod, National
 Semiconductor Corp.
Stan Meresman, Silicon Graphics
 Computer Systems
Bob Puette, NetFrame
Bill Raduchel, Sun Microsystems

Rudd Roggekamp, FMC Corp
Sid Sapsowitz, MGM/UA
Rob Selvi, Cooper & Chyan

Rick Sessions, National
 Semiconductor
John Staedke, Hitachi/EDS

Mike Steep, Lexmark
Tom Zusi, AlliedSignal

PREFACE

This book stands at the intersection of management and money, the place where modern business fundamentals and current finance principles come together.

Business managers have traditionally used accounting-based financials that looked backward, at the wake—showing where the organization had been; today, they are learning to use financials that look forward toward the horizon.

In the following pages, twenty-plus insightful business leaders reveal their tools and techniques for seeing "beyond the numbers."

Visionary corporate managers and executives no longer limit themselves to asking for financial data that shows where their organization has just been but, rather, insist on measures with the predictive power to show where the organization is going.

Leaders for the 21st century demand to know more than just the value of current assets; they want to judge the ability of those assets to produce wealth in the future.

Company business-unit managers and line managers typically measure results without taking into account the cost of equity or the cost of debt; this overstates returns, leading to decisions that can destroy shareholder wealth.

We see leading companies today adopting powerful measures like RONABIT and turning to some form of the "new metrics"—economic value added (EVA) and cash flow return on investment (CFROI), sometimes called value management.

These newer financial tools are being adopted as a more aggressive and more accurate way of determining which actions and choices will be most likely to increase total shareholder value—the share price of the stock multiplied by the number of the outstanding shares, a measurement of corporate strength that is accepted as the most powerful in the current business environment.

Told in the words of insightful business leaders, this book is designed for all managers, executives, and leaders who sense that their financial judgments

Return on Net assets Before Interest & Tax

and decisions may not be fully informed. The book explores the measures that tell what's really happening in the organization—providing a basis for solid decision making in today's highly competitive global marketplace.

Also included are guidelines for strategic planning and for designing a compensation plan that motivates executives to make decisions that will increase shareholder value.

ABOUT THE INTERVIEWS

The principal text of this book consists of personal interviews with 20 CFOs, CEOs, corporate executives, and authorities on finance.

All interviews have been edited for clarity and flow. In addition, the interview subjects were invited to amend and expand the text as needed to protect confidential information and to ensure that their ideas are clearly conveyed.

wls

FOR YOUR REFERENCE:

AN INFORMAL GLOSSARY OF
KEY TERMS USED IN THIS BOOK

A glossary usually belongs at the end of a book, and those who look for it will find one there.

But not all readers who come to these pages will have a business school degree or a finance or accounting background. What follows is for those who don't yet have a working familiarity with terms like "RONA" and "inventory turns," or who know the terms but don't appreciate their significance.

I'm indebted to Arun M. Kumar, who compiled these explanatory notes. Arun is with KPMG Peat Marwick LLP's World Class Finance Consulting practice, in Palo Alto, California.

Margin

Revenues less expenses.

> An income statement item, and often considered the key word on the income statement; an old adage says that "profit occurs at the margin." Most companies make a net profit of less than 10% of revenues. An improvement in margin of 1.5% of revenues, by reducing either costs or expenses, will often translate, after taxes, to an improvement in earnings per share of 10%.

Gross margin

Revenues less cost of goods sold.

> Increased gross margins are a basic measure of return on manufacturing or purchase costs.

Return on assets (ROA)

Net income as a percent of total average assets, which means assets before accumulated depreciation.

> ROA measures the effectiveness of a firm's original assets to create profits.

Return on net assets (RONA)

Similar to ROA, except that the denominator is net assets (total invested assets less accumulated depreciation).

> This measure better reflects the amount of capital tied up in an asset, since the Net Asset figure on an existing asset such as a factory lowers with the passage of time due to depreciation. RONA favors the use of existing assets over investment in new assets.

Return on net assets before interest and tax (RONABIT)

Profit before interest and taxes (operating profit), as a percent of net assets.

> An operational measure that focuses managers on the operating profits they

generate using assets assigned to their businesses, and excluding the effects of taxes and finance costs.

Return on noncash assets before interest and tax (RONCABIT)

Profit before interest and taxes, divided by average total assets less cash.

> A return-on-assets measurement. By removing cash, the measure provides a look at the efficiency of the capital invested in operations (for example, factories, equipment, and real estate). This measure can be especially effective at the business-unit level, since most operating managers in large corporations are not responsible for cash management, which is a treasury function.

Return on capital employed (ROCE)

Net income as a percent of capital employed.

> This measurement is typically favored for industry benchmarking.

Return on investment (ROI)

The income from a project divided by the investment in the project.

> A measurement used to evaluate the performance of specific investment projects.

Return on equity (ROE)

Net income divided by stockholders' equity.

> ROE has often been used as the best measure of the performance of a company or business unit.

Cash flow on cash invested (cash on cash)

Cash flow compared to the total cumulative cash invested in a project.

> A measure of cash on cash is payback—how quickly the cash invested is recouped in incremental cash flows from a project, usually measured in years.

Hurdle rate

The minimum rate of return that a proposed project must earn in order to be accepted by management for investment.

> Expressed as a percent.

Internal rate of return

The discount rate that makes the present value of cash flows of a project equal to the initial investment in the project.

> A measure of the profitability of a project or investment. The calculation yields a result that can be judged against the cost of capital to determine whether the project is justified.

Receivable days

365 divided by accounts receivable turnover, where accounts receivable turnover is sales divided by average accounts receivable.

> An indirect measure of the speed at which a company turns receivables into cash.

Days sales outstanding (DSO)

The total amount owed by customers, divided by the sales for the preceding month or quarter and normalized for days.

> Abnormally high DSO may be a symptom of customer satisfaction problems and

the quality of order fulfillment—customers not paying on time because they are not happy with what they have received.

Inventory turns
The cost of sales for the period (or, if forward-looking, for the subsequent period), normalized for an annual basis, divided by the period-end inventory.

> A measure of how rapidly inventory is converted into sales. If the inventory at the end of the month represents one month's cost of sales, the inventory turns for the year would be 12. The higher the inventory turns, the better.

Free cash flow
Net income plus depreciation, less capital spending and changes in working capital.

> The residual cash flow left after meeting interest and principal payment, and providing for capital expenditures.

Discounted cash flow
The stream of future cash flows, discounted back to the present, to account for the time value of money.

> A method of estimating an investment's current value based on projected future revenues and costs. However, the results are only as accurate as the estimates used.

Cash flow return on investment (CFROI)
The cash generated by the business, discounted (as in discounted cash flow), divided by the investment employed to generate the cash flow.

> CFROI looks at the true amounts of cash invested in a business, and takes into account the effects of inflation. This provides a more valid basis for judging the value of investments. (See Chapter 2.)

Total shareholder return (TSR)
A measure that combines cash flow generation with the rate of growth of assets and the contribution to free cash flow.

> TSR reflects the extent to which a business unit of a company is contributing to the capital gains and dividend yield to investors of the overall company. This measure, however, does not account for differences in risk.

Economic value added (EVA), or economic profit
The profit that remains after the opportunity cost of all capital employed is subtracted.

> A measure that encourages managers to return income to investors greater than what they could have obtained from their next best business risk. (See Chapters 3 and 4, and elsewhere in this book.)

CHAPTER 1

A CALL TO
ACTION FOR FINANCE

An Interview with Prof. Patrick Keating,
the Graduate School of Business,
San Jose State University

Prof. Patrick Keating focuses on the structure and organization of finance departments and what makes them successful. He is the coauthor, with Stephen F. Jablonsky of Pennsylvania State University, of Changing Roles of Financial Management, *the best-selling book in the 50-year history of the publisher, FERF Research.*

We met in Keating's office on the 8th floor of the Business Tower on the San Jose campus in the heart of "Silicon Valley," California. The conversation quickly turned to a project Keating had done.

THE STATUS OF FINANCE

Your research must sometimes take you deep into little-examined parts of the corporate structure. I suppose that what you find is sometimes as much a surprise to the company itself as it is to you.

PAT KEATING:
There was one company I was doing a study for—a major computer company—where we found a desire on the part of some finance people to play a new and different role. But it became clear that this was a software/hardware engineering culture; marketing came in a distant second. From there, finance was an even more distant third.

When you've got that kind of status structure, it's very tough for finance

1

to have an influence on the business unless you've got a really strong CFO who's going to exert solid leadership with line management.

From what I can tell, the man who was then CFO was pretty influential at the senior management level, but he didn't seem able to translate that influence down through the finance organization.

The company now has a new CEO, and it will be interesting to see what he does, because he's got an understanding of how it all has to fit together financially. Whether he feels he'll need a stronger finance organization or not, he already has a good idea of how things are put together.

FINANCE AS A BUSINESS PARTNER

What were you aiming to achieve in the research project?

The research was based on companies like Boeing, Ford, Merck, and AT&T, and we identified some of the kinds of changes that those firms were making; these clearly suggested a move toward the concept of finance as a business partner.

We put together an assessment instrument that we have administered to over 2500 managers, both line and finance, which basically allows us to gauge what the role of finance is in the business.

We're now doing a new study commissioned by the CFO of Boeing, who had just been appointed to that job when we did the original study. On the earlier go-around, Boeing came out in a mixed light. It was an interesting kind of split because at the business-unit level, such as at Boeing Commercial or Boeing Aerospace, they were trying to make the shift in roles. At the corporate level, the attitude was, "Somebody's got to play the corporate cop; we'll do that here." So finance was exhibiting different behaviors at different levels.

Overall, what the study showed was that finance staffs tend to see themselves as partners and players and advocates, while line people tend to see finance as corporate cops.

That seems to suggest that finance people haven't done a very good job of changing costumes.

I think there's a whole array of different reasons for this failure. A lot of finance people think they're doing strategic work when they're not—they're busy running numbers, and they think that they're doing something else.

One real obstacle right now, I believe, is the financial systems. They're so fragmented that, even though the finance people want to be doing all this sophisticated support of business, they're still busy running the numbers. They're gathering the data from the different systems and enforcing the marching orders of top management. So they just haven't been able to make the shift.

But I think it's also because we're captives of history. A lot of finance organizations have made some of that move, but they're still stereotyped by the line people.

And then there are many companies today where the CEO still wants finance to play the traditional role. So there are some departments that don't want to make that "costume shift," and don't even think it's an appropriate shift to make.

THE ROLE OF FINANCE

There seem to be three ways of looking at this issue—what the CEO wants finance to do; how the finance people see their role; and how the rest of the organization views the finance operation.

What we find when line people evaluate finance is that oftentimes they'll give finance people good marks for saying the right words and having the right vision . . . but when it comes down to asking the question, "What do they do?" the perception of finance is still that it serves the policeman/scorekeeper type of function. Everybody in finance can speak the words, but they're not sure how to make them a reality. So there's a shortfall between commitment and capability.

Finance organizations basically fall into one of three types—command and control; conformance; or competitive team. Each of those types of organizations has a particular pattern of involvement in the business. The command-and-control type is the corporate cop; the conformance type is the bean-counter/scorekeeper; and the competitive team actually plays a role in running the business.

We found that when people fill out our questionnaire, they actually tend to identify two patterns, rather than three. We ended up saying that most organizations fall into some combination of either command and control/competitive team or command and control/conformance; we call the former the business advocate, and the latter the corporate policeman.

The changeover really comes about as a function of changes in the competitive marketplace and in deregulation. There are two things going on. One we can consider historically—if you looked at the 1980s, when we were all wringing our hands about the Japanese "eating our lunch," you'll remember all the arguments about U.S. companies being too managed by the numbers, taking the short-term view, not investing for the long term. A lot of that blame was laid at the doorsteps of finance—it was *too* dominant.

One thing that was going on in certain companies at the time was a kind of pulling back, based on a sense that finance had a stranglehold on the people who really should have been running the business—the engineers and so on. Ford is the classic case of an organization that was dominated by finance staff, who didn't run the business but were still in control. It's interesting that Ford has made significant strides to balance the financial and management perspectives.

So one of the forces was to get a better balance between operating people and line people. Yet there were other companies like AT&T—when it was trying to transition from being highly regulated to operating in a competitive environment—where the finance people didn't know how to run a business that had to compete in the marketplace.

The banks are another example. They were highly regulated, and they didn't need to know much about making money because it had been guaranteed. And that has all changed.

ADOPTING A STRATEGIC VIEW

How do you get a finance organization to take a more strategic look at things, a longer-term look, when the market is evaluating the company in terms of what your last quarterly earnings report said, and whether it represented the anticipated level of growth?

The $64,000 question. There's a lot of debate about that. I think, for the most part, the market does value strategic action that has long-term focus.

If you look at the research, when companies announce major investments, or R&D programs, those tend to bring very favorable reactions in the marketplace. So I think it's wrong to say that there's an antipathy—that the marketplace values only short-term action, short-term strategies. I don't think that's true.

We sometimes have held the Japanese up as exemplifying more successful business methods. Yet it's something of a misstatement to say that Japanese companies are all focused out on some horizon that you can't even identify; they're looking for one- and two-year paybacks on their investments, too.

DOWNSIZING AND FINANCE,
DOWNSIZING IN FINANCE

In this process of redefining the financial organization, is there a backlash of criticism in some companies saying that finance is becoming too large and running on swollen operating budgets?

If you look at the benchmarking data that various consulting firms produce—as a percent of revenue or even finance staff as a percent of the total head count in the organization as a whole—what you find is that costs are coming *out* of the finance organization, partly because there's so much room for improvement.

And, to the extent that finance is an information-processing function, technology is there waiting to replace people. If there was a backlash, it would be the type of backlash that occurred at Ford, where the finance people became too dominant.

To go back to your point about finance strategies and short term/long term, I think some of those criticisms arise when financial criteria are used without a really good understanding of the business, and when qualitative factors somehow can't be brought into the decision-making process—for example, in deciding whether to invest in this particular plant or technology—then you can have some real problems. If the company is run like a conglomerate—just a portfolio of assets to be sold and divested—then you can run into problems.

So that's where the backlash would be. Not so much *costs*—I think costs are successfully being wrung out of the structure right now.

But how much basis is there for the criticism in some companies that the finance department is swelling while everybody else is supposed to be downsizing? Is that condition actually widespread?

You can do certain things to replace people with technology. But if you're going to attack some of the really fundamental costs of operating an organization, you have to change management's underlying operating philosophy—including the way finance participates in the business. You want to get rid of all those non-value-added players who are just checking up on what everybody else is doing.

At the same time, if you've got a management style where nobody trusts anybody, what happens? The CEO hires more finance people to be looking over the shoulders of everybody else.

So it becomes partly a matter of trying to change the influence of finance and also wring costs out of that part of the organization, which in turn requires a shift in the roles.

CAN YOU MANAGE BY WHAT YOU MEASURE?

A shift that might require getting people to change what they measure?

In your book *Profit from Experience,* you say that you can manage by what you measure. I think that needs some qualification.

The point is that what gets measured gets focused on and therefore gets done. The flip side is: What gets measured, gets distorted.

Measures are easy to game—give me a measurement system and a target, and I can probably produce the number . . . as long as you don't ask me how I got there. If you manage through measurement, people will behave according to the measures, but you may not get the kind of results you're actually looking for.

So it almost seems as if management has to precede measurement. You have to establish the rules of the game, people have to understand what's going on, and there has to be a sense of trust and fair play.

Then you give people measures and say, This is what we're going after.

"THE MARGINAL UTILITY OF SOPHISTICATION"

How do the financial approaches we use in the U.S. compare to what's being done elsewhere?

The answer is probably not what you'd expect. On a study mission to Japan with a group of CFOs and other finance types, we were trying to understand how the Japanese manage themselves financially versus U.S. companies. When you compare the numbers of finance staff that the Japanese have as a percent of the total to a U.S. staff, the Japanese are very lean.

The first reaction of a lot of people is, "The Japanese seem to have their act together—maybe we really don't need all these finance people running around." But when you look at their financial systems, you see that they're much simpler. They don't have all this sophistication.

Mario Cordi of Nestlé coined the phrase "the marginal utility of sophistication." There's a point at which sophistication doesn't buy you anything whatsoever.

Where that point is—where more sophistication gives managers better tools to run the business and where it becomes just too much and really gets in the way—that's the art of management. No one is really sure where that breakpoint is.

At the traditional end of the scale is what's called the DuPont model—a model that was formulated by a man named Donaldson Brown, who was the head financial person for DuPont and then GM back in the 1920s. It's the fundamental accounting model for any organization, which says that your return on equity is a function of your profit margins, your asset turnovers, and your financial leverage. These are the three fundamental drivers that affect your return on equity.

That's how any good manager should be managing. Those are fundamentals of accounting.

When you get into cash flow, and shareholder, and EVA, there's a part of the new metrics that makes very good sense. You have to know your profit margins, asset turnovers, and financial leverage, and you have to know what drives those. What are the success factors that drive your margins, your asset turnovers?

There's a lead/lag factor at work here. You have a financial model—National Semiconductor wanted 40% profit margin, 20% return on equity, and so on. In order to get those, the company has to achieve certain asset turnovers, and so on.

But then the question is: What drives *those* numbers? So you need an economic model that says: Here's what actions will result in these kinds of non-financial measures that also will have this impact in terms of our financial model of the business.

Traditionally, American companies haven't had that; they should have, but they haven't. Everything has been managing *by* the numbers. You can't simply say, "These are the numbers we need. Go do it." But people really don't understand all the different actions that lead to those numbers.

So a metric system needs to come along with some sort of a model that says: These kinds of non-financial actions will lead to *these* impacts on our overall financial performance. Then the process begins to make a lot of sense.

I think you can get a manager's attention through the metrics. And at the business-unit level, I don't think you have to put in place supersophisticated frameworks; I just don't see that that's where the real value is.

So there are cultural issues and behavioral issues the company has to address if it's really going to make that measurement system work. You have to make sure you have that infrastructure of attitudes and behaviors and organizational structure so that people can actually make the right decisions and have the right tools and knowledge, and be able to generate the targets associated with this new measurement system.

THE NEW METRICS:

MEASURING THE VALUE-
CREATING POTENTIAL

CHAPTER 2

CASH-FLOW METRICS AT NATIONAL SEMICONDUCTOR

An Interview with Donald Macleod, CFO, National Semiconductor, Inc.

Don Macleod is the kind of CFO that CEOs dream about: a prototypical numbers man who has managed to go beyond financial management to what is now recognized as the higher plateau, where he is able to adopt methods that let managers see whether they are being successful in creating shareholder value, and in making decisions that promise to enhance it.

Born and raised in Scotland, Macleod speaks with an accent so thick you almost hear bagpipes.

We met in his modest, glassed-in office in the National Semiconductor executive suite.

Part I—Overview

CHANGING CORPORATE GOALS

You were here when a new CEO came in at National. From the finance perspective, what changes did that bring?

DON MACLEOD:
When Gil Amelio arrived in May 1991, he first talked about building shareholder value as a prime objective. Frankly, I don't think we understood what this was; we all talked about the share price.

Were the things he was asking for quite different from anything National had done previously?

Like every other company, we had an inbred culture that determined what we did and what numbers we looked at. Gil brought a new perspective, a way of looking at things from many different angles; that was somewhat challenging.

For example, the phrase "business partner" galvanized the creation of a finance organization that moved away from the old controller-style role, which focused purely on the P&L.

RONA

Were the early changes partly in terms of what metrics you were using?

Our business is capital-intensive, and we needed to incentivize people to make the right investments. We had been overcapitalized—too many facilities. And one of the CEO's very early goals was to turn us around from a profit-oriented, pure P&L, bottom-line-oriented management team to one focused on return on net assets—RONA.

We chose that because of the two items—the return, and the net-asset base. By improving the return, which is a profit result, you would improve RONA. At the same time, by *reducing* the asset base, you would also improve the calculation. So you could work on the numerator and the denominator at the same time.

In this situation—where we had too many factories because, in the past, we had over-invested and weren't now getting the return—we had to do two things: we wanted to get better return, and at the same time to narrow our investment base.

The investment base isn't just factories. It's inventories, it's receivables, it's all the conditions that go into the net assets on the balance sheet.

And considering RONA led to some different decisions than you might have made otherwise?

We closed some factories, but we also *sold* some factories. For example, we sold our Bangkok assembly and test plant, but we set up a contract to continue to use its capabilities.

The RONA behavior encouraged the general manager to get the asset off his books but still have use of the facility. Okay—you're paying someone else a profit when before it was all yours. But the RONA calculation encourages you to get that off your books.

Our wafer-fab [a plant for manufacturing the "wafers" of computer chips] in Israel was sold, but we kept an interest; we also gave the new owners a contract that let us continue to buy the wafers. So, here again, we got the wafer-fab off our backs, and we got the commitment to invest in the future off our backs. On these two items of RONA, we reduced the asset base.

ROE GIVES WAY TO ROI

Line managers typically look at the profit and loss, not the balance sheet. Were you trying to change that?

Yes—and I'll give you another example. The CEO said, "My proxy for shareholder value is going to be return on equity. If we get a better return on equity, we'll get better recognition from the stock market that we're doing the right thing."

He set a goal that we get to 20% ROE—because companies doing that well or better on a consistent basis are considered, in general, to be the top performing companies. In a context where the company is losing money, that's an admirable goal.

But as you improve, all the dollars not paid out in dividends go to increase the equity base. So to an extent, with ROE, you're chasing your tail because as you do better, you're forced to continue to do still better—you increase the equity this year, so next year the profit or earnings have to go up by the same ratio just to keep the same ROE.

We accepted that at first, and then, subsequently, we started talking ROI—return on investment.

But we discovered that there was no good correlation between share-price performance and return on equity. We started looking for a theoretical correlation between economic performance and total shareholder return; TSR [see Glossary].

INTRODUCTION TO THE NEW METRICS

What led you in the direction you took on this?

We talked to people from a compensation consultant when we were developing the long-term incentive plan for the company, which had been tied to return on equity. They mentioned the Boston Consulting Group's cash flow–based performance measures.

When we met with BCG's people, they went through a presentation, and one exhibit really hit us right between the eyes: they showed us a chart

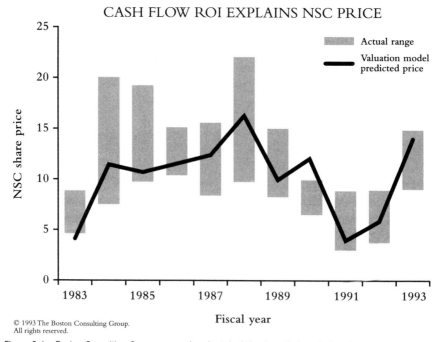

CASH FLOW ROI EXPLAINS NSC PRICE

Figure 2-1   Boston Consulting Group prepared a chart depicting how their cash flow–based measures would have predicted National's share price over the previous several years. Each block shows the range of share price during the year; the black line is the share price as predicted by the BCG metrics.

of the correlation between our share price and what their model predicted the share price would be [Fig. 2-1]. With only one exception, BCG's chart showed a very reasonable correlation between the predicted stock price and what actually happened. The BCG people said, "We have a tool here that you can use to value your prospective forward business performance."

We thought this offered an opportunity to drive our division business managers to optimize their business decision making in a way that focused on cash-flow return on investment, and therefore directly on share-price performance. Through this linkage, they could also determine what portion of National's future share-price growth their division could account for.

Planning is most often seen as a tactical tool—but you seem to be talking about making it a strategic tool by using shareholder value as a bottom-line concern for planning. That sounds like a valuable approach. What happened?

Each division, when it made its strategic plan, would make the usual decisions about levels of capital investment, levels of research and development spending,

14

levels of spending in the factories to improve quality, decisions on pricing, decisions on products. All of these decisions rolled up together resulted in the business plan.

Using this tool, we would then value that business plan and determine what that individual portion of the business would contribute to share price over time. We could then make managers focus on those choices that had maximum impact on share-price growth—hence, shareholder value.

When you add up all the divisions of the company, that would be the theoretical share price of the company over time. The view was that the general managers pressing the right levers—making the right economic decisions, correlating to shareholder value—would maximize shareholder return over the future.

Obviously, you've got to go back and say, What *is* the right rate of return over the future to maximize shareholder value? So we then did another study, in which we asked: What constitutes superior economic performance? We looked at the last 20 years for the S&P 400 and the Value Line Semiconductor Index, and looked at the performance of the top third—breaking it into blocks of five years—each year with the previous five years, not five distinct blocks.

From this, we were able to say: Here's the premium that's required to be a top-third performer. If this model predicts a certain rate of return over time for the company, based on history, National should then be a top-third performer in the future. Of course, the stock market doesn't behave so predictably, but, based on our historical look, that's what you'd have.

What we had is shown in the chart [Fig. 2-2]. Each of the division general managers knows what he's expected to contribute to the improving stock price over time if he achieves his plan.

Today we're in the middle of fiscal '96, and our stock price is about $16 or $17. When we made this plan, our stock price was $12; we've been up as high as $30. The blips of pricing over time are gravitating around a rate that this model predicted quite well.

PHASE I ENDS, PHASE II BEGINS

What changes in approach did you need to make when National returned to profitability?

In Phase I [the initial phase of National's corporate transformation], the things I've been describing represent good behavior. Our RONA focus was very appropriate. In Phase II [after the return to profitability], they do not array

15

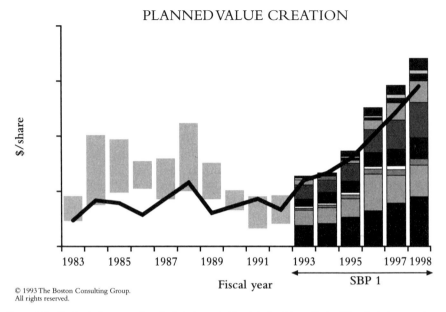

PLANNED VALUE CREATION

Figure 2-2   Similar to the preceding chart, but now looking into the future. Each of the shaded segments represents a specific division of the company.

so well—because what you may be doing is limiting your capability to grow in the future.

RONA motivates you to reduce your asset base, but every time you make an investment, you *add* to your asset base, which impacts your RONA.

So, as we entered Phase II, what we wanted was a tool that, in a capital-intensive industry like ours, would encourage people to make appropriate investments based on their cash-flow generation capabilities and hence their impact on future share price.

What financial measures were used to arrive at the decision that the Phase I goals had been reached and it was time to transition to Phase II?

We had set up what we called the "Five CBIs"—critical business issues. The fifth was financial, and there were three aspects to it: breakeven, gross-profit improvement, and return on net assets.

Now, clearly, breakeven is a fact—once you're making money, you've passed breakeven. We still use breakeven as a percent of sales as a key metric—so we haven't thrown away the context, even though we've moved beyond that issue.

16

Gross-profit improvement—we said we wanted to go from 24% up to the mid-40s. Once we passed 40%, we could say we were achieving our success model [see Chapter 12].

When we got to the point where return on net assets was enough to get us over 20% return on equity, we had reached an acceptable RONA.

So the transition from Phase I really occurred when we got to these points. Breakeven came very early. A couple of years down the road, 40%-plus gross profit came, and so did the achievement of our 20% ROE target.

At that point, we moved beyond the Phase I financial CBIs; they're all good CBIs, but you lose momentum and interest in them when you get to the point of satisfactory or success-model performance. You need to move on to the next phase, which we defined as being focused on quantum revenue growth.

Aiming at breakeven, you need to manage your below-the-line spending to make sure it doesn't get out of balance with revenues. In Phase II, to grow revenues faster, you need to invest in resources and assets, and you're making decisions about investing in your below-the-line spending—R&D, selling, marketing, administration—to allow you to generate future revenue growth.

Part II—"National Semiconductor Value Management"—National's Cash-Flow Tool

Under the guidance of Macleod and his team, the Boston Consulting Group tailored a version of the cash flow–based approach that they called CFROI, cash flow return on investment. The resulting tool, designed specifically to address the needs and preferences of National, is known as National Semiconductor value management, or NSVM. Its name reflects its orientation: the whole point is to gather information about, and model the way toward, increasing shareholder value.

THE PREMISE OF THE CASH-FLOW APPROACH

What's the basic premise that underlies your cash-flow tool?

National's NSVM model is fairly complicated, but basically what the model does is to value the investment and the cash flow. The ratio of these two,

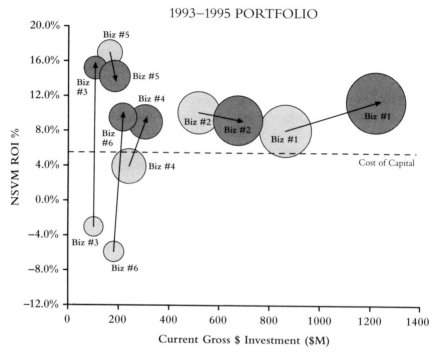

Figure 2-3   A graphic representation of the change in NSVM ROI (cash-flow ROI) over a two-year period for six of National's divisions: 1993, lighter circles; 1995, darker.

with appropriate multipliers, is the CFROI of the division. The NSVM model incentivizes you to make the right investments because it values those investments and also the cash-flow returns from them in the future.

When you want to move from a RONA-based approach to an asset-incentive approach, this NSVM tool is appropriate in that it values the impact of these investments to shareholder value creation, allowing our general managers to choose and justify appropriate investments.

Some of our divisions are very capital-intensive—we need the most leading-edge wafer fabs, we need heavy capital intensity up front, and we depreciate pretty quickly. But there are other divisions that don't need a high degree of capital intensity. And our dilemma is seeing which of these businesses are the right ones to nurture and improve on. It always sounds good to grow the units that need the capital investment. But this industry is littered with examples of overinvestment in wafer-fab capacity.

The problem is how you can look at your businesses on a level playing field when they have such different conditions of capital intensity. The NSVM tool allowed us to take a portfolio approach to these different businesses [Fig. 2-3].

The 1993 version shows Business #2 producing a return on investment of about 10%. By the end of 1995, the rate of return had somewhat diminished but was still above the real cost of capital. *Any returns above the real cost of capital are incremental, and create shareholder value.*

We also found that we had some businesses that were returning less than the cost of capital—in other words, destroying value. What did we want them to do? You don't want their management teams just to focus on an outmoded, textbook effort to "grow out of the problem"; you want them to move up on the chart over time, first improving the rate of return on their existing asset base, before any increase in the investment rate.

On the other hand, the businesses that are returning better than the cost of capital are businesses that you do want to be investing in. Take the example of Business #1, the biggest business returning above the cost of capital; over this time frame, we were investing in it as referenced by the growing gross investment level. Clearly the right choice!

So there are two different behaviors that we're looking for. When we evaluate a division's plan, we say, "Are you returning better than the cost of capital? If so, are we investing appropriately in your business? If you're not returning better than the cost of capital, what are you doing to improve your rate of return?"—which for them needs to be the first and only priority.

So this is our level playing field tool. We look at two things in our NSVM—total shareholder return . . . and ROI, in the form of cash flow ROI. So, again, the tool gives us a way to look at our portfolio, a way to prioritize and value appropriate capital investment.

When you're planning, you can always show a good return on paper; this tool can test whether your assumptions are likely to work out over time with regard to their impact on shareholder return.

The tool helps general managers press the right levers so that their choices can correlate with the creation of total shareholder value.

BENCHMARKING THE NSVM APPROACH

Were you able to get any guidance or insights from other companies while you were creating this?

Indirectly. In the move from Phase I to Phase II, we all recognized that there were certain trade-offs we'd need to make. We would need to rapidly increase the rate of investment in wafer fabs. And perhaps we'd need to change our "success model" in R&D—spend more in R&D up front, to kick-start the strategic market segment focus that we'd adopted.

19

We decided to look at other companies that have gone through this dramatic growth phase; if we were going to be, let's say, a $10 billion company by the end of the decade, in roughly five years, we wanted to look at other technology companies that had grown $8 to $10 billion in about this same time period. What trade-offs did they make to achieve this? Could we learn from them?

We found a block of time when Hewlett-Packard, Compaq Computer, Intel, and Motorola were able to achieve that growth. So we took apart the numbers to see what trade-offs they had made. For example, Compaq Computer had reduced its margins dramatically, had changed the marketing and channel focus, and had grown because it had become a larger-volume player instead of winning by staying just one step ahead of IBM as it had in its early years.

Intel invested massively in wafer fabs, to provide the volume to dominate the microprocessor market.

We then applied our National Semiconductor value management model. First of all, we looked at the *actual* TSR creation: What share-price improvements occurred in the period when they grew dramatically? Then we simulated, using our model. What shareholder value should have been created? The results were enlightening.

In the case of Hewlett-Packard, when we took our model and looked at the share price—the TSR they should have created versus what they actually did create—it looked as though the market wasn't recognizing the momentum. The stock was then about $75. Afterward, it went up, and it split, and it's now at about $90.

Within four or five months after we did this calculation, the stock had moved from $75 to $120. If we had had enough confidence in our own model, we would all have bought Hewlett-Packard stock!

But the reason we did this analysis was to develop case studies on our growth aspiration, look at the trade-offs, and see if, in fact, these trade-offs resulted in integrity from the stock market's point of view. We then went back and presented this to our executive committee, which led to a debate that concluded with a decision to increase our rate of capital spending and increase the rate of investment in R&D; for example, this year, fiscal '96, we'll spend $80 million more on R&D than we spent in '95. That's about a 25% increase, a significant change. We also spent over $600 million on capital expenditures in FY96, more than double the rate in FY94.

We consciously made those decisions a year and a half ago, as part of a transition to Phase II.

In hindsight, we were perhaps a bit too aggressive, given the abrupt slowdown in the semiconductor industry market today. But these were the right decisions in the context; if you want to grow that revenue line, you have to make some trade-offs.

So we applied our model, we looked at case studies, we looked at correlations, and we made our investment decisions using our model to influence how we should proceed.

EVALUATING NSVM AT THE DIVISIONAL LEVEL

Sometimes the sophisticated metrics used at the corporate level don't play very well with the business-unit managers. It sounds as if you didn't have much problem with this.

What we started off with first was using the tool as a way of looking at the corporate business division portfolio and having the divisions relate their plans to share price. Our first strategic plan had only these two things in it. In other words, the divisions really just valued the plan; they didn't say, "If I do it *this* way, I'll get a different result; if I invest more in R&D, I'll get a better rate of return." As they planned details and choices, the division GMs didn't necessarily optimize for CFROI; they just looked at the results of the plan for the company and, after the fact, how it looked in potential shareholder value terms.

But, the next year, we decided to conduct an economic value discovery process in some of the divisions. With three divisions, we held a training session for each general manager and his staff—talking about the concept; going through the correlations; going through the behaviors; talking about cash flow, investment rates, and how you tie it all together.

One of the divisions dropped out—the staff went to the classes but never really used the tools. Of the two remaining divisions, the staff of one went through the value discovery process but really couldn't convince themselves what the market adoption rates for their new products were likely to be. So when they developed their models for value creation, in particular, they really didn't have enough confidence in the projected revenues.

They came back to the executive team and said: We're not very certain that there's going to be a return from this investment. We talked it through, and eventually we significantly reduced the rate of new investment and rolled the whole business into our Local Area Network Division, redeploying the staff and the other investment resources.

That's interesting because it's not necessarily the kind of decision you'd expect a cash-flow model to lead you to.

Right, but it was clearly the appropriate decision in the circumstances. And without the model and the formal value discovery process, we probably wouldn't have seen that.

So, two down without much success. How did the third division fare?

The third division went on with the detailed value discovery study on one of its major units, a commodity business running very mature factories that were almost fully depreciated. This is a "cash cow" business area for the company—that is, it produces positive cash flow and positive returns, with little attention, and it gets no new investment.

The staff used the NSVM tool to go through scenario analysis, considering looking at questions like—If we invest more in R&D, can we improve the cash flow? If we upgrade some of the factories, what will that do to our shareholder value creation? If we lower the price, what will the impact be on the cash flow ROI?

They analyzed different scenarios that would result in improved NSVM and ROI and total shareholder value; they presented these to management as a whole set of options.

We chose to invest selectively in some R&D; we chose not to invest in upgrading the facilities, but instead to take a more price-aggressive posture in the market.

So, these were two ends of the spectrum. A mature business with a relatively predictable cash flow and a totally new high-technology communications business with a very unpredictable, very difficult to understand future. We applied our model and got highly valuable results. We felt good about that. So also did the general managers, and their value discovery teams.

But, for the division that learned to use NSVM in depth, were the benefits much greater than the benefits you'd get from just using sound business judgment?

Everyone always talks about "More R&D produces value," and things like that. But in the context of their specific business, the GM and his staff were better able to understand what the real economic value drivers were for them.

THE NEED TO FOCUS ON GROWTH

In Phase II, we also asked ourselves, "What is superior performance for the company, from a TSR point of view?"

At that time we had two operating groups that were an intermediate organization between the company and the divisions. We told the two group heads, "In our upcoming planning process, we want you to focus on producing superior shareholder value performance," and the measure we asked them to address was to develop a plan to produce a consistent TSR of 20%.

We said, "We're not going to tell you what your sales numbers should be for the five-year plan, and we aren't going to tell you what capital spending you can have. We want you to come up with a plan that will give 20% TSR over the plan period. And tell us how you're going to do it, so we can address the necessary resources required to achieve that plan."

They came back and presented a plan that was pretty good but, in retrospect, was not well focused on our revenue growth objectives. Although we drove value, we perhaps did it at the expense of top-line revenue growth.

We perhaps misunderstood that, at the end of the day, value in our business is derived much more from revenue growth—or, at least, the prospect of sustaining revenue growth in the future—than we may have recognized in our model.

So, in our most recent strategic plan, we spent a lot of time looking at, for example, how our competitors are performing from a TSR point of view, to keep us focused on the revenue growth and market share imperative.

There are a lot of other issues to consider, as well. For example, for the period 1987 through 1993, we looked at all the competitors and asked how we were performing. We looked at the impact of sales growth versus value growth—Did the TSR of our competitors come from investing in assets or from pure sales growth driving profits? So we've got a lot of perspectives.

We were also able to describe to our board of directors what we thought were the value drivers in these other companies and contrast that to where *our* value should come from in the future. In other words, our tools gave us the basis for a much more meaningful dialogue on value creation options with our board.

COMPLEXITY

As you know, metrics like CFROI are criticized for being too complex. Has that been an issue at National?

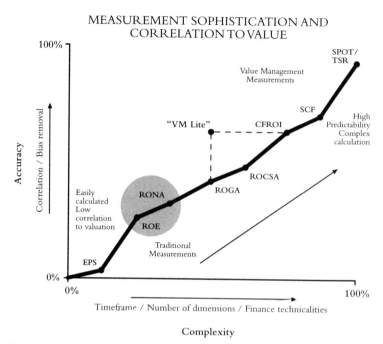

Figure 2-4   Accuracy vs. complexity. The chart attempts to depict the relative accuracy and complexity of a number of financial metrics, including those used in the National Semiconductor cash-flow approach.

From a portfolio-management aspect, we can discuss our model and its results without everyone necessarily needing to understand fully the nuances of the model and the TSR correlations. But when we're looking at economic value discovery in the division, we do have an issue of complexity; the model can become very, very complex.

We have a chart [Fig. 2-4] that addresses this issue—showing the ability of different measures to predict share-price performance. As we go up the scale, there's better correlation between earnings per share performance and shareholder value. There's low correlation on ROE, but it's better than EPS, and so on.

There's better correlation in return on *gross* assets, and still better correlation in return on *current* gross assets—in other words, restating assets for depreciation and current replacement values. Our CFROI model gets good correlation, but that comes at the expense of greater complexity.

We developed a tool we call "VM Lite," which is a very simplistic tool we use for some of our smaller divisions and newer business units, as well as for some of our decisions on a day-to-day basis. And we actually used this in an incentive plan for one of our innovative divisions. The idea here, of course, is that you're sacrificing complexity but, also, to some extent, you're sacrificing correlation. But it was a trade-off that we developed to continue the VM ROI momentum to the next-level business unit.

Do you expect eventually to have NSVM used widely throughout the company?

That's a question everyone has asked: To what extent will you push this further down the organization? We will not push it down the organization any further. NSVM is not a tool for day-to-day business decisions; this is a tool for strategic planning, and asset allocation in a strategic planning context. People will tend to use it more to value results and less to value choices.

We're relatively comfortable with that—we recognize that pushing it further would be difficult. Even our finance people find it difficult to comprehend fully all the implications of the model. We've run many different training courses and find that the M.B.A. graduates from Northwestern and Stanford and Wharton understand it, but they're in the minority. So, when you think in that context, there's no point in pushing it down when its implications are not evenly understood by all.

So, how do you get managers at the working level to take the strategic view you're trying to get?

We haven't changed our metrics—we continue to look at the same items. NSVM gives us a way to take the collective result of the metrics and study the impact on shareholder value.

The whole suite of key metrics that we look at, at a macro level, all roll up to revenue growth and profitability for each of our divisions.

EDUCATING THE BOARD

Every year, National has a strategic retreat for the board, usually a one-day session in April, where senior management presents and debates strategy with them. One of the things we started doing early on was that, the night before that session, we would have product demonstrations for the board, where they could get the flavor of some of the new products that we're working on; two years ago, among those product demonstrations, we had a PC set up to demonstrate our NSVM tool.

Frankly, having Boston Consulting Group's name attached to the model also made our board feel comfortable that, in a strategic sense, it was obviously a credible partner.

25

RECOGNIZING THE NEED FOR NEW METRICS

National seems to have come to an understanding that some new approaches were needed, while a lot of other companies in similar predicaments have continued struggling with old solutions. What does it take for a company to become convinced that it needs to begin using some more powerful financial metrics?

I don't think we came to an understanding here; I think we were just more rigorous in looking at what shareholder value implies in terms of business behavior. And I think we were more rigorous in trying to remap our compensation structures, to put in place compensation vehicles—at least, for those at the highest level in the company—that had a correlation to real shareholder value. Other companies try to do that by talking about how compensation may be related to shareholder value—but they often don't actually have a tool and structure in place, as we have, that links behavior at the business-unit level so directly with shareholder value. [For more on compensation, see Chapter 18.]

A MODEL FOR THE LONG TERM?

The bottom-line question: How successfully has the model been working for National?

If you take a long-term view, it's working; if you take a three-month view or a six-month view, people can always tear it apart.

But it all boils down to this: If you can demonstrate that what you're doing is generating sustainable cash flow, you can get value for that. This is what business is all about—getting sustainable, free cash-flow return from the investment choices you make today. Investors will clearly give you value for that, if you do it right!

That's why it was good for us to do the models, using a commodity-product business on the one hand, and one of our most technology-intensive businesses on the other. We showed that you could apply our cash flow–based model in both contexts.

It also showed us that there's still room for mature businesses in the semiconductor industry. In fact, those businesses can clearly provide more predictable returns in the long run if managed properly, although without the glamorous growth.

One of our goals at National is to use the resource base of our mature businesses, to position them to support our core capabilities—which is focused on our "analog and mixed-signal" capabilities. One of our most efficient fabs supports one of our mature businesses, and over time we will position that business to support the core business of the company. So these assets are there for us to redeploy, in addition to providing sustainable cash flow for the future.

This gives a flavor of the completeness of our model. We have divisional-level models and divisional-level behaviors. We have corporate-level portfolio approaches. We have corporate- and divisional-level TSRs—share-price models.

Our CEO not only supported this effort but kept reinforcing it. When presented with business and investment choices, he always asked, "Have you guys looked at the NSVM on this?" If we were doing incentive plans, he would insist that they have a value-management context. Too many leaders have a flavor of the year, and the next year it's something different, and you get no sustainability. Something like this really is long-term. You can't just do shareholder value one year and look at your plan and then forget it.

We get lots of calls about what we've done with value-management financial planning, because we've made it integral to how we manage and measure the results of our business strategy.

We endorse the approach because we made it work.

DON MACLEOD

Personal Perspectives

CFO WITH A MANAGEMENT BACKGROUND

Did you start out intent on a career in finance?

My degree is in economics—monetary economics—totally irrelevant!

In the United Kingdom, people get into finance through public accounting; in the U.S., it's an M.B.A. I became a Scottish chartered accountant [the U.K. equivalent of a C.P.A.], and my first job was with KPMG Peat Marwick in Scotland; National Semiconductor was one of my clients.

In time, National brought me on board, and I had a marketing position in Europe for a couple of years. National has a group called the IBG, the International Business Group, which is split into four geographic regions. In the European region of the IBG, I was the number two person, running the Standard Products business, which at the time was about a quarter of a billion dollar sales portfolio.

I was responsible for marketing, logistics, planning, information systems, warehouses—a broad portfolio of general management. I spent three weeks out of every four on the road visiting our customer base as the company's representative at a management level.

Then Charlie Sporck [National's legendary former CEO] asked me to come here from Europe in the fall of '90—a few months before he retired. With him, I went through our first restructuring, in 1990.

Charlie determined he was going to fill the CFO position internally, and I was the only one considered who was outside the finance organization. Because of my exposure to our products and customers, I was given the position; the background gave me a better perception of what the company was trying to do, rather than just what the finance function was trying to do.

The other day on television [during the 1996 Presidential primaries], Steve Forbes was talking about the money he was spending on his campaign, and he said, "Like any good Scotsman, I won't spend one penny too much"! And I thought, "Well, that's part of who I am, too."

CHAPTER 3

THE ECONOMIC VALUE ADDED (EVA) APPROACH AT HARNISCHFEGER

An Interview with Francis M. Corby, Jr.,
Executive Vice President of Finance and Administration,
Harnischfeger Industries, Inc.

Harnischfeger traces its history back to a machine shop launched in the mid-1800s by German immigrant Henry Harnischfeger and a partner. The corporate headquarters in Brookfield, Wisconsin, outside Milwaukee, stands on property known as Bishops Woods. It seems a peaceful, serene setting, but a stand of trees outside the window masks a busy freeway—a situation which you can read symbolically if that's your inclination.

Fran Corby looks distinguished and very fit and, though he's beginning to gray, appears younger than his 52 years. He has an undergraduate degree in philosophy, and an M.B.A. from the Columbia University Graduate School of Business in New York.

The interview conducted for this book has been expanded with remarks made during a benchmarking site visit organized by the American Productivity & Quality Center, of Houston.

ABOUT THE COMPANY

I'd like to start with some background on the business that Harnischfeger is in.

FRAN CORBY:

We're organized in three main business groups: production mining equipment, both underground coal mining machinery and surface-mining equipment, such as large electric shovels and draglines. We also produce paper-making machinery and systems. And the third business is materials handling, which consists of products such as the overhead cranes you see in factories and warehouses, container cranes, and a variety of hoist product lines.

All three of these businesses produce very high-technology equipment. And it's a global business, in about 50 countries. Market share is number one or, in a few cases, number two—a leading market position.

The business is cyclical because the paper-making side rides the ups and downs of the paper business.

What's the size of the company?

This year [1996], if you annualize our first-half results, we'll do about $2.8 billion, with about a 40% growth rate. We've had two acquisitions so far this year—both very much EVA-driven.

BEFORE CHANGING THE METRICS

Before we talk about the metrics you're using now, I'd like to ask about the main financial approaches the company had traditionally used.

We were your classic American company, with the focus on driving growth, both at the top line and the bottom line. We were very much an income statement–driven company, very focused on sales levels and operating results. Our operating people were generally more concerned with P&L than with receivables, inventory turns, fixed assets, or any other measures like those.

We ran the company using the classic budgeting approach—an annual operating budget. But, over the years, we had ended up with a very large balance sheet, a lot of capital built into the business, and a lot of inventory stashed in consignment, work in process, and raw materials.

Many of us felt that we had too much investment for the returns we were generating.

Looking back, are you satisfied with the way the capital budgeting was being done—or was that one of the problems?

We would decide early in the year that we were going to spend, say, $50 million. We didn't necessarily allocate that in any kind of scientific way; we might simply say: This operation has half of the business, so they get half of the $50 million—allocating by revenue size rather than by the value of the projects. And the money that was allocated would, of course, always be spent because, if you didn't spend it, you looked like you didn't need as big an allocation in next year's budget.

And, often, after an expenditure, we didn't go back and analyze whether the equipment was performing the way it should be in financial terms. We were falling into the trap of spending a lot of money on capital items that, perhaps, we really didn't have to.

What measures were you primarily relying on at that time?

In terms of our capital budgeting in the past, we used internal rate of return analysis and discounted cash flow analysis [see Glossary].

The difference was that folks would go through the exercise and justify spending capital money on the basis of these great returns that they were going to get out of a machine tool in the future. That's okay, but it's highly dependent upon how much work you're actually going to put across that tool. So, your assumptions have a very, very great impact on your decisions.

If you're in a situation where you're budgeting your capital and you're purchasing a long list of machine tools for manufacturing every year, and you're justifying those machine tool purchases by internal rate of return and discounted cash flow analysis, these things become financial issues, and they're dealt with by the financial people.

Because they're too complicated for a line manager to deal with?

Exactly. The controller who prepares the capital request does the calculations for you. But there's no tieback afterward because, a year later, when you sit down to do your operating budget, on which your bonus is going to be determined, you start all over again—because the situation has changed, and the market's different. And you totally ignore what you committed to do a couple of years earlier.

The problem was that it was viewed as just a financial matter—"I know I need the machine tool, and my divisional controller has to justify it for me."

A COMPENSATION PLAN THAT DIDN'T WORK

So your compensation plan was tied to the budgeting process, too.

Incentive compensation was tied to the operating profit budget; when a manager achieved his budgeted results, he got a good bonus. Because of that, you saw the budgeting process effectively focus on negotiations—people knew they were paid on their achievement compared to the budget, and so, if they were able to negotiate the right budget, they'd get a better bonus. Below 80%, they got no bonus; above 120%, they got a maximum bonus.

So, historically, it was almost institutionalizing poor behavior—because the people who got good bonuses were oftentimes the people who had negotiated low budgets. And then they didn't have the incentive to perform better than 120% of their budget. So they operated at a number within that 80% to 120% band. And they really didn't use the budget enough for planning purposes.

Because bonuses were tied to budgets—this is an overstatement—but, essentially, the people who got the best bonuses were the greatest negotiators or the greatest fibbers. When you're in a cyclical business, if you can convince people you're in the downside of the cycle, you can get a low budget, high opportunity, and high incentive.

RECOGNIZING THE NEED TO CHANGE

How did the awareness come about of approaches that might get the rest of the management better focused on things that would be good for the company?

Many of us here felt that we needed to have more focus on management of the capital employed in the business and that the best way to do this was not to have the financial types—that is, ourselves—bugging people for day sales outstanding or inadequate inventory turnover, and so on.

Instead, we wanted to find a way to get participation from management at all levels in doing a better job managing the balance sheet. That's what really got us interested in making a change.

One of the motivators we had was that a lot of people were unhappy that our stock wasn't performing better. For a long time, the excuse was: Wall Street doesn't understand us, we're a capital business, we're a cyclical business—there were more excuses than you can imagine. Finally, back in the early '90s, we looked in the mirror and said: If they don't understand it, maybe we're doing something wrong.

And because many of us felt that the investment tied up in working capital and even in our fixed assets was just too much, we first and foremost wanted to find a way to get more people involved in managing the balance sheet better. It looked as though there were things that could be done if we changed our incentives, changed our focus somewhat to get more bang out of the same level of investment.

And, at the same time, we were looking for approaches that might give us longer-term growth in terms of shareholder value.

SELECTING A NEW METRIC

When did you start looking for some other approach, and how long was it before you decided what the approach would be?

We had started looking at different alternatives in 1991. However, in 1992, there was a change at the top of the company. The chairman retired and he was replaced by the president and chief operating officer, who had been my predecessor as chief financial officer. This was an opportunity to make some real changes.

The prior CEO was a very good leader, but his focus over time was more on managing that P&L—again, leaving the balance sheets to the financial people. We really had a chance to make some significant changes by engaging others in balance sheet management.

Some of us were quite familiar with EVA. I had first become exposed to Joel Stern and Bennett Stewart [founders of the EVA approach] years ago when I was with Joy Manufacturing Company, which is now one of our subsidiaries. Our financial group looked at a number of alternatives, but EVA was an approach that was consistent with what we wanted to do. We liked the relationship of EVA to market value, and it had the elements we wanted to focus on—a combination of capital and return.

We did the EVA comparison, and our return on investment was lousy compared to our cost of capital. Our market value did not compare well with our book value. When we found that out, it confirmed what we had already figured, that we had to do something to improve our return and our capital utilization.

And then, as we looked at some of the empirical data that had been put together by folks at Stern Stewart, we became favorably impressed with what that data suggested in terms of growth in shareholder value over time: if you can continue to produce returns over time that exceed the weighted average cost of the capital employed to get those returns, you can increase shareholder value.

Were you concerned at all about selecting a method that might be understandable only to the people at the highest finance levels while the rest of management would be left in the dark?

That was very, very important to us because we wanted to make a very significant cultural change. To do that, we had to have something that could be put in very simple terms and could be understood across the whole spectrum of our management group, down to the first-line managers.

And so we were looking for something that would not only focus attention on managing the balance sheet better but would be easy enough to sell to a lot of people. It would be something that they would be very much encouraged to take up themselves, which gets into the whole area of incentives.

LAYING THE GROUNDWORK FOR EVA

How long was it before the company was using EVA more or less effectively?

1992 was a year of introspection, of what we were and what we wanted to be, long-term.

We had gotten away from the concept of the grocery store—you know, you count your money at the end of the day and, if you've got more than you started with, you've made money. It doesn't matter what you've got on the shelf—you can't spend the groceries, you can only spend cash.

So we had to make the change in measurements, but more than anything, we had to change behavior—and not just at the senior levels, because that's not where you get the impact. You've got to change behavior down through the organization, through the operating levels.

We went through a rather deliberate and very important process of selling different groups within the company on the concept—first our management policy committee, which consists of the CEO and those of us who reported directly to him, and then a larger group of senior managers from all over the world.

We took it to two different committees of the board—the finance and strategic planning committee, and the human resources committee—and then to the full board. And then to the senior managers; we spent a good part of '92 and '93 running training classes.

BEGINNING TO USE EVA

Once you had gotten all the buy-in and had done the initial training, what was the process of getting up and running?

We wanted to put in this program in the downward part of the cycle, so that natural operations would allow for good improvement, because we wanted to be able to show success in the first year or two of the program. We didn't want people to be able to say, "New program, no bonuses, another way of cutting back." We wanted to institutionalize the behavior, and we didn't want to have a failure the first year out of the box. If that had happened, people would not have adopted the program as a part of their working lives.

In fiscal year 1993, we initiated EVA as a performance measurement tool. But then the idea was that in 1994, we'd go full-bore to an incentive plan that was based entirely on EVA. And that's what happened—for the first time, it was the only tool for incentive compensation.

That's long enough for you to have seen some improvement. Do you have some numbers that are reflecting whether it's actually working for you?

There's a lot of evidence to suggest that it's definitely working. For example, at the end of fiscal year 1992, the beginning of the process, our stock price was at 18; today it's at 36.

We also found a very close correlation between actual EVA production along the way and our stock price—so much of a correlation that we put a chart in our 1995 annual report that tracked this.

Also, we went from a position of negative EVA—our running rate in the fourth quarter of 1992 was in excess of $100 million negative—to positive EVA in the fourth quarter of 1995. So, that was a huge change in EVA.

TRAINING ON EVA

You talked earlier about the training program. I'd like to ask you to describe it in a little more detail.

When starting out, we wanted to make sure that the senior financial executives, who were going to be the agents of change here, were well versed. These were my direct reports, including the top financial executives of our main business groups, who reported to me on a strong dotted-line reporting relationship.

We had Bennett Stewart come in himself, not so much to actually do the training but to make sure that we didn't have any unanswered questions. After that, the senior financial executives participated in the design of our system.

Then we extended to a larger group of financial executives, bringing in group controllers and divisional controllers. And we had Stern Stewart do that training—it's about a one-week program. While this was very useful, we learned we could really do that ourselves, and so, from that point forward, we set up our own training. Basically, it was driven by the financial organization. We've trained a great many people since then.

We offered classes to anybody who wanted to sign up. And most people did, because they realized that this was the direction the company was taking. We had sales people, inventory control clerks, purchasing agents, systems people—the whole range of operating people, who wanted to understand what these concepts were.

Realistically, I think that's the only way you can do it. You've got to get the operating people who are managing those resources at the lower levels to bring it into their operations. It doesn't make any sense to preach to them—that's not going to change anything.

It's now gotten to the point where it's training on demand, responding to requests from different operations, particularly new businesses that we acquire, to provide this kind of training. At this stage of the game, it's no longer something being pushed on the operations by corporate financial management but, rather, it's being demanded by the operations.

EXPLAINING EVA

Obviously, Harnischfeger has been successful in explaining the concepts of EVA through the company. What's the terminology you use to explain the basic notion?

EVA is not rocket science. It's really a very simple concept. Whether or not you're performing well in terms of managing the balance sheet is something that you don't have to be very smart to figure out.

What we use to describe it is simply the following. We just say that economic value added is simply the difference between the net operating profits after taxes and the cost of the capital employed to produce those same profits. That applies whether you're talking about a division, a subsidiary, a company, or a decision, acquisition, or divestiture—whatever the case may be.

That's all it is—the difference between the net operating profits after taxes and the cost of the capital employed to produce those same profits, utilizing a weighted average after-tax cost of capital.

EVA FOR BETTER DECISION MAKING

You've mentioned a couple of times using EVA to provide the right incentives for managers. Do you recall an example where EVA consid-

erations led a manager to make a different decision than he might have otherwise?

Yes. In our surface-mining equipment business, for instance, we had consignment inventory held at customer sites in overseas locations. Our international sales people always said that you can't sell equipment overseas unless you have consignment inventory on site. We put EVA into effect and we still had consignment inventory overseas, but the managers gradually reduced their inventory investment by 50%.

They reduced the amount of inventory on hand?

Exactly. And it wasn't a decision that was dictated by corporate—which was the point of all this. It showed we had found a way that encouraged people to make good decisions that took into consideration the cost of capital.

Another example: After an EVA training session, one of the sales executives said, "I'm going back to my office and I'm going to change my sales terms," and he did just that. He had realized that there probably would be little problem if he reduced his sales terms from net 60 to net 30; he didn't think it was going to cost him anything—but to him personally it was worth a percent after tax in EVA.

Also, if you just look at the company as a whole, our capital employed for those businesses went from a little less than $1.2 billion to a little less than $900 million—down by over $300 million, in a three-year period—during which time our sales increased.

We're at the point now where there are no budget negotiations related to incentive compensation. It's truly on automatic pilot, where a business unit's target is driven off its last year's results. And even though we're a cyclical business, we'll continue to do that, because we have to manage well, on the capital side and on the income side, on the down part of the cycle as well as on the upward part.

There was a lot of concern that this program would reduce compensation and that it would take a lot of the judgment and negotiation out of the process—so we didn't put EVA in place for compensation purposes until a year later, in '94. We gave the business-unit managers a year to figure out how the program works and how they would do better under it.

For nonbargaining-unit people in the U. S., this also replaced our profit-sharing plan. We set a target percentage for everybody at 3%. In other words, if we do just what we're supposed to do according to the EVA target, everybody will get an additional 3% of salary in profit sharing. If we do worse, they might get 1%, or even nothing. If we do better, they can get more.

Last year, the profit-sharing payment ranged from 3% to 8%. My secretary got a check at Christmas for 6% of her salary.

COMPUTING THE COST OF CAPITAL

I'd like to get into some specifics of what you are actually doing in your EVA calculations, so that people can understand what it might mean for them if they decided to explore this approach for their own companies.

Our approach has always been to keep it as simple as possible because, again, we wanted to influence a lot of people to change the way they did things.

So, for example, we very carefully calculated our weighted average cost of capital, using the classic calculation. We began with our most recent long-term debt issue which, at the time, was 8.9% for 30-year money. From that we determined the after-tax cost of debt.

Then, to determine the cost of equity, we looked at the 30-year U.S. Treasury bonds and asked: What has been the stock market's historical return over and above the 30-year U.S. Treasuries? We went through the records back 50 years. We found that the stock market has historically outperformed long Treasuries by 500 basis points [5%], and so we added this amount.

Then we factored in the most recent calculation of our beta [a measure of the riskiness of a stock; a beta of 1.0 indicates the same risk as the overall market]—because the investor is not buying the stock market, he's buying our stock, and we had a different risk characteristic.

From all that, we ended up with a cost of equity that was approximately 16.2%.

Next, we addressed our target capitalization mix; we wanted to be at a debt-to-capitalization ratio [the ratio of a company's debt to its total capital; the higher the ratio, the greater the risk of investing in the company] between 20% and 40%. At that ratio, we were highly comfortable that our rating agencies would continue to rate us at the same investment grade level they had been rating us at previously. We took the midpoint of that range, 30%.

That gave us 30 parts debt, 70 parts equity; the debt had an after-tax cost of 5.4%, the equity was 16.2%. Factor that all together and we ended up with 12.9%.

But we used 12% even, because all the sales executives would know that sales terms for an extra 30-day are going to cost them 1% after tax. So they ought to be able to get it back somehow; otherwise, they may not want to give that up.

Another reason we moved cost of capital down from 12.9% to 12% is because we felt that, if the company did have good solid growth, we would be permitted a less conservative mix going forward in the future, which would reduce our weighted average cost of capital. And in fact, that really is what has happened. Our cost of capital has come down and would now be closer to 12% anyway.

ADJUSTMENTS TO EVA

One of the factors in using EVA that seems to concern people is deciding which of the many possible adjustments they should use. What governed your decisions on this?

Our budget performance was always focused on operating profits. So we began with operating profits, and we just added a few adjustments to take it down to net operating profits after taxes—which meant we were using as a starting point something that all our people were comfortable with already.

For the purposes of the EVA calculation, we make a number of adjustments, including things like R&D expense, which we capitalize and take over five years.

And there were other adjustments like that, not more than a dozen. The only kinds of adjustments that we considered were those that were material in our case, and that were theoretically correct. In the Stern Stewart methodology, there would be many, many more adjustments that you could take.

Would you share the list of adjustments that you make?

I can tell you what the key ones are. To make it simple, let's take one of our businesses.

We start by adding back any interest income that would be generated by foreign operations—because the U.S. operations have their cash stripped; our cash-management system is such that we don't keep domestic cash balances in any of our operating entities. But in the overseas subsidiaries, we do. So, to the extent that the overseas subsidiaries say that they need X amount of cash on their balance sheet, they're going to be charged for that since it's invested capital; they're charged 12% after taxes from an EVA standpoint, but they get a credit back for the interest they actually earn.

Goodwill amortization is another adjustment. In terms of capital employed, we go back to the original purchase price of an acquisition. So if we buy a company for $200 million and $100 of it is the net assets of the company and the rest is goodwill, that acquisition, to be EVA breakeven, has got to earn 12% after tax on $200 million.

Also, changes in other long-term liabilities are added back. All warranty is considered to be, if you will, "non-economic." In other words, any changes in warranty reserves, even if they're not long-term reserves, are adjusted out so that operating profit for EVA purposes is only negatively impacted when a payment is made, not when an accrual is made in the warranty reserve.

In terms of things that are added back, that's the extent of it.

Then the subtractions. We have the amortization of the capitalized R&D—because, remember, we're capitalizing R&D and amortizing it over a five-year period; so this is the flip side of that. And then, finally, cash taxes—this is not our book taxes; these are cash taxes paid.

When we're finished with this exercise, we've gone through maybe a dozen adjustments and ended up with net operating profit after taxes, which is the first step that's taken in terms of EVA calculations.

Capital employed can be viewed in our case in one of two ways. If you look at it from an asset standpoint, it's basically total assets minus current liabilities—with an adjustment that adds back amortized goodwill.

So, one way of looking at your capital employed is total assets, minus current liabilities, plus amortized goodwill. If you want to look at it from the liability side of the balance sheet, it's debt, equity, and what I like to refer to as "free liabilities," which are long-term liabilities like warranty reserves and LIFO [last in first out] reserves, and so on. And that's it—as simple as that.

Do you deal with market value added as well?

We do, but we frankly don't pay a lot of attention to it. We believe in it, however, and I would argue that that's one of the reasons why our stock price increased: We produced better and better economic value added performance as we went from a negative $100 million to breakeven in that couple-of-year period. But we don't track market value added.

Is EVA something that your people can grasp in terms of the kinds of measures that they're more familiar with using? Do they understand the connection between EVA and ROE, and so forth?

Yes, but more than that, EVA has made it more direct—they can understand much better now the impact of a decision on EVA and on the factors that impact the stock price.

Overall, I suppose it would be fair to assume that you're a champion of EVA.

We said that we would achieve EVA breakeven in five years. We were at breakeven last year, which is three years ahead of schedule.

We started measuring our operations with EVA in 1992; at that point, we were about a $1 billion company. Today, we're at almost $3 billion and much more profitable. So, yes, it would be fair to say it's working for us.

FRAN CORBY

Personal Perspectives

BACKGROUND

Were you educated in finance?

My education includes a B.A. in philosophy, and an M.B.A. from Columbia University, with a concentration in finance and international business.

You're a New Yorker?

No, I grew up in the Chicago area. I was interested in going to Columbia because, at the time, I felt that it offered the best concentration in international business.

I went to work for Chrysler Corporation right out of graduate school and was there for close to 11 years. The last job I had with Chrysler was as vice president and treasurer of Chrysler Financial Corporation. While I was with Chrysler, I lived in Detroit three times, in Mexico City twice, in Lima, Peru, and in London.

From Chrysler, I went to what at the time was Joy Manufacturing Company as corporate treasurer. I was in that role for three years and then was made vice president and corporate controller.

Then again I was approached by a search firm to come to Harnischfeger as chief financial officer, which I did in August of 1986. A couple of years ago, I was made executive vice president for finance and administration.

ON MANAGERS LEARNING FINANCE

If you were advising some younger people who had promise or interest in moving up to senior management positions and executive positions, what kind of advice would you give them about equipping themselves with a working knowledge of finance?

It might depend to a certain extent on how you define *finance*. But I would say to managers and other key operating executives who want to move up the ladder that it's very important that they learn enough about finance so as not to be intimidated by it. The bottom line is that it's not very difficult. But it has to be demystified for a lot of people.

And what's the best way of doing that? How do they get over whatever for them are the hurdles to understanding finance?

I think they have to keep asking questions until they understand the issues.

And who do they ask questions of? Their business–unit finance person—is that what you're suggesting?

Absolutely. And they should never walk away from a discussion not understanding, because it isn't that difficult. People make it sound that way sometimes, but it just isn't.

CHAPTER 4

NEW METRICS
AT FMC AND
R.R. DONNELLEY

An Interview with Cheryl A. Francis,
Executive Vice President and Chief Financial Officer,
R.R. Donnelley & Sons Company

Cheryl Francis is a walking contradiction—hard driving, hard charging, fast moving, but at the same time athletically trim, stylishly dressed, very soft-spoken, and looking much too young to hold a position of great importance. Once she gets talking about her subject, though, you take her seriously, concentrate on staying focused on her train of thought, and quickly figure her as an odds-on favorite to become one of the very few women who will lead a Fortune 500 company—and probably sooner rather than later.

FMC, where Ms. Francis worked until a few months before this interview, is a $4.5 billion company producing chemicals, defense systems, and machinery used in the petroleum, airline, automotive, and food-processing industries. The company also mines gold and silver in the United States and Latin America.

R.R. Donnelley, her new employer, is an international printing company with 1995 revenues of $6.5 billion. The company's printing output ranges from advertising inserts for Toys 'R' Us to the National Enquirer newspaper, from corporate annual reports to best-selling books.

The interview took place in the Donnelley corporate offices in downtown Chicago, which are decorated in the kind of impeccably tasteful style that makes Chicagoans proud and executives of other companies envious, with antique furniture, museum-quality paintings, and splendid sculptures, including rare Chinese pieces more than 2000 years old.

BACKGROUND

I'm always interested in the route people take to reach the executive level, so I'd like to begin by asking you to describe the path that brought you to the CFO's job.

CHERYL FRANCIS:
I actually haven't stopped at very many points along the way. After getting an M.B.A. at the University of Chicago, I went briefly into a consulting role as a corporate finance consultant for an organization that was housed within a commercial bank but did advisory work on things like valuation, capital structure, and dividend policy.

As it turned out, I didn't stay there very long before going to FMC Corporation in 1979. I started in corporate development and planning. My mission initially was to bring in a performance measurement system that could be applied well within a diversified company environment so that the top people in the company could start to make some portfolio decisions about where to invest.

I worked at FMC for about 16 years prior to coming to Donnelley, with some time out for teaching at the University of Chicago.

What were the qualities Donnelley was looking for when they selected you as CFO?

I don't know too much about that. My predecessor retired and here I am. But I think the management team was ready for some financial discipline.

CFROI AT FMC

What kinds of metrics did FMC use while you were there?

We actually evolved from one measurement system to another. We started with cash flow return on investment, which we used in a planning context. Later, when we decided we needed to roll it out into internal reporting, we switched to something we called *net contribution,* but you would be more familiar with it as *economic value added;* we did that in 1982.

What was it about the cash flow metrics that worked as an effective tool when you used them, and then why were they given up?

We didn't give them up initially, we continued using them in the planning context for a while, side by side with net contribution. Eventually, we did give them up, but it was several years later when we thought we were getting the same information from the two systems and it wasn't worth running them in tandem.

But the beauty of CFROI is that it's truly a valuation context. It causes you to look forward and then discount back so that you have a sense of the market value of the businesses that you're running. Based on that, you can start to make some decisions by asking yourself: Should I hold this, or would it be more valuable in somebody else's hand? Should I combine it with something else along the way? If I change the projections for the future, how does that impact the valuations?

It's a very nice tool to have in a planning construct when you're trying to figure out what your alternatives are and where to position the businesses.

But it doesn't translate very well into an operating environment because it's more of an "internal rate of return" calculation. It's dependent upon pushing things forward and then discounting them back. We used to call it "progress, not perfection." It was pushing people in the right direction but, in the end, the extra 20% of value you got from CFROI was not viewed as worth it.

SWITCHING TO EVA AT FMC

And you went to an EVA type of approach instead.

In an EVA kind of a situation, you get most of the same context simply by giving all managers responsibility for their own balance sheets and charging them for the assets that they utilize. And that just flows right out of a P&L kind of a framework that everybody in the operation is very familiar with.

Net contribution has elements of EVA, but it uses a slightly different definition. It was actually very interesting because we did it all on a current-cost basis, so that inflation adjusted all the assets—which is part of the methodology falling out of CFROI.

That was important to FMC because, first of all, we were in so many different kinds of businesses with different asset intensity—the chemical businesses, for example, had very old assets. And some parts of the business were very asset-intensive while others, like defense systems, had very new assets and were not as asset-intensive. We also operated in a lot of international environments, like Brazil, where inflation was a big factor.

And so it really levels the playing field to inflation-adjust everything and then do all the calculations with real discount rates and real effective rates of return.

But, about three years ago, we ended up abandoning that at FMC because inflation had come down to the point where it was no longer so important a factor, and the assets were turning over. We found we weren't getting any different signals with this additional level of complexity.

That's the first time I've heard the suggestion that the rate of inflation might have a bearing on the type of metrics you decide to use.

You need to be clear about whether the rate of inflation needs to be an important consideration in your investment and financial decisions. If it doesn't, then a current-cost EVA or CFROI approach may be more effort than you need.

EVA AT DONNELLEY

And you're now using an EVA type of approach here at Donnelley, right? Because it isn't as complicated for line people to understand?

It's very simple. The only complicated part comes if you do the full rollout that the Stern Stewart group would recommend; then you make 130 to 160 adjustments to normal accounting. But you can get extremely close by making half a dozen. And that's what Donnelley is doing. We're taking just normally recorded accounting measures and making about six adjustments to get us pretty close.

THE SIX ADJUSTMENTS TO EVA

And what are those six adjustments?

The big adjustments are that we're putting the leases back on the balance sheet, so we capitalize them. And we're giving everybody complete responsibility for goodwill, and it never leaves—so, if you make an acquisition, then you have goodwill associated with it. It's yours forever and you have return on that, year in and year out. Those are the two biggest adjustments.

We also are capitalizing the start-up—the negative EVA related to starting up a new plant—so that we don't discourage reinvestment in the business. And it doesn't go away; it gets built into your balance sheet. Later, when you start to make a return, you have to return on that investment as well.
The complete list is:
Start-up capitalization.
Inventory FIFO.

Leased assets.
Goodwill.
Asset disposals.
Cash taxes—we charge people taxes based on the actual cash taxes that
   would impact them as opposed to some kind of an accounting number.

You list "asset disposals." What are you doing there?

This refers to disposing of an asset that would be leaving your balance sheet
and you get a gain or a loss on it. What we're doing is not giving the business-
unit manager credit for the gain or the loss but just removing it from the
balance sheet so that the manager gets one benefit as opposed to two.

So, how is it handled?

We simply capitalize it. When a business manager brings in a pro forma and
gets a capital plan approved—say, to put a new press into one of the magazine
plants, then he has immediate cash flow out the door. After the press goes
in, it takes about a year to get up and running before it begins to create profit.

You simply take that piece, capitalize it, and make it part of the asset
base—and you don't penalize the business for it. Pretty simple concept, but
how you execute it can be complicated.

That's important for the line managers so that they're led to make the right business decisions?

Exactly, right. And, then everybody is on cycle for EVA purposes, and the
balance sheet reflects the true cost of the assets—at least, as close as we can get.

Those are the big adjustments that we make.

You said that the amortization was complicated.

The capitalization of the start-up costs is.

How do you help the line managers overcome those complications?

First of all, you only do it when it's significant; if it's a relatively small project,
you say: Forget it—it's not worth the effort.

For the purposes of Donnelley, what's significant?

About $5 million. So, for the bulk of what people are spending money on,
they don't have to worry about this issue. When it's bigger than that, they're
going to worry about it because their incentive compensation is based on EVA.

ROLLING OUT EVA

We're still in the learning phases of how we're implementing EVA, so we have a kind of recipe book that we've sent out to people. We've had a lot of education around the concept.

But as we put our budget together this year—which was the first time people really had to internalize all these concepts—we held people's hands all the way through, and it took us about two to three extra months to get the balance sheets for the budgets really nailed down. But we think that was a good learning process.

Just to give you some background, Donnelley's adoption of EVA has been an evolutionary kind of thing. This [1996] is the first year of a full rollout but, in 1994, we parceled working capital back to people's business units and charged them for that.

In 1995, they got the fixed assets along with it, but the charge was on a pre-tax basis. This year, for the first time, we've incorporated the six adjustments, including the goodwill, which is important to us because we have a fair amount of intangibles. And now we're doing all the calculations on an after-tax basis. It's rolled into all the incentive schemes. This was the final step.

SELECTING THE RIGHT METRICS FOR YOUR SITUATION

Would you say that different types of industries, different types of situations, call for different measures?

Absolutely.

And what guidelines would you give for that?

I think you just go back to the basics of what drives your business and then figure it out according to that. Quite frankly, that's one of my concerns about Stern Stewart—they have been very successful, and they are very bright people, but now they have an almost canned program and, when you talk to them about tailoring it to your business, they are not as receptive as I would like to see them be.

So, I think you just go back to the basic economics of the business and figure out what it is that drives it and how you can get people aligned around those issues.

Do you see EVA as a solution for everybody?

I think a residual income kind of an approach—which is all EVA is—is a very powerful tool in some form for just about everybody.

And, as for cash flow return on investment, are there industry groups where that makes more sense?

CFROI is particularly good as a planning tool because it's somewhat forward-looking and because it's more economic in terms of the outcomes it gives you than something based on an accounting model. So, it's useful in a certain environment, but it's really hard to get to the people on the plant floor and get them excited about it.

A lot of companies, of course, use one set of metrics at the executive level for corporate planning and a completely different system where the people are really doing the work.

Which I think is a terrible idea, by the way. That was how we started at FMC, and it just caused paranoia because everybody thought that the corporate people had a black box they were looking at. Nobody else could see it or understand it. How do you get people aligned in a place like that? How do you have ownership? You can't.

So, it may be working, but the perception of people is that there's something going on that they aren't permitted to know.

It works at a certain level in terms of assessing the businesses but, for us, it didn't work at the level where we needed it to work: to change people's behavior and the way they think about their business. So, it's incomplete.

That's why a residual income approach like EVA or a similar kind of a measure is much more compelling in terms of the ability to really change a corporate view.

DRAMATIC INSIGHTS AT FMC

Do you consider the use of EVA at FMC successful?

There's a history of how dramatically it changed people's view of the businesses.

And that showed up in the numbers?

Oh, sure. Within two years, we had squeezed $400 million out of working capital. Since that point in time, almost every year, FMC has run with negative working capital—the liabilities are larger than the current assets. The customers are financing the company! It's a wonderful situation; it changed very dramatically.

And that was largely due to giving the managers measures that have sent them in the right direction?

That's part of it. I'm not one that says measures and incentives are the solution to all of this. I think they can support—they can add an exclamation point to—the emphasis that management is putting on certain measures.

I just have this philosophical problem that makes me ask: If I hold a carrot out, will that be the only thing that somebody's going to look at? I don't think that's what happens. So, yes, EVA is very supportive of getting people to think differently about their business.

But you say that's only part of it. Then there's something else going on there that accounts for the success at FMC?

Let me tell you a little bit about that. FMC is a very diversified company. Basically, the fellow who became chairman in 1972, Bob Malott, had inherited a lot of problems—a result of his predecessor's making lots of acquisitions because they wanted to be big and they wanted to be diversified.

He was left with a portfolio that didn't make sense and he had to rationalize it. That's why we used CFROI. It helped us make trade-offs and get out of businesses. Then, when we got to the point where those problems were behind us, we adopted for internal reporting this metric similar to EVA. That got people really focused on managing their balance sheet and creating cash flow, which gave us the $400 million out of working capital.

All of a sudden, we started to see land appear as assets that could be sold. You know, acreage that somebody bought when they built a chemical plant and now they realize they don't need "the back forty."

In the case of FMC, managers were being charged at market value for land because everything was at current value and we'd appraised the land. You know, if you're operating a defense business in San Jose, California, you turn around one day and realize that it's become very valuable property. Or our research property in Princeton, New Jersey—why do I need that land? I can sell it and let somebody put houses on it or a factory or something. And so, all these assets started to turn up—hidden assets we didn't know we had, creating the opportunity for a lot of cash flow.

That's a great benefit brought about by a change in perspective. In 1984, CFROI had been in place for two years, and there was lots of cash coming in the door. The corporation had investment alternatives to face, but not nearly enough to absorb all the cash that started to appear. So, at that point, we bought back a third of our shares.

The next year, in 1985, we did the five-year plan and began to look forward. All of a sudden, we saw that we were investing in the businesses to keep them healthy, but debt was going to be gone and cash was going to be $1 billion, and what were we going to do about it?

So, what FMC did was to recapitalize the company. We went out and borrowed $2 billion, turned around and paid it to our shareholders, and leveraged ourselves to the hilt; we had negative equity to the tune of $600 million. It dramatically shifted the model.

And, because the management knew how to run the businesses very effectively for cash, we were one of the very successful recapitalizations that occurred in the 1980s. We came out in very fine shape afterward. FMC was back to an investment grade company by 1992.

That must have been a nervous-making time.

It took a lot of guts. And the same chairman was there throughout the entire period.

He must have had good financial advice, and a great deal of confidence.

Bob Malott's one of the best financial people I've ever worked for. And, at the time, we didn't have a CFO—Bob was effectively his own CFO.

He knew what questions to ask.

He's very smart. And he had a good advisor—Warren Buffett was a good friend. When we were trying to figure out what to do, Bob flew to Omaha and got some advice from him.

In the case of FMC, the stars and the moon were aligning, and the CFROI measurement system helped—particularly with the advance education, so the thinking process was in place before we started to make some of these dramatic changes to the capital structure.

What was the impact of all this on share price?

In 1982, on an equivalent basis and adjusting for splits, the stock was trading at about $5, and today it's at about $67. A lot of that happened during the recapitalization, and I had the experience of being part of the team that did that.

So there's a story here about the power of the way you think about things and how you measure things.

It's powerful, but I'm not going to tell you it's the only method out there. People have to have good business judgment, really understand their customers, figure out how to make the model of the business profitable—that's equally as important. And also the sense of ownership by the business managers—you know, "This is mine; I'm going to make it work."

That's a very good story.

It's a wonderful story. There was a Harvard case study written about it.

ESTABLISHING EVA AT DONNELLEY

So your time at FMC was dramatic. What's going to happen here at Donnelley?

It's going to be dramatic here, too. The people here just don't understand how far we can go, but they're going to learn, and we're going to learn together.

What are you seeing so far?

We're seeing some really interesting things. The culture at Donnelley has a wonderful track record of strength. It's more monolithic than FMC; it's very focused on print and has first-rank stature in everything the company does—extremely strong market positions, very strong competitive positions, strong customer relations, and so on, all the way down the line.

But, you know, you always get in trouble when you start to believe your own press, and so I think the sense of urgency needs to be heightened, but I think we're getting there.

How are you getting there? What is it that's changing people's perspective?

The competitive horizons are changing. There are some things happening externally that are clearly sending messages we need to pay very close attention to. And we need to be very aggressive about what our competitive advantages are and to maintain them and improve them in the world in which we operate.

Is there something changing the competitive picture?

Sure. All you have to do is read *Business Week* or *The Wall Street Journal*. It's the whole question of the printing industry versus other formats for receiving information—the electronic world and how that could be impinging on us.

And then we just happen to be in a depressed time for printing right now, for three reasons: Paper costs went up 30% last year [1995], the cost of postage went up 14% and, as everybody saw during Christmas, consumer confidence took a dip. So, if you're producing catalogs, you're downsizing them and you're sending them to fewer people and only the people that you think will really give you an order, not the prospecting list.

If you're producing a magazine, the same thing—you cut down the trim size so it's less costly to manufacture on the paper side and less costly to mail. All of that has impacts on our business. And it's not just us; everybody in the print sector has had a fairly difficult time in the first quarter.

In a way, that's good, because it's causing us to really wake up and think about being as efficient and as effective as we can within each of our businesses.

NEW DIRECTIONS FOR FINANCE
AT DONNELLEY

What are the things you're working on right now?

Donnelley has spent a lot of money over the last five years, and the returns on investments are not where we would like to see them or where our investors would like to see them.

But the philosophy seems to have been more one of growth. Now, we're charging the managers of our business units every time they invest a dollar.

The victory is not getting the board to approve the spending; the victory is starting to actually earn returns on the spending—because the cost is now embedded in your balance sheet and you're going to be measured against it forever.

That message is getting through. So, we're seeing things like this: The people that run our directory business wanted to buy a new press. We said, "We don't have a lot of money to spend; isn't there an alternative to this?"

The directory people thought about it in EVA terms, and they said, "Yes, we'll simply move in the press that's under-utilized at this other location; the utilization is going to go up fantastically, and we're going to be able to meet all of our customer needs, with no incremental investment to the company." We should always be thinking about those things and now we're beginning to.

Working capital is another one. We're going to see some real improvement there. It's an exciting time to be at Donnelley because it's an excellent manufacturer and a superb sales and marketing company, but the finance function hasn't yet had the effect that it can.

GETTING STARTED WITH EVA

If a company learns about the EVA approach and decides that it makes sense for them to look into it, how do they go about getting started?

There's a real body of evidence out there—so many companies are using a similar approach. You could start by talking to companies you respect that have a similar kind of measurement system in place, as a basis for thinking about what the value would be in your own company.

If you decide to go ahead, at some point, you're probably going to want some help in facilitating the process of installing EVA or whatever you decide on. We happen to use Stern Stewart, but there are many people who can help you with similar kinds of measurements—from Big Six accounting firms to consulting firms of just about any ilk. It's not that complicated, but it's helpful to have somebody that you have confidence in, come in and facilitate.

So, in many cases, businesses could ask their accounting firm.

To help them think it through—right.

But you have some reservations about the Boston Consulting Group approach. It's more complicated, but you suggested there was another reason.

It doesn't translate well out into the operating units. It's a different framework than people are used to thinking about.

Having run those kinds of numbers ad infinitum from 1979 to 1982, I feel that it's really not that complicated, but it can be hard to explain, and it's not something people are used to working with.

★ ★ ★

(For insights from Cheryl Francis on the use of derivatives, see Chapter 7.)

APPROACHES TO
FINANCE FOR
THE 90s
AND BEYOND

CHAPTER 5

PLANNING, DECISION MAKING, AND DEVELOPING PEOPLE AT GENERAL ELECTRIC

An Interview with Dennis Dammerman, Senior Vice President, Finance, General Electric Company

Visitors to the main corporate headquarters of GE are dazzled—some might say "assaulted"—by a lobby in reds and blacks: a black stone entry leading to a sunken reception area that is carpeted in fire engine red. The receptionist's desk is 12 feet of stone in matching red, topped in black marble, and behind her, on a vast expanse of wall, is an eye-popping 15-foot abstract oil by Robert Motherwell, said to be his last work. The predominant colors of the painting fight the colors of the room, a mal de mer clash. Still, the overall impact shouts vibrancy, a willingness to take risks, to be daring—but at the highest levels, with the best of judgment.

Dennis Dammerman's office is what you'd expect—large, light, understated, with an antique desk and a connoisseur's selection of art.

Dammerman merits a large part of the credit for making GE one of the world's most successful companies in terms of the growth of shareholder value. And, as made abundantly clear in these pages, that measure has become the most valid yardstick for determining whether a company is succeeding.

It's interesting that the two most successful companies in creating shareholder wealth are in one respect exact opposites: Coca-Cola has a single product, while

59

GE defies logic by operating a dizzying array of businesses, from the manufacture of lightbulbs, washing machines, jet aircraft engines, and huge railroad locomotives to running the NBC and CNBC television networks.

For one of the most important executives in America, Dennis Dammerman is surprisingly warm, engaging, and relaxed. Having agreed to spend an hour and a half in the middle of a busy working day, he is clearly committed to giving this his full attention, as if he had nothing more pressing to do at the moment.

GE is one of the most successful firms in the history of publicly owned companies in terms of increasing shareholder value. Clearly, the company has found effective ways to track and encourage behaviors that support value creation. What's the basic approach behind this?

DENNIS DAMMERMAN:

I think the world—the investment community and everybody else—is gaining more and more appreciation for cash, particularly if you try to invest around the world.

I was looking at some charts today that compared stock market valuations in continental Europe, the U.K., Japan, the Pacific Rim, emerging markets in the United States—and you really can't do that on a price/earnings basis. You really have to go to price/cash, because it's a common denominator.

There's a lot more emphasis today on cash, in addition to earnings per share, and in terms of our own compensation measurements as well as the external world's view of what are important measures.

We are a U.S. company, and the majority of our stock is held by U.S. investors. And earnings, even on a quarterly basis, are very important in the U.S. market. As long as that's true, we're going to pay a lot of attention to earnings, and we're going to pay a lot of attention to how much we make each quarter and each year, and how it compares to how we did the year before and the year before that.

But we're also paying a lot more attention to cash. When I started this job, *speed* was not something we talked a lot about—measuring how fast we do things was not something that I spent a lot of time looking at. Today, it's part of our lexicon; we talk it all the time, and we judge people's business performance in part by how fast they do things.

We've got a big effort on quality at the moment—measuring it, using the 6Sigma approach. In the past, it was "Zero Defects" or "Go for Quality," with those posters of a little gopher running around with a hat on. You always had those things, but this is a much more *disciplined* approach.

VALUE MANAGEMENT METRICS AT GE

What form of the "new metrics" is GE using?

Market value added, economic value added, and so on—those are certainly things that we track. But unlike some companies that use EVA or MVA for all their internal measurements, we don't do it as much. Obviously, we worry a lot about it, since we're the largest market-capital company in the world.

Still, I personally have a hard time communicating economic value added all up and down the chain, from the person on the factory floor all the way to our shareholders. Explaining what it is and how what they do impacts it is not easy.

INPUTS AS METRICS

My view is that it's very important to give the same message to everybody. I don't think you should be telling an hourly worker a different story than you're telling your largest institutional investor. We believe we're better off, at this level, understanding how the inputs—quality, customer satisfaction, speed, and all—translate into economic value added. When we talk about flow technology, or about cycle time, or about speed, or about quality, we need to understand how the input affects the output.

So it's our job as the leadership of the company to understand how the inputs influence EVA. But our message to everyone else focuses on the inputs. I *can* give a speech to hourly employees about speed and the benefits of being fast and how customers like it and what it means to their business. I can get the workers excited about it. But it's hard to give them a speech about economic value added and get any excitement.

We have a very diverse company. Getting somebody who works in a lightbulb factory to understand how they impact economic value added, at the same time you're trying to make the same message understandable to somebody who works at NBC or an aircraft factory—it's a hard speech.

But if all those other things are being handled right—speed and quality and customer service and so on—then you're creating economic value added.

FINANCIAL AND NON FINANCIAL METRICS FOR BUSINESS MANAGERS

How far down in the organization is EVA being used? For example, what are the presidents of the business units looking at?

I'm not saying this is right or wrong, I'm just saying that this is the way we run GE—the presidents would be looking at more traditional measures. They're looking at cash flow, they're looking at return on total capital, at net income. For non-financials, they're looking at speed, quality, and customer satisfaction, and at employee satisfaction.

We get all the presidents of the business together and we talk about economic value added and what the results are, about what we did and why we did it. But it's not something that we put in front of them every month.

You then expect that they'll interpret the EVA information and understand what they need to do to improve on the measurements they're tracking.

Thinking about return on total capital works quite well as a surrogate—because, basically, economic value added is a return above your cost of capital. So if you know what your cost of capital is, and if you know what your return on capital is—on an interim basis, without making all the adjustments that you have to make for economic value added—return on total capital is not a bad surrogate in the short term.

FOCUSING ON THE INPUTS

General Electric has done such a phenomenally good job of increasing shareholder value—people wonder what the secrets are. Do you have some key items you track that other people are overlooking?

One key thing that I keep looking at are the *inputs*. Where does it start in the process? And how do you manage those inputs—speed or quality or labor expended—how do you make them more efficient and better, and then relate them to how they influence the output—cash, earnings, sales, and so on?

Understanding how the inputs relate to the outputs is a big part of our job. Previously, accounting spent most of its time measuring the outputs. We have to spend more of our time in finance focusing on the inputs; the whole business team does.

The ideal goal would be some day to be able to worry just about the inputs, knowing that if you do a good enough job of this, the outputs are going to be just fine, thank you. If you've got the best quality, you're the fastest, and you've got the lowest cost, then you should have good market share and you should have a profitable business.

(Laughing) Granted you've got to pay attention to things like, Are you in a market that's worth being in? If you have all those wonderful inputs and you're making buggy whips, then you've got to ask yourself why you're doing that.

ON NOT FRITTERING AWAY THE GAINS

I think it's a much more activist role for finance leaders of a company to be having an impact on the inputs. But they also have to make the bridge to ensure that those good things coming about because of the progress on the inputs are falling through to the bottom line instead of getting frittered away somewhere before they get there.

You know how that sometimes works: You've got a big project on quality and you're going to save $2 million. You've got to make sure that the $2 million gets reflected somewhere in the P&L, or it doesn't do you much good to have made the savings.

In other words, is it really a saving if it doesn't show up somewhere!

Right. And it's not always as easy as it sounds to track those things. "I know I told you it saved $2 million; what I didn't tell you is, I had to spend *this* to get it and I had to spend *that*." Or, "I saved $2 million but I spent $1 million of it to work on my next project."

MANAGING FOR THE SHORT TERM
AND THE LONG TERM

These sound like short-term goals. But the success of GE makes it clear that you must be concerned about the long term as well.

We are unabashedly a high-performance, high-pressure company, and we see it as our job as leaders of the business to manage for the long term as well as the short.

We've been growing earnings every quarter since 1975. Our contention is that we've been successfully managing for both the short and long terms because, if we hadn't been managing for the long term, that string would have run out.

Emerson Electric has been doing this for 35 years. Coca-Cola is another very good example; except for a couple of hiccups brought on by some ill-fated long-term decisions, it's done this very successfully as well.

EDUCATING THE MANAGERS

Do you find that your business-unit managers have grasped these concepts fully, or are you looking at an ongoing learning process?

They're very astute—again, because of our diversity.

When you're talking about Seinfeld or Jay Leno versus a CF-6 jet engine or a topmount, no-frost refrigerator, about the only way you end up with commonality is to express it in some sort of numbers—cash flow, earnings, capital, and the rest.

I would say that, on the whole, our top management team is extraordinarily adept at thinking about balance sheets and financial statements and the impact one has on the other, the impact that this action over here has on that financial number over there.

My observation is that on the financial front, management in the U.S. today is much better than even five years ago. But, again, I think GE is on the leading edge of that because of the search for commonality in terms of expressing ourselves in financial terms. And also because a former chairman—Reg Jones--had previously been a CFO.

And Jack [Welch] is extremely astute with financial analysis and balance sheets and operating statements. He expects, when he's talking with our associates, doing a budget review or a strategy or operating review with them, that they're able to answer questions without turning to their left or their right to ask their finance manager about it. They only have to go through one or two of those experiences before they get the message that they're expected to know those things.

FINANCIAL METRICS AS A COMMON LANGUAGE

Listening to you creates a sense that GE has become a leader in the way it handles its finances *because* of the diverse nature of its operations.

Financial measurements end up being the common expression for all of us. You can't compare Seinfeld with a CF-6, but you can express how much the Thursday night schedule makes us at NBC, and how much the CF-6 produces in cash flow, earnings, and market share . . . and, therefore, you achieve some commonality. So we end up talking a lot in financial expressions.

We look at our plastics business, our appliance business, our locomotive business, and we understand what their return on capital is, and their cash flow and earnings, and we understand how they contribute to EVA.

INFORMATION SYSTEMS TO SUPPORT FINANCE

It would seem to be a given that, for a finance organization to operate effectively, the information systems people have to be extraordinarily responsive and flexible, so that they're providing timely information and meeting the changing needs. But I don't hear this spoken about very much in connection with finance.

I think it's a whole *business* need, and I am genuinely excited about an announcement that was in the paper today [April 9, 1996]. For the first time ever, we have named a chief information officer at the senior vice president level. As you might expect, it's a man who's been with us for some time— Gary Reiner.

He can help us move into the next stage of technological thinking. If you have an emphasis on speed and an ability to move quickly and you're taking your order-to-delivery cycle from 18 weeks to three days, then you have different information technology and information systems needs than you did before.

And it's not a matter of bigger and faster computers.

Right. It has nothing to do with bigger and faster computers. In fact, maybe it's *less* data!—because you don't need all these things that tell you what the market is going to be like 18 weeks from now. You can't possibly sit there and say, "I'm pretty confident that four-and-a-half months from now, in Northern Indiana, there's going to be this great demand for pink refrigerators with purple polka-dot liners." But if it's three days, you have at least a shot at saying, "They're asking for them now; so, why won't they still be asking for them three days from now?"

How can information technology lead that parade? Doesn't the CFO have to tell them what's needed?

I'd say no—because I think the CFO is too narrow; I think the *business* has to tell them. Sure, a CFO who has a good all-across-the-business view can play a big role. But the information officer has to be listening and understanding the business needs.

Embarking on a three-year development project for some information system is crazy because you know that, in today's world, by the time you get it done, it won't be any good anyway. You cannot let yourself do that. You cannot be out there developing new information systems.

All the MRP [materials/manufacturing resource planning] systems that we installed in the '80s and early '90s—we're just rolling them up right and left because they're not any good anymore. We've got to replace them with something that gives real-time information.

LEARNING FROM WAL-MART

GE seems like a very self-sufficient company. Do most of your operating ideas develop internally?

We have a whole initiative we call "quick market intelligence"; it's something we learned from Wal-Mart!

Wal-Mart holds a weekly "pace of the business" meeting for its managers from all over the country. The managers all fly back to Bentonville [Arkansas].

They take action across the board. "Lava lamps are hot in Milwaukee this week"—so they get every lava lamp in the inventory and send it to Milwaukee.

There's no rocket science about this, but you better know whether you have any lava lamps, and how to get them there, and when. You better have the information systems to do that, and give you the answers quickly enough, or those opportunities are going to be lost.

PRICE AND SPEED

In your years in the business arena, what are some of the key changes you've seen taking place?

One is that, in today's pricing environment, you can't wake up in the morning and say, "I think we ought to raise prices 5%." Those days are gone, and the only hope you have of getting a good price in today's market is to have something people want and nobody else has. If you do, and if you're fast enough to respond to that need, then you can ask for a price premium.

After the World Trade Center bombing, one of the things the Trade Center people needed to get the place back running was some huge air-handling equipment, because the equipment was in the basement and it had all been blown up. They were getting bids from everybody in the world that makes air-handling equipment, and they were being given delivery offers of six months, eight months, a year.

American Standard said, "Would next week be okay?" You think American Standard didn't get paid extra for that? Of course they did.

It's in those kinds of situations that you find the opportunity to get rewarded for the value you're adding in today's world. But you need information technology not just to follow you there, but to *lead* you there. Because it's information technology, and knowledge, and data, that are going to provide the ability to respond in situations like that.

THE CFO AS A PEOPLE-MANAGER

I have 30 direct reports, and Jack [Welch] has a comparable number. I obviously don't have half an hour a day to spend with each one of them; neither does he. And he's very good at spending time with people—he's the best I've ever seen at making time available.

What that situation forces you to do is to constantly challenge yourself to make sure you have the very best people doing the job. People have always asked me, "How do you spend your time?" I start reeling off this list, which always adds up to 400%.

THE FINANCE PROPOSAL AT GE

When a business manager needs to get approval on a major project, what's the process like—how much documentation, and so on?

As a company, we're relatively informal, but that doesn't mean that a proposal is not thought through. And it depends on what it is; some of them may be not much more than three pages with five bullets on a page.

We're capable of making some pretty fast decisions here. I remember one of my early experiences, long before I became CFO. I worked a year and a half on making a $34 million acquisition—and then we were unsuccessful . . . (laughing) probably because we spent a year and a half on it!

A $1.5 BILLION DEVELOPMENT PROJECT

Out of this culture—high performance, high pressure, high expectations—we believe that each one of our businesses is better for being a part of us–because we can provide them management talent and financial resources.

In the middle of the worst recession that anybody has seen in the commercial airline industry, as well as the military side of aircraft engine manufacturing, we embarked on the biggest development program in the history of our company, the GE-90 engine.

We're spending $1.5 billion to develop a brand-new engine, and we made the decision in the context of that depressed environment.

We could do that because engines aren't the only things that we have; we have other things that we can balance it with.

What does it take to make a decision of that magnitude? Is it strictly a numbers decision?

Whether it's right or wrong, only time will tell. Considering the pricing environment in the market at this moment, it's hard to get excited about the wisdom of the decision. But, as we sat around and looked at it, I remember the remark that Jack made as we were chewing our fingernails and wondering, Do we move forward on this? The projections show cash flow crossover about the time my one-year-old grandson will graduate from college; that's when cash flows will start being cumulatively positive.

Jack's statement at the time was, "If we think the aircraft engine business is going to be a good business for the next 50 years, until 2025, and if our successors are going to be in that business, playing a prominent role, then we have to move forward with this engine development."

It's a very long-term decision, but that's one of the benefits of having this great big, powerful, wonderful company, with a great big balance sheet, and great financial strength, and a long-term history of earnings performance—you can make those kinds of decisions. And even if they're wrong—as devastating as that might be—you haven't bet your company.

"BETTING THE FARM"

How does that translate to a working guideline for someone who's running the financial operations of a $100 million company?

We make decisions here on development programs, and new-product programs, just like anyone else does in the context of their $100 million company.

Some of the best entrepreneurs and businessmen have believed enough in what they were doing and how they were moving forward—whether it was Henry Ford or Steve Jobs or Bill Gates—to get them up and running. But you do sometimes have to make decisions where you're betting the company.

You need to be careful that you aren't making too many of those at one time. We got ourselves in that bind maybe 25 years ago, when we had made three really big decisions—on nuclear power, on computers, and on jet engines. We finally reached the conclusion that, as big a company as we were, we couldn't take the swing on all three of those. And so we got out of computers; maybe that was the wrong thing to get out of, but we did.

I think it's very hard to generalize, but anybody sitting there with a $100 million company that wants to make it a $1 billion company, by definition, has to make these decisions, he has to take bets like that.

THE ROLE OF INTUITION

Making that kind of bet takes good information; what else does it take?

People ask us, "In a company like GE, with all its diversity, how do you run it without having huge mechanisms of bureaucracy?"

Part of the answer to that is low turnover of people. When people start moving into the leadership ranks of this company, they'd better plan on staying around for a little while. Because to make decisions as quickly as you have to make them in today's world, you really do need what I'll call "intuition."

I don't think intuition is one of those things you're born with or not born with; I think it's an accumulation of experiences. When you have something presented to you, you crank it through your head, ask the three right questions, and make a decision. You're able to do that because you're reasonably intuitive about the business environment.

You're suggesting that intuition grows out of experience.

That's my view. I know that I'm a more intuitive business person today than when I took this job 12 years ago and that I'm better at making, or helping to make, decisions on behalf of the company.

If intuition is just an artifact of experience, how does intuition differ from experience?

I think you have to be able to take all these experiences and learn something from them. I suppose you could say that, if you can't absorb the experiences and make some logic and reason out of them, then you're not gaining in the ability to respond intuitively. It has to do with an ability to process what you've learned.

Personally, I may not be very intuitive about locomotives, but I know I'm a lot more intuitive about our locomotive business today than I was 12 years ago. I don't claim to be an expert in the broadcasting business either, but I know I'm more intuitive about NBC and that industry than I was when we acquired it.

WHO DOES GE ENVY? SMALLER COMPANIES!

Obviously, size brings a lot of benefits, but it must bring some tough disadvantages, too.

We are envious of people in smaller-sized companies because, to us, it means that they're closer to the customer, they're faster, they're not burdened by as much bureaucracy. As much work as we've done to get rid of bureaucracy, it still exists.

When I talk to people in smaller companies, I tell them, "As you become more successful, you have to change the way things work." Everybody can't be involved in everything anymore. But the thing they have to work really hard at, as they get big, is continuing to think small and protecting all those things that were valuable to them when they were a smaller company. The closeness to the customer, the closeness to the market, the ability to make fast decisions because you're close to everything—you have to keep that edge.

DAMMERMAN'S TWO METRICS FOR THE SMALL COMPANY

What's your recommendation to the leader or financial person in this smaller company you're talking about? What two metrics would you tell them to look at?

If a small company is going to have only two measurements that it worries about, they ought to be cash flow and customer satisfaction.

And it should do everything it can to keep that small-company character. Don't start trying too early to think like a bigger company. I've seen so many companies all of a sudden start infrastructure, adding businesses, doing all these things.

But how does a company grow larger without falling into that trap?

Take advantage of what you have. Of course, as you grow larger you have to change, but don't put in things that artificially, unnecessarily remove you from the action. Don't put in layers that are supposed to be there for control but instead really just filter. Don't lose what is your real advantage; if you've been growing with the business, your advantage is how intuitive you are about the business, what your instincts are. Don't sit there and have it filtered fourteen times.

What we've done here at GE is to spend the last fifteen years trying to eliminate those things that were filters, and get back closer to the action. Instead of having nine layers between the bottom of the company and the top, we have four—we're getting closer.

People in a small- or medium-sized business that's on a growth path have all this intuition, all this knowledge; they can make fast, intuitive decisions. But they can't if they don't even know that something's happening out there, if there isn't a mechanism to get information up to them quickly. Because you'll have bureaucracies analyzing the problem fifteen ways to Sunday. You get layers of questioners. And then you lose what you brought to the table.

It's a tough balance, but you've got to remember what brought you to the dance. If you're a small company on a growth path, it's this small cadre of people you've put together—that's what brought you to the dance. Don't lose the knowledge and the feel and the gut.

DENNIS DAMMERMAN

Personal Perspectives

Did you have finance in mind from the start?

When I was in college, I didn't have any idea what I wanted to be. I got an economics degree from a small school in Iowa [University of Dusquesne, class of '67] and planned to go on to graduate school for a Ph.D. in economics.

But then the draft deferment was dropped for students in graduate school, so I went job-hunting instead. I had two job offers—one was from GE, in the financial management program, and the other was from United Airlines, in a brand-new entry-level training program. I told the United man that GE had offered me a job in the FMP program, and he said, "I'd really like you to come to work for us, but if you've got an offer from FMP, you'd be crazy not to take it."

I really wasn't very attuned to finance, even though I'd taken a couple of accounting courses. But I liked it—I found a lot to stimulate intellectual curiosity, and I was learning on a daily basis.

Some people enter a finance job, get stuck in a cave of numbers, and never again see the light of day. That obviously wasn't your experience. Were you doing something differently early on?

When I was a cost accountant, for example, I spent more time out on the factory floor than I did back in my office because I wanted to know what all those things were that I was costing; I wanted to know what they were made of and what they were for.

They were thrilled to have somebody who was curious about that. It got to the point where I could take people on plant tours because I knew enough about the manufacturing processes. In GE, people are still like this.

Finance, I found, got you involved in all the functions of the business. You at least got a look. Then, when I was in marketing financial analysis, I got the chance to learn a little bit about marketing, and so on. So I found it a great way to get to know about a business.

72

Is this the exception today or the norm?

I've seen a dramatic change all across the finance function of America in terms of what the CFOs and the finance departments see as their role—how they've evolved from being "backward-oriented" to being a lot broader.

By and large, I think GE has been one of the leaders of that movement, and I think people are moving more and more in that direction.

I think, for a young person getting out of school today, finance is a terrific place to work. Although there's this sense that the grass is always greener over in an operational job, we find that, while people enjoy time spent in a cross-functional assignment, when they get back into a big finance job, they remember the experience of being able to look across the whole business and have an impact on the whole business.

So, we're finding that they want to go out and get the cross-functional experience, and then they want to come back.

It takes a different breed than it used to—and it's one of the things I think C.P.A.s have to worry about a bit—that the experience base the accounting firms provide their people is very much attuned to the older model rather than to the newer one.

But they're making changes, too. KPMG, our accountants, used to get 75% of their new employees right out of college. Today, they hire about 75% with one or two years of business.

CHAPTER 6

TRACKING SUCCESS WITHOUT COMPLEX METRICS: CASH FLOW AT ALLIEDSIGNAL

An Interview with Tom Zusi,
Vice President of Finance and Chief Financial Officer,
AlliedSignal Aerospace

Recent years have been good ones for AlliedSignal. While the company's revenues have increased by only 20% from 1991 to 1995, net profit turned around dramatically, improving from losses of $273 million in 1991 and $712 million in 1992 to a positive $875 million by the end of the period.

In the time that Tom Zusi has been CFO of the Aerospace Division, contracts from a major customer, the federal government, have continued to decline; net profits have nonetheless been increasing—a tribute to management's decision making.

The interview was conducted in Zusi's office at the division's headquarters just south of Los Angeles.

THE BUSINESSES OF ALLIED

The corporate name, AlliedSignal, doesn't really give much of a clue about what businesses the company is in.

TOM ZUSI:
Basically, we are a $14 billion business, in three primary areas: aerospace, automotives, and engineering materials.

In automotives, we have a little shy of $4 billion revenues, basically in friction materials, an aftermarket that includes AutoLite and Fram filters, and a turbocharger business.

Engineer materials have also grown to just $4 billion. That's really the nucleus of the old Allied Chemical, which is what started this company. We have stayed in polymers and fibers, tire fibers, carpet materials, and plastics.

In aerospace, which is our part of the business here, we are the largest supplier to the commercial aircraft industry. There's no plane that flies that doesn't have a part of ours on it: avionics, environmental controls, auxiliary power units, turboprop and fan-jet engines, executive jets, and regional jets.

DON'T HIRE INDUSTRY EXPERTS

When you first got to the Aerospace sector, what were some of the changes you made in the finance organization?

When I came and tried to re-energize this organization, I avoided recruiting people out of aerospace, because I didn't want their paradigm. I wanted people from the Pepsis and Motorolas of the world. I hired a fellow from GE Capital Leasing; well, what does he know about aerospace? I don't care. He has the fundamental skills.

I'm a great believer in that principle. Even when I went to oil and gas, they said, "What do you know about oil and gas?" and I said, "What do I need to know?" I can go to a class and learn what I need about the fundamentals in a couple of days. It's the broad skills that one brings that are going to carry the day, not knowing how you drill or what types of navigational instruments an airplane needs.

Is that wisdom that applies only to the finance department?

No. To me, the ability to be a leader transcends all functions—the ability to be a good listener, a good problem solver, a person who can bring action and energy to a company and push it into areas that it hadn't thought about. Those are the skill sets I look for when I do my recruiting.

FINANCE SYSTEMS: KEEP IT SIMPLE

That's the people side of what you've been doing here; how about the processes and systems of the finance operation?

We do not have state-of-the-art systems. I don't want to create financial systems. What I want to do is to make sure we have world-class processes that will generate sufficient information for me to manage my fiduciary responsibilities, and to generate what the business people need in order to be successful. So I'm not going to put in a set of stand-alone financial systems.

People say, "Let's put it in a cost system." I wouldn't put it in a cost system, especially after having seen what the Japanese are doing. All I want to know is ins and outs.

We used to build massive cost systems because we had all this inventory. No one wants inventory anymore. If you have just-in-time one day of inventory, you don't need the massive systems that we've had in the past. You need very simple ones.

I asked the president of one Japanese company about inventory, and he said, "I know every day where my inventory is. I know how much we receive because I pull from my suppliers only what I need to produce on the floor, and I know what we ship." And then he said, "Except for one supplier, and that happens to be my American partner—he doesn't ship on time, so I've a buffer for that!" Which was humorous.

The Japanese talk about one-piece flow. They had a machine in one place we visited that was very complex, did lots of operations. And our host said, "That's the next thing we do an analysis on." If you just look at the fact that this machine performs so many operations, you say, "That's great; no one has to touch it." But it's very complicated to maintain, so you've got downtime, and you've got maintenance costs. What was very interesting was that, as you look at their processes and their one-piece flows, their view was toward the simplistic.

In the same way, I would say that, in financial systems, we are going to have to go toward simplicity. We tend to make things much more complicated than they need to be. That's why I'm opposed to these heavy cost systems—we get information that I'm certain we don't use at all. It certainly doesn't help us make better business decisions, it certainly doesn't help us reduce the cost, it certainly doesn't make our relationship with our customer any better. You have to think it through and see how simple you can make it.

Another example: We're working today on activity-based management, and people say, "Why don't you put that in as a cost system?" I say, "No, it's a tool."

VARIABILITY AS A NONFINANCIAL METRIC

What metrics would you have on that list of things you most need?

We need to know the major input items that have variability. For example, in procurement, we need to know what hits the dock and what we've ordered, so that we know what ultimately is going to come rumbling through the process.

We need to keep track of our labor base—what we're doing with overtime, what we're doing with temporaries, etc. They have both a cash flow and an income implication.

You focus on the areas that cause variability in the manufacturing process. If scrap were the biggest item, then I'd probably want to find a way to capture what we're doing there, and so on.

In the past, we always tried to assign variability to a product. I might make the argument: Let's capture the variability of our manufacturing performance—and that relates to the manufacturing process, not to the product. What we need to do is, using activity-based management, to validate periodically what it really costs to produce a product, or what it should cost, and that's our model.

So, for purposes of looking into the price/life cycle of the product, what are you going to sell it for today, what are you going to sell it for tomorrow, what do you have to produce?

But notice that I don't need to know individual product cost. I don't need standard cost by every one of the components. All I want to do is to make sure that I get all the variability out of the manufacturing process. That's a whole different kind of concept.

I don't need to look as often at the things that don't have variability. They're going to be reasonably predictable, and I don't need to look at the fixed costs—I know what's going to happen.

So, you create a simple model just by going back and saying: What are the key variables? Let's capture just those on the level that's appropriate. With just those things, I can pretty well tell you how my business is doing.

If I were to tell you my vision of what a cost system would be, I would describe something quite different than you might expect. I might start by asking my manufacturing people to tell me what they need to know. If you think about the manufacturing process, really, it isn't so much that this widget cost you $1.20 and the next one cost you $1.25. What that represents is the variability in the manufacturing process. So, track the variability.

OTHER NONFINANCIAL MEASURES

In the nonfinancial area, what are some of the key things that you're providing to your managers?

It's interesting. We now, as an organization, are disseminating information quarterly. Each quarter, we do what we call an operations excellence review with [corporate CEO] Larry Bossidy. I participate in it, as do the manufacturing people, the material people, and the quality people.

We basically came up with a very simple chart and we said, "Our customer is number one. Here are the metrics we need." The chart features what we need to focus on in order to grow and integrate: revenue growth, productivity, cycle time reduction, cost of poor quality, our financial commitments—cash flow, net income, working capital turns—and so on; also safety and employee satisfaction.

Basically it becomes a very simple process. Each item on the chart is color-coded red, yellow, or green—obviously, you know what those mean. What's key is that we establish targets with each business-unit manager. You say where you are performing and where you're not.

Those that aren't green, we need to know more about, and we spend time working those issues. Basically, we start a "drill-down process," going deeper on the red and yellow items until we identify what level the problem is at.

What this process does is make you think today what's going to go wrong in the next quarter and the quarter after that. And then you know you need to figure out what you're going to do to correct it or compensate for it. Because the problems will occur—there's no question about it; the only question is, which ones, and how soon?

The big thing with Larry has been the ability of AlliedSignal to perform consistently. We just reported that we've now had 17 quarters in a row of earnings improvement at 14% or greater. That's how you get P/Es. This is not magical—earnings growth translates into stock performance.

THE IMPORTANCE OF CASH FLOW

You seem to be doing well without using EVA or another of today's more powerful financial tools. What would the argument be in favor of using them?

I think EVA may help a manager understand how cash translates into shareholder value. I find at AlliedSignal—and I don't think we're the exception—that managers down through the organization don't fully understand cash flow. And, to me, until you master an understanding of cash flow throughout the organization, going to the next level up with EVA isn't going to work.

EVA is probably a good tool for senior financial managers and strategic thinkers to take a look at, but I'm not sure it's going to be useful down through the organization.

CASH FLOW AND INCOME

How do you explain cash flow so that people at the working levels understand it?

I try to explain that cash flow is about generating cash, and knowing how to save it, and when to spend it. When you try to think of it in other terms, you only cloud the issue. Some people get confused when they look at net income and cash flow because the numbers don't match up quarter to quarter.

But, over time, net income and cash flow will always be equal. They don't look the same because it takes time before an investment makes money for you; then the cash comes back in.

For us in AlliedSignal today, the thing that drives stock price, more than cash flow, is income. It's what's left after we sell our product, pay out what it costs to produce it, pay interest, and pay taxes. Smart investors would say that the cash a company generates is the ultimate measure of success. Companies that are truly successful learn how to generate income in the short term, as well as plenty of cash flow to reinvest in the business. And those companies will be the premier companies of the future. That's why, at AlliedSignal, there's such a passion over generating both income and cash.

There's also a misconception that only a few people can affect cash flow. The fact is, every employee can impact it.

Most employees are good at managing their own money. They know how much comes in, and they plan how much to spend and how much to save. The amount they save is their cash flow. They use it for investments such as a home, retirement savings, and so on. What we'd like employees to do is to apply their personal cash flow skills at work; that is, spend the company's money as they spend their own.

CHANGING EMPLOYEE ATTITUDES
ABOUT CASH FLOW

What will it take to get the cash flow message clearly communicated?

We are maturing in trying to change the whole behavioral pattern. Companies struggle with this because, by the time you start thinking about cash, it's really too late—the only things you can do are basically out of your control.

We're trying to go to a rolling 13-week cash flow forecast. I'm actually trying to drive our financial reporting to weekly reporting. The intent is not traditional closing-the-books weekly reporting. It's selective—limited to the items that are really important, the things that will tell me and the business people what they need in order to know that the business is running okay and the cash is okay. That's all I want to know.

The thing we've seen that's most difficult in cash is that it doesn't coincide with the income time frame. When you're halfway through the quarter, you've basically finished the cash cycle because you've shipped all the product you're going to ship on which you can get paid before the end of the period.

The materials people said last November, "Oh, but inventory will be down by the end of December." I said, "Okay, now where is it going to go?" "We're going to ship it," they said. I said, "Are you going to get paid by the end of December?" "Well, no," they said. And I said, "Time out—you haven't helped me with cash." So, we've modified the cash flow cycle. We've gone to weekly cash flow calls with our management team.

Is that explanation getting across throughout the organization?

I think we're succeeding in getting our people to understand that, without cash, we can't spend money on engineering, we can't fund new capital equipment, and we can't buy companies that will help strengthen our strategic position. Cash allows us to reinvest in the business. It's our lifeblood.

I wrote an article in our quarterly newspaper that basically says: "Everybody contributes to cash flow." And we're in the process of rolling out a five-minute video that we can deploy all the way down to the shop floor. We hope, by the end of this year, that everyone will have seen the video.

It has a workshop with it that basically says to managers, "What are the things that you do that influence cash flow?" We want them to be able to reply, for example, "If I order parts and pull more inventory in, someone's got to buy the finished products." "If we spend more money than our department budget, that hurts us." "If we don't get the product out in time, the customer won't pay for it in time for it to show in this reporting period."

I went out to one operation that was a captive manufacturing unit, and I asked, "How are you doing in cash flow?" The manager said, "We're captive, we have no cash flow." I said, "Wait, let's sit down; bring the team in here."

I asked, "Do you order product?" "Yes." And I said, "Well, you have to pay for that."

I asked him, "Do you ship product?" "Yes."

I said, "The sooner you ship it, the sooner we can collect it."

So, as in any other company, we have people who are just thinking in terms of what they do, not in terms of how they can change the cycle time of cash by changing their behavior.

How well are you doing at meeting your cash flow goals?

If we look at our cash flow performance for 1995, we did very well in generating income, collecting from our customers, and spending less than anticipated. So we did all the things to help bring in cash.

But cash flow disappointments really showed up in inventory. Specifically, we didn't make sure that we only brought into our factories the things our customers wanted. We also spent too much money on overtime pay, supplies, and so forth.

All these things show up as inventory. We continue to work on the problem of having the right material and getting it through our manufacturing processes and out the other end in the shortest time period.

Do you have some specific receivables goals that you're working toward right now?

We'll be taking past-due receivables down by 25%.

CASH FLOW METRIC AT THE EXECUTIVE LEVEL

Are you also using cash flow as a metric at the executive level of the sector?

The president, manufacturing, materials, and I get on the phone 15 minutes a week with each business to go over all the basics. What materials did you bring in? Did you ship what you were supposed to ship? In fact, one of the units back in the fourth quarter said that it would give its employees an extra two days off if they shipped everything they needed to by Thanksgiving, because if they shipped by Thanksgiving, they knew we'd collect the receivables by year-end.

Tell me the revenue stream and how many employees I have. That's pretty easy. These are very simple metrics one can look at and know the well-being of the business. That's where I think we need to improve the most—getting the information we most need, on a timely basis.

BEING SEAMLESS TO THE CUSTOMER

We used to do business with one airline that had to deal with 17 different businesses in AlliedSignal. They got 17 different invoices, which they paid to 17 different places. Well, that's not very friendly.

Our strategy today is to be transparent to the customer and to be one company. We've got to be seamless to the customer.

WHAT THE BUSINESS MANAGERS NEED FROM FINANCE

Our business people need information that isn't just financial. They need information that the competitors don't have, that maybe tells them to adjust their price, or to try to figure out how to solve a cost problem—but information that allows them to do something different than the competition will do.

If I look at our financial systems today, it takes too long to close the books because we've got these humongous systems that are cranking out all this data that really doesn't tell you everything. So, I'm launching a revolution, if you will. It's a revolution saying I'm not going to put in financial systems; I'm going to try to lead and drive world-class process and systems improvements. I will make sure there is only the minimal financial information produced for finance to execute our fiduciary responsibility.

But the focal point is getting the right information to the right people. Some of it will be financial, and some of it will be operational in nature, such as defects per thousand units. That's a whole different mind-set than how we've managed in the past.

TOM ZUSI

Personal Perspectives

ZUSI'S BACKGROUND

Did you have an accounting background before coming here?

I started in public accounting at Price Waterhouse. AlliedSignal was my major client, and the Allied people enticed me to join them. I've been with Allied 15 years and I started—no surprise—as the director of audit. I've basically moved up through a series of positions in finance.

LEVERAGED BUYOUT

I also spent a couple of years at Allied's oil and gas business in Texas as the VP controller. While I was there, we did a leveraged buyout in which KKR [Kohlberg, Kravis, Roberts & Co.] purchased half the company. In what was at the time a rare situation, Allied retained a 50% interest and KKR had a 50% interest.

That must have been a wonderful place for you to be sitting at that point. You got to take part in a very unusual kind of transaction; it's not that uncommon today, but most people who go through a finance career never have the chance to see one.

We leveraged up a business with $1 billion in debt, with the oil price at $22; within three months, oil was at $8. It was very humbling because, in a leverage buyout, cash is king—not the earnings you report. You have to realign your skill sets to be well focused on cash generation.

We went from a very internal organization, within the safety blanket of the corporation, to a company that had lots of money at risk, where we had large borrowings; we had to operate and behave differently because we were trying to survive. It wasn't just the LBO—it was an LBO in which the marketplace had eroded substantially, which created another dynamic on top of the LBO. It was a great experience.

The controller's job was a change from what you had been doing in the department?

When I went down there as the controller, it was in the traditional subsidiary kind of role within AlliedSignal and, though cash flow had a place in the pecking order of importance, it wasn't as critical to success. But when you do a leveraged buyout, obviously, the play is cash. You need to pay down the debt and get to a position where you can spin off some stock—or whatever exit strategy you choose.

It requires a different perspective—you can actually see management operate differently, even within a $2 billion business. Although, ultimately, with the decline in oil, it ended up being about a $1 billion business!

Then, after I had been there a couple of years, the position of controller of AlliedSignal opened up, and I was asked to take on the role. I moved from Texas back to Morristown, New Jersey, and was the VP and controller of the corporation. I held that position for over seven years.

Dan Burnham [president of the Aerospace Division] had been after me to come to Aerospace and help develop the finance function here. Not that I didn't have a chance to play that role as the corporate controller, but there's a big difference between what you can do on a day-to-day basis when you're closer to the action, versus what you can do when you are trying to do work at the top, where a lot of your time is spent with the investment community, the board of directors, and so on.

CAREER LESSONS

Looking back on your career, have there been one or two major incidents or events that you feel gave you especially valuable lessons in working finance?

Besides the LBO, I think the other most valuable experience was having a chance to watch Larry Bossidy come in and mold the company.

If there's any one area that he would bug me about—both in my old role as his controller and in my new role as the CFO of this business—it's the quality of my team. He knows his executives can't get the job done individually; he knows the next level down can't do it all—so you have to start cascading down to identify talented people who can help drive the business. We are only as good as our people.

Larry places a significant responsibility on the finance people. If things don't go well, he's as likely as my boss to kick me. That's the role we play.

He expects us to be constantly challenging the organization, purging out the problems, being the coach, being the cheerleader, and doing all those things. He believes that, without setting high expectations and bringing in a world-class team, you're never going to get there.

I think just watching him for those two years was probably a career by itself. It was a tremendous opportunity.

ON THE CHANGES IN FINANCE

In an overview, what are the changes you see happening in finance today—not just at AlliedSignal but elsewhere as well?

In finance, we spend too much time looking backward; we need to spend way more time participating. When Larry Bossidy came, he caused us to look more forward—and that was a struggle because he set some very ambitious goals for us.

For us, maturing is our ability to constantly be ahead of the game. As Larry would often say, "What you need to worry about today is tomorrow's problem. If you are only worrying about today's problem, you will always be worrying about today's problem and you will always be behind."

Finance is losing a lot of its definition, not because it's not bringing value to the company but because we're aligning ourselves with processes. My view is that the finance function in the future will have only very few people that are "financial." What you'll have is people disseminated throughout the organization in manufacturing, in materials, on the distribution side, that have very good financial skills, that are comfortable with numbers, that are comfortable with doing analysis, that can help the business people, the process leaders, be successful. That's basically how we're deploying our resources.

Will finance come to be called something else as its mission changes? I don't think that will happen.

We rarely talk about where this profession is going. Traditionally we had a transaction orientation, and we focused on the past. We need to spend time focusing on the future.

"THINGS I WISH I'D KNOWN EARLIER"

Are there one or two key financial metrics or approaches that you wish you had known about earlier in your career?

Without question, cash flow. Not that I didn't know about it, but we weren't driving it the same way. Actually, at one point, when we were struggling to generate the level of cash we wanted, I said, "I'll tell you how you change the behavior. Don't measure income anymore; only measure cash. Everything is cash."

However, we've got to go to the Street, and we have to have earnings. I believe that, if you generate cash other than by liquidating the company, the likelihood is that you're going to generate healthy earnings. You can't get the cash without earnings.

Even in my days back in the LBO, we were focusing on cash, and maybe that's how we survived, yet it never really resonated with me. I think now, without any question, that if you have a mentality of growing and developing a business and you put great emphasis on cash, it will all come together.

When Larry Bossidy came to AlliedSignal, cash was clearly second fiddle. And of course, whenever you put a metric second, you don't have to guess what the performance will be relative to what's first. What you measure is what you get.

CHAPTER 7

RISK MANAGEMENT AS SEEN FROM STANFORD BUSINESS SCHOOL

An Interview with Darrell Duffie, Ph.D.,
Professor of Finance,
Graduate School of Business,
Stanford University

Darrell Duffie earned his undergraduate degree in Canada and his master's in Australia; his doctorate, in engineering economic systems, is from Stanford University. He has worked in industry as an engineer and is the author of three books on securities and futures markets. His many articles have appeared in such works as the Journal of Mathematical Economics, *and* The New Palgrave Dictionary of Money and Finance.

Despite his impressive credentials, Duffie belies the image of the university professor as stuffy and remote. He showed up for our meeting wearing a polo shirt and carrying a backpack and helmet: he had bicycled from home to join me for lunch at the Stanford Faculty Club.

Although his expertise covers a variety of areas, he's a recognized authority on risk management and the use of the sometimes suspect instruments called derivatives. These subjects were the focus of our conversation.

THE BASICS OF RISK MANAGEMENT

Probably the most widely known kind of risk-management instrument is the derivative. How do you explain the basic principle of derivatives to people who are unfamiliar with their use?

DARRELL DUFFIE:

A typical definition of derivative would be a financial contract whose payments are keyed to some other economic indexes, usually the prices of other underlying assets. For example, an option on an interest rate would give you the right, but not the obligation, to borrow at a certain interest rate.

Or an option on a foreign exchange would give you the right, but not the obligation, to buy a given quantity of, say, deutsche marks at a certain time and a certain price. In these cases, the derivatives are keyed to some underlying index like the interest rate or exchange rate. The index is usually the price of some other financial security, though not always.

And in teaching a course on derivatives, what you're teaching is how to evaluate the risk in a particular situation?

Yes. At Stanford we have two courses in this area. One teaches how these derivative markets work, what the instruments are, how they're priced and, in a more narrow sense, how they're hedged. In other words, the course addresses how one would control the risk of a derivative position; it centers around the derivatives themselves.

Then we have a more advanced course called Corporate Financial Risk Management. This has a much more managerial focus, which takes what students learn in the derivative market course and applies it to particular decisions by corporations. So, if you're with an international corporation—for example, Merck, the global pharmaceutical company—and the company is receiving billions of dollars every year in foreign revenues, what would you do to set up a system to control that financial risk by using derivatives?

What are the accounting implications? What incentives do you need to create with your managers? What are the regulatory implications? What kinds of instruments might you want to use? What kinds of software might you want to use? These are the sorts of questions addressed by this second course.

TYPES OF RISK-MANAGEMENT INSTRUMENTS

What types of risk-management instruments are we talking about here?

You could break derivatives themselves into two classes, one of which is exchange-traded, and that would be the one that you're probably most familiar with—futures contracts, or exchange-traded options contracts. When you see a TV news scene of a commodities exchange, these are the things that you see people on the exchange floor yelling at each other about.

Then there are the over-the-counter derivatives, which are bilateral contracts negotiated between company A and company B. So, for example, I would pay you every six months such and such an amount if you promise to pay me in return whatever the current six-month interest rate is for the next five years. And we'll set up that arrangement in our contract.

That's called a *swap,* which is by far the most common kind of derivative. That's an over-the-counter derivative, not traded on an exchange.

And then there are other risk-management products that are, in essence, one-off contracts. It could be a securitized asset or liability. For example, insurance companies are getting interested now in selling bonds whose coupons are keyed to the liabilities that they face through the insurance claims. They would control their financial risk by virtue of issuing these special products.

Or there could be credit-card receivables that are securitized and sliced in various ways. Those products are sold into the marketplace, usually to relieve one party of certain kinds of risks. So these might not really be called derivatives, but they're structured products that are used in the management of financial risk.

Those are the principal kinds of risk-management instruments.

USING DERIVATIVES: CAPITAL-INVESTMENT EXAMPLE

How about an example that makes it clear why a derivative product might be used and how the deal is worked out.

Let's suppose that I was about to set up a factory in Japan. I've asked you to be the manager in charge of making that decision. You know that your success in this firm depends on how good your decision turns out to be. You'll be going through a thought process something like this: If you set up this factory and the Japanese yen depreciates dramatically and we lose our shirts, people are not necessarily going to be able to sort out that it wasn't your fault, that it's just an exchange-rate movement that nobody could have predicted or controlled.

I may find I've just built a factory that isn't making enough return to earn the cost of capital.

Right—and the possibility that this might happen presents a risk to you personally. So you won't set up this factory, even though you know that, in principle, it's a positive net present value project and would therefore add value to the firm. But in this situation, where you have to take this risk on your own shoulders, you're just going to avoid it.

Since you know more than anyone else about whether the decision is right or wrong, you're not going to be held accountable for avoiding the situation.

The company is just going to accept that I've determined that the investment in the factory is not justified.

You're not going to be blamed for making an inappropriate decision.

Yet, all things considered, it's not the right thing for you to do.

But suppose you happen to know that you can control the risk associated with the depreciation of the Japanese yen. You can do this by taking offsetting derivatives positions. Now you can capture the positive market value of this project and not be subject to this risk of the yen.

In this example you've given, what sort of derivative instruments might work to protect the investment?

This sort of thing may be a foreign exchange swap—a commitment of your firm to pay a certain number of U.S. dollars every six months, and receive a certain number of Japanese yen in return. You'd select a term for the swap based on the life of this project. It could be three years, or five, or ten.

So the rate of exchange is fixed in advance. But doesn't this require that you find somebody who thinks the yen is going to move the opposite way?

Yes, but that's usually not a problem because there are banks whose business it is to locate those counterparts for you. In this case, they'll charge a small premium because it's a fairly liquid contract. If it was something more exotic, then you would want to consider as well the cost associated with the transaction fee. It might be large enough to dissuade you.

CORPORATE BORROWING EXAMPLE

How about a situation that doesn't involve foreign currencies?

Let's suppose I'm running a corporation that needs to borrow from time to time. The market is uncertain of the risk that it faces in buying my bonds. The market doesn't know what the extent of my exposure is to various financial indexes and believes the volatility of my stock is fairly high in the market. There's concern that the market may not get paid back. So what would happen is that it would be willing to buy my bonds only at a lower price or a higher interest rate.

Now, if I could undertake some risk management to control my risk, the market volatility for my stock would go down. The market would perceive that I've got my risk under control, and I might be able to borrow at more attractive rates.

But Nobel prizes were awarded to Franco Modigliani and Merton Miller for showing that simply transferring risk by trading financial securities, unless there's something else going on, is not going to make the situation better. It's not going to improve the market value of the firm. However, in the example I've described, it's the fact that the issuer of the debt knows more about the situation than the investor in the debt that makes this work.

It also presumably reduces the prices the investors are willing to pay for the bonds. The investors don't know as much about the situation.

And that's why the risk management may help. If you can see that the stock price is fairly non-volatile, even if not entirely smooth, then you might be willing to pay more.

But, in an ordinary transaction, the investor wouldn't have access to information about what kind of risk management was being practiced.

But they could see in the marketplace how your stock has been behaving—has it been very volatile or not?

And the volatility tells you how risky the stock is. So a company may be able to command improved stock prices if it can cut down on the volatility simply by using risk-management techniques.

But this is not an easy example to model clearly with the available economic theory, and my comments are quite speculative in this case.

RISK MANAGEMENT FOR THE FIRM
WITH HIGH DEBT

How about the situation of using derivatives for the highly leveraged firm?

In a highly leveraged firm—in other words, one that has a lot of debt—there's some risk that a change in market conditions may drive you to the brink of bankruptcy—for example, through an increase in your commodity costs.

You can reduce the risks of the situation in many cases by taking risk-management measures. So, for example, if you're subject to the cost of energy, you can buy options that allow you to lock in the maximum prices you would have to pay for your energy input for the next three or four years.

That's a very common product on today's energy markets. The New York Mercantile Exchange, among others, sells oil futures contracts. If you buy your oil in advance at a price you know you can handle, energy costs are not going to drive you into bankruptcy. The market sees that you're doing this; it'll bid the price of your stock up because it knows the stock's no longer subject to financial distress costs, and everyone's better off.

RISK MANAGEMENT FOR THE SMALLER FIRM

What's your advice for the smaller firm?

I would say the ideal situation, even for a small firm, is to get involved only to the extent that you can control and understand what you're doing. And sometimes the control aspect means having an independent auditor, which could be your auditing firm, making periodic reviews of positions, and imposing accounting controls and execution controls so that no one is allowed to trade on behalf of the firm without proper independent authorization, and so on.

When I speak about getting outside help, I don't necessarily mean hiring some other firm or consultants to actually run the operation; I mean help for this oversight only. A firm should only get into this business to the extent that it understands what it's doing.

These instruments that we're talking about are often very highly leveraged, and it's easy for mistakes to occur—as in the Bankers Trust and Proctor & Gamble case. I'm not laying blame, but it's alleged that the agents at Bankers Trust acted with a conflict of interest, in that they were both in charge of execution of the positions and, at the same time, to some extent responsible to management for overseeing the degree of exposure.

The oversight can be handled inside the firm but with advice as appropriate from independent sources.

WHEN RISK MANAGEMENT GETS
OUT OF CONTROL

As a result of some of the headline incidents in recent years, I think a lot of people have probably gotten the impression that derivatives

make about as much sense as taking your corporate bankroll to the gaming tables at Las Vegas.

Most of these derivatives disasters have occurred with what one would think of as a large, sophisticated organization that is certain to have a big treasury function, with plenty of resources to put to work controlling this problem.

But in many cases it's simply a lack of control or oversight. I'd say that's the most common source of this problem. It isn't simply that the organization has too big an appetite for risks or, as an organization, has unrealistic objectives about what it can do with these products to generate profits. I think, in most cases, it's one individual who has a false impression that he or she knows what's going on in financial markets and thinks he or she can generate a huge profit. The organization sometimes buys into this idea. Or sometimes a "rogue trader" acts with the approval of the organization. And then disaster strikes because the organization hasn't set up the proper counterchecks to prevent it from happening.

When there is policy and monitoring, when every position has to be tagged "This is an investment" or "This is a hedge," after the fact you'd be able to establish whether this person had simply made an imprudent investment.

OUTSIDE OVERSIGHT

You mention the CEO and CFO. Do they have to do this oversight themselves? Who actually does this?

Inside the company, oversight can be handled by an experienced senior finance person who understands the instruments being used. Sometimes that means the CFO, and sometimes someone else.

But there needs to be oversight from outside as well. Many of the major consulting firms have the capability, in addition to their standard auditing and general accounting work, of coming in and giving a readout on whether the activities in the risk-management area or derivatives area are appropriate. On an ongoing basis, are they meeting the stated objectives and the policies? How big are the positions at the moment? Are they losing or are they not?

Sometimes an additional task like that can be put into the relationship with an auditing firm. And that's a good place to have it, because of the independence of the auditor.

93

So, when does a company call on an individual consultant—somebody like you? Why are you brought in?

There are mainly two kinds of situations. One is that there's a system already in place, and the company needs someone to come in and compare it to the most sophisticated state-of-the-art practice in the areas of risk management that it's involved with. My job would be to make suggestions for improvement, and also to use my reputation in the area as a signal of quality.

In other words, I can send a letter saying that I've reviewed the system and that it meets the requirements for a system of this variety.

To reassure management.

That's right.

Here's another kind of project: A company may say, "We have this particular exposure, and we need some assistance in designing a strategy to defeat it"—that is, to reduce the risk. Or, "We're thinking about marketing a financial product, but we're not sure exactly how to design it, or how to price it, or how to hedge it." I would then go in and set up models in that area.

Those are the two main situations in which a company benefits by bringing in an authority whose expertise includes keeping up with the latest developments.

DARRELL DUFFIE

Personal Perspectives

Do you have some of your own personal guidelines on how a company should use derivatives?

One is: Decide in advance why you're using them. Another is: Establish a system that monitors whether they're being used to meet those objectives.

"Why you're using them"—what's the range of whys? Are there a lot of different possibilities?

Let's take two basic cases. There are situations in which a firm may wish to make investments in a certain area by taking a derivatives position. So, for example, a copper mining and smelting firm that is very knowledgeable in the copper market decides, on the basis of its own excellent analysis of the copper market, that copper is a very good investment this month.

The easiest way for the company to take a position would be through a derivative contract, with no muss, no fuss—it's just a phone call.

On the other hand, risk management may, and often does, include reducing risks associated with the indicated copper prices. Your objectives of risk management in this area must be carefully defined, so that you've decided in advance which trades are designed to reduce risks and which trades are designed to take advantage of temporary opportunities in the market for investment purposes.

The principle is: Make sure you establish a clean distinction between speculative or investment-based derivative positions versus risk-reducing positions.

CHAPTER 8

POWER METRICS AND THE USE OF DERIVATIVES AT FMC AND R.R. DONNELLEY

A continuation of the interview with Cheryl A. Francis, Executive Vice President and Chief Financial Officer, R.R. Donnelley & Sons Company (For background on Cheryl Francis and descriptions of FMC and Donnelley, see the introductory notes to Chapter 4)

Cheryl Francis' reputation in management circles is built in part on her success in dealing with derivatives. Her comments on the subject add real-world experience to Professor Duffie's remarks.

USING DERIVATIVES

What size does a company have to be before it can begin to think about using something as sophisticated as a derivative?

Well, first of all, many derivatives are not very sophisticated. Secondly, it's not a size question, it's a question of the kind of business you're in and the risks that you're trying to manage—because it's just one tool that you have for risk management.

It's just like managing risks through insurance, or by partnering when companies get together to share risks.

In the international environment, derivatives offer one way to protect yourself for currency hedging.

Perfect example: FMC was in the gold business. We sold forward our gold because we knew we were going to be producing it at a certain cost and we knew we could sell it in the open markets however many days hence. And so you sell the gold in the ground, and you get a little extra value as a result of that.

So it depends on the business you're in.

In that case, how far forward were you dealing?

In the gold business, we would sell half the production out to two years, and then, as we got closer, we would up it to about 80% within an 18-month window.

But it had to do with our confidence in our mining plants and our ability to be able to predict the amount of gold we would be producing. It doesn't have anything to do with size.

Did you at some point look back to see how much better off you were for having approached things that way?

Yes, and it always depends on the time period that you pick. Generally speaking, I would say it was a good thing to do, but in an economic sense, not a compelling thing. What it did do was give us a lot of predictability about what the cash flows and earnings would be from that business.

And protection against the unexpected.

Yes, although that didn't prove to be the biggest challenge.

We buy fire insurance not because we expect a fire but to protect us against a calamity.

The place I think we have to be careful with instruments like derivatives involves the same issue. You have to understand the business and match the product that's doing the risk management to the actual risk inherent in the business. When you don't, you're basically speculating.

How about using these instruments in a company that has a lot of cash to manage and is just looking for better ways of increasing the earnings on the cash?

That depends on how you define *better*. If you don't have the matching going on, you're putting more risk in place because you're creating more expected returns. And so, in effect, you've created more of a possibility of a fire rather than just buying insurance. It's a different product then; it's an enhancing product rather than an insurance product.

So your own perspective, I gather, is to use derivatives for risk balancing rather than for earnings.

That's my perspective. We're not in the position of having a lot of excess cash assets, but, for an example, in the pension fund at Donnelley, as was true at FMC, we have very little exposure to people who actively use derivatives and hedge funds, who try to get that extra piece of return through a derivative product.

Are you using derivatives here at Donnelley?

We use them to a very limited degree here—primarily around currency transactions.

The way you describe it, your use of derivatives at FMC was, in a sense, just the natural course of buying insurance in the business.

Because FMC was such an international company, the most active use of derivatives was in the hedging program. What we always tried to do there was to zero out at the end of every day, to match currencies. And the most liquid market to do that in is the derivative market.

What do you mean by "to match currencies"?

We need to get back to dollars—the owners of FMC and the owners of R.R. Donnelley tend to be U.S. investors—dollar-based people. When you're running a business in France that's selling into Italy and you've got certain liabilities that are coming in lire, you need to get that back to a functional currency in French francs. But, eventually, what our investors are concerned about is dollars, and so we have to net to dollars periodically, preferably frequently.

I suppose that's especially true in a country like Brazil or Argentina.

The problem is that you don't have liquid derivative markets. It's so in Mexico as well. Everybody hated to see the peso devaluate the way it did. There's no efficient way in the derivatives market to put an insurance policy in place that's cost-effective—so you're paying one way or you're paying the other. That's just a cost of doing business in Mexico.

If it makes sense for a company to use derivatives and the responsible executives understand how derivatives could help them, but its staff aren't really sophisticated enough themselves to do it, can they turn to an outside source with confidence to advise on that?

Probably, but I wouldn't. If you don't understand it, you shouldn't be doing it. It's not that hard to understand if you're using it simply as a risk-management tool.

It's not hard for the typical finance officer to understand?

The CFO should be able to understand it. Again, you don't have to turn to your investment banker or commercial bank; you can turn to some of your colleagues in the industrial community who have policies and practices in place that should be fairly transferable, if you're trying to use it just to manage the risk of the business.

CHERYL FRANCIS

Personal Perspectives

SHAPING A CAREER: CHERYL FRANCIS MAKES A "NO" INTO A "YES"

Has there been some particular event that became a defining moment or a career-changing moment that dramatically affected your outlook?

Yes, but I'm not sure it's related to what your book is about.

I have two children and had been going great guns at FMC while they were small, up until the point when they were one and four, and then I ran into some real issues at home about child care that if you're a parent, I guess you can understand. It was important that I be home at that point to stabilize things.

So I quit my job, and the people at FMC said, "We want you to do that because you obviously need to, but don't make any decisions about your career; you're not in any position to do that." They asked me to keep talking to them through this period, which I did.

I ended up just taking a leave of absence and eventually coming back part-time. That was interesting, but it didn't go well because I was working with these high-quality people who were used to being able to call on me 24 hours a day, seven days a week. I was supposed to be part-time, so it just didn't compute.

We went through what was for me a very painful period trying to figure out what was realistic.

What sort of role were you supposed to be playing?

Director of investor relations, three days a week, plus I was doing a merger for the gold company at the same time, so I was kind of juggling a few balls—all in three days a week.

It actually worked pretty well from the outside world's perspective, but it drove the chairman and other members of top management completely crazy. And so they drove me crazy.

100

I had to find a place where I could continue to learn and contribute but be in more control of my time. That's when I went to the University of Chicago. I met with the dean and asked, "Do you ever have non-Ph.D.s teach in the business school?" He said, "No."

But there was an "except": "Except if there's an area in the curriculum where we have a gap—a subject where we don't have faculty qualified to teach."

So, on my way out of the dean's office, I grabbed a curriculum guide. I defined a course for them that was not being covered and that I was uniquely qualified to teach.

And that was?

It was called "Finance as a Catalyst for Change."

Then I came back and talked to a dozen of the people on the faculty over lunch. The conversation started by them saying, "What do you mean, 'We have a gap in the curriculum'?"

I took them through exactly what the plan would be and, by the end, the people from the accounting area wanted the course in their curriculum, the people in finance wanted it in theirs, and the people in business policy or strategy wanted it in theirs.

Then I went back to FMC and explained what I had done and why, and that I would be leaving within about a six-month time frame—to give them time to reposition around the investor relations job, which was pretty tough to fill.

It turned out that I never really left FMC, I acted as a consultant for them—on a much more profitable basis, I might add—but on my own clock, while teaching at the university.

The thing that really changed my perspective was that, after I arrived at the University of Chicago, the first day I got six phone calls from people saying, "We had no idea you were leaving; we would have loved you to work part-time on this, or do this project for us." or "Couldn't you think about doing thus and so?" And I found out I had more options than I could possibly have imagined.

So, I was sitting in this box because I was so focused on what I was doing that I didn't understand how many choices were out there. Now I feel very free because I know I'm able to do what I think is right and, if it turns out that it's not right for Donnelley, I have other choices. That's a very empowering feeling.

101

Would you recommend to other people in finance that they consider teaching for a while?

Yes, it's a tremendous exercise for anybody because you have to really know what you're talking about in order to convey it to others in a way that helps them learn, so it's a good learning experience. And it's a very gratifying experience.

CHAPTER 9

SELECTING PROJECTS TO FUND, THE "RONABIT" METRIC, AND BASING DECISIONS ON THEORY AT SUN MICROSYSTEMS

An Interview with William J. Raduchel,
Vice President, Corporate Planning & Development,
and Chief Information Officer, Sun Microsystems

Sun Microsystems started in the classic image of Silicon Valley high-technology companies: it was launched by a group of college friends (the name is an acronym for "Stanford University Nerds"—really!) and has become a $6 billion developer of computer equipment and software. Their modern "campus" is located south of San Francisco in Mountain View, California.

Bill Raduchel, who holds M.A. and Ph.D. degrees from Harvard, served as the CFO of Sun from 1989 to 1991.

Raduchel has a friendly, relaxed laugh that masks one of the keenest financial minds in Silicon Valley. We met in his office, adjacent to the office of Scott McNealy, Sun's CEO and one of the original "nerds."

CHANGES RADUCHEL MADE IN SUN'S FINANCIAL SYSTEMS

You took over as CFO at a time when Sun was in trouble. What metrics were the company using then, and what metrics did you go to?

BILL RADUCHEL:

Our CFO resigned in June of '89. It was the only quarter in which we lost money as a public company. We were in the midst of negotiating a private placement in lieu of doing financing; we delayed signing the private placement to get better interest rates, and then the quarter didn't deliver as planned, and we were sued.

So, basically, we had no cash, we were losing money, we had litigation, and the CFO quit. And I got to be CFO.

We then did $1 billion in financings in less than a year.

The problem was that there was a financial process, but it was slightly disconnected from the operational process. And so, when you went into a meeting, there were always two sets of numbers. There was a set of numbers that the finance people were using, and a set of numbers that the operating people were using—and they had nothing in common.

Today, there's only one set of numbers. The operating and finance people both speak from the same book. That's not a difficult principle, but it wasn't true in Sun at the time. And, by the way, there are lots of companies where that's still not true today.

Finance tends to be after-the-fact reporting, as opposed to managing day-to-day what's going on. We had no way of knowing what we did as a company until 20 to 30 days after the quarter closed. Today, we know revenue, margin, and so on by 10 o'clock each morning.

I had been hired to be VP of planning, and we were just starting our first real planning process at the time. It's hard to manage a company when you don't know what you're doing—there were no real management processes going, no outlook process. When we committed to products, there was no supply/demand process.

Most of what I did as CFO was to engineer process. That, and hiring people. In the end, it was hiring great people.

ABOUT RONABIT

I keep hearing about RONABIT [return on net assets before income and taxes—a metric that Raduchel has become known for because of his use of it at Sun. The term is commonly spoken with the accent on the first syllable.] In Silicon Valley, at least, a lot of people seem to associate that metric with you.

Sun was in trouble; and because we were in trouble, I had the luxury, or the risk, of being able to make a lot of decisions and not have people complain about them. So, we put in a bonus plan that was tied to RONABIT, which had been talked about at Sun for a couple of years but never used.

RONABIT is just return on net assets, and the BIT excludes interest and taxes—so it's an operational measure. And we paid people based on RONABIT.

Sun was a company that had treated cash as free. RONABIT paid people for not using cash. So, overnight we took this company from a cycle time of 273 days in 1989 to 137 days four years later.

And that was because of changing the incentive system?

And a lot of other things. It was a complex change in culture; good compensation was clearly part of it. By changing to RONABIT, we made people think that cash was valuable, and we succeeded in driving people's behavior.

We did hundreds of projects to get our cycle time down. We generated $1 billion in cash on operations—A billion dollars in cash on operations! That's not profit, that's reduced inventories, reduced accounts receivable. That's a huge accomplishment!

What are the other key metrics that you use as a guideline—not just what the company's using at the top management level, but what's filtering down to the general managers and their people?

We use RONABIT—we pay everybody on RONABIT. We did not have a complicated message. It was a very simple message: If we made our plan, you would get X amount of money and, if we beat our plan by a particular amount, you would get two X. And the plan was basically established in such a way that people could beat it; it really took extraordinary performance to do that, but it was certainly doable, and people went off and did it. We came close to doing it the next year as well, beating it to the max.

You've got to help people win. Part of what we did was create an incentive plan and set up goals and financial metrics so that a lot of people could win. And in winning, the shareholders won even more—the share price between '89 and '91 more than doubled.

COMPENSATION BASED ON RONABIT

Does it seem to you that using RONABIT the way you do is something that applies in other industries as well?

We don't use RONABIT today. We actually pay people based on a chart that has revenue growth and EPS [earnings per share] growth on it . . . although there are some things around cash that basically bring RONABIT in the back door.

But we have RONABIT up at 50% to 60%, and it's hard to get it a whole lot higher in our business.

It depends on the situation. I'm a firm believer that in business there are no rules. [Laughing] Except maybe mine!

The moment you think there are rules, you're going to get into trouble. You've got to be able to change the rules. You could be the ardent defender of RONABIT as the only metric in the world . . . and, a year later, you're going to change it because that's not the appropriate metric for you anymore.

I believe in comp plans that are simple and straightforward. [For more on Sun's compensation approach, see Chapter 17.]

DECISIONS ON FUNDING PROJECTS

One of the challenges facing business leaders is defining the capital budgeting process so clearly that managers know the elements required to get a yes on a capital expenditure or a new product, or whatever. It seems as if it should be just a matter of saying, "When you use the right formulas, when you give me the right answers, when you can show that what you're asking for is going to be good for the company, then the answer is going to be yes." That should be straightforward, right?

Yes. But human nature being what it is, that means that, nine times out of ten, you say no.

I remember one occasion when I said yes and, as a result, we now have a very good line of servers [computer data-storage devices]. The engineer who got that yes is now a vice president. He came to me in August of 1989 when we had no cash, no money, and everything was controlled; he came to my office at five o'clock, and he didn't know who I was, had no idea who I was. And I didn't know who he was.

He walked in and he explained to me why he needed money to go buy a bunch of machines that can simulate servers.

And I gave him the money. Without that, we would not have had the 2000s and the 1000s [successful products in the Sun line].

On what basis did you give him the money?

One, he had a good presentation but, two, he got money for the same reason that maybe I was able to get money for Sun; at the end of the day, banks do not loan money to companies. People loan money to people.

If there's one lesson I learned from being a CFO, it's that companies don't matter; it's all people things. Analysts buy stock based on people. Banks loan money based on people. All business is people to people.

I believe that—but if this engineer had had all the same things on paper but had not been able to explain very effectively, if he'd been, like most engineers, so bogged down in detail, it wouldn't have gone anywhere.

He wasn't necessarily very articulate; it was just that he was very sincere. And I had been around engineering and I knew the business pretty well. I knew what he was trying to do, and I was convinced that this guy would go and deliver.

Was that right or wrong? I don't know. In retrospect, it was a fantastic decision. And, by the way, I'm not giving you selective memory because that was the only capital improvement I ever approved! (Laughs).

So I'm quite sure I said No to things I shouldn't have.

SAYING YES

But you didn't say Yes at that initial meeting.

[In reply, Raduchel simply smiles.]

Oh, you did! That's a fascinating story.

IN SOMEONE ELSE'S PROJECT PLAN, HOW DO YOU KNOW IF YOU CAN TRUST THE NUMBERS?

But how do you come to believe the numbers that people are showing you when they want you to fund something? What do you require of them to be sure you're getting numbers that make sense—sales projections, for example?

I think you have to do a couple of things. In the end, it's people to people—so you have to have a loyal staff. We operate in Sun on a functional principle, where all the people in finance work for the CFO, no matter where they are.

We say that the relationship to us is a thunderbolt, which means that, if they don't break a rule, the reporting line is invisible. But if the line appears, it's stronger than any other line on the chart.

It's basically a principle that says, "Look, if you don't break the rules, you pretty much function as part of whatever organization you're working with. You break the rules, you're now considered part of *my* organization and we will have a conversation about what happened." So, you've got to know the business; you've got to understand.

The management process we use at Sun is largely still the same one I put in as CFO. There's a group called FMG, the financial management group, which is the VPs in finance and the CFO; we meet every week for a couple of hours to talk about the business and where it's going, so that everybody is aware of what's happening.

The people sit down and look at the numbers. They all have some content knowledge; if you have no content knowledge, you're dead—you can't tell if the numbers mean anything. We've had a couple of finance people come through here in our history who never knew the content and they would stand up and make a presentation that was almost laughable.

It was sad, laughable but sad, because they were sometimes presenting numbers that were just so clearly wrong. If you understood the way the business flowed, you could look at the numbers and realize that there was no possible dynamic that could yield that outcome.

In terms of market share, that sort of thing?

Bookings, revenue, shipments—they all flow from one another. You learn after a while. That's why I say an academic bent is helpful—analytical thinking. You should be able to look at the numbers and say, "Hmm, A, B, C, D, E, F, G, it can't work. There are patterns that just aren't possible." But you've got to have content knowledge to do that. You've got to have experience.

Is that all knowledge, or is there a certain kind of intuition that makes you good at that?

I don't know that it's intuition. It's certainly analytical skills. If you don't have any analytical skill, you can't get to first base. That's why everybody doesn't make a good CFO. In all these jobs, you've got to have a mixture of skills to be able to do them; there's not one simple thing.

BASING DECISION ON THEORY, NOT DATA

Joe Dionne, the CEO of McGraw-Hill, taught me a lot during the time I worked for him. One of the things he said that I have never forgotten is that you can't run a business based on data. You can only run a business based on the theory.

And this appeals to me because, as a trained statistician, I understand that data proves nothing. Data can only confirm or deny a theory, but it's still a theory. You've got to have a theory of how your business works.

It's easy, as a CFO, to get lost in the data. And I think that great CFOs understand that running a business is a mixture of theory and data. You do collect the data, and you can go and test theories by looking at the data, but, ultimately, you have to run a business based on the theory.

You invest money the same way—based on a theory. The data's never going to tell you whether it's a good investment or a bad investment, except when it's too late. It's a theory; you've got to constantly build the theory.

So, I think that to be successful today in any corporate-level job, you've got to be somebody who's comfortable making decisions based on a theory.

That may be the chasm. And that is a huge chasm, because it takes a degree of intellectual self-confidence that probably borders on arrogance. But if you don't have it, you're dead.

There's a tremendous temptation to look for evidence and, by the time you have the evidence, it may be too late. If you're looking to the data to tell you the answer, you will kill the company.

That's why you need theory. Your company can prosper only if you base decisions on a theory.

109

BILL RADUCHEL

Personal Perspectives

You became Sun CFO at a time when the company was in some trouble. What made them think that you were the person who could get the company out of that predicament?

Scott [McNealy] and I are old friends; he was originally a student of mine back at Harvard some 20-odd years ago. I don't know—maybe he thought Sun was going to find a new CFO and I was only going to be in the job for a couple of weeks. And maybe nobody realized how serious the situation was.

And why you? What was it that you were doing at that point?

I was Sun's vice president of corporate planning and development, but I had been at Sun for only nine months.

GIVING UP THE CFO JOB

A lot of the financial people who will be readers of this book have their eyes on some day becoming a CFO. You _were_ a CFO, and left it for a different job. What was the motivation?

I loved being a CFO. But at one point we did an audit and all these problems came out, and the audit recommended that the board create a full-time CIO with accountability. When we did the evaluation, the decision was that I was the best candidate for that job. This just happened to be a more valuable job to the company in Scott's view, so he asked me to do it.

Though my job title is chief information officer, I'm not really CIO in the usual sense. We're a systems company, and I'm the debugger of the product strategy. I'm the one who sees how it all comes together. I'm also the vice president of corporate planning and development, which is actually very complementary with my role of CIO because I get to use all our products. That makes me very knowledgeable about where they are and where they're going.

In a sense, you're a customer at the same time?

I'm a customer at the same time.

Given your druthers, would you still be doing financial things or do you look forward to getting back to it maybe at some time?

As the vice president of development, I still do a lot of the financial things. I still do relations with investment bankers, any M&A [mergers and acquisitions] activity. Some of those things would sometimes belong to a CFO, sometimes not.

THE ROLE OF THE CFO

How do you see the function of the CFO in today's corporation?

CFO is a very tough role. I remember that when I was teaching at Harvard, I was talking one day to one of the kids who was a great goalie and who always sat by himself at the back of the team bus. I knew him pretty well, so I went back one day and I asked him about it.

He said, "If you're a good goalie, you can't afford to be friendly with the players on the team because to be a good goalie you have to assume that any one of them will let you down. You really have to assume that any one of them, when he's coming down the ice, may not make the play that's going to prevent the shot. So, therefore, you really have to stand back and stay away."

The CFO role is basically a goalie role. It's a very hard job personally, I think, for the people who are in it. It's hard to be popular if you do a good job. Two years of being CFO taught me that, ultimately, you have to accept accountability, and I think I'm a much better executive for my stint as CFO. Much better. I'm much more realistic about the hard line because I was forced to it.

I can tell you about the day that I arrived in New York off the red eye, walked into a room, and realized that I was about to borrow $180 million. And there's nobody else there from Sun—it's just me. I get to sign my name and borrow $180 million and sign off to a whole set of reps and warranties. You're very much alone.

And you're very much alone when you're on the phone with your bank explaining that you may break a covenant and that you're going to have a problem. Being under fire teaches you a lot of things.

I believe in that. I believe that being CFO made my tendency to think worst case, worse. I mean, I am very strong and quick to think worst case.

I have one friend who argues that the price of being CFO is that I never married—because it had made me so worst case–oriented that I'm reluctant to marry. I don't know whether she's right or wrong.

111

I spend a lot of time talking to other CFOs, and what I've found is that you tend to get a pretty cynical view of human nature. You learn that people come in and tell you things that just aren't true—extremely optimistic predictions of what might happen. Or people walk out of the room not having told you a part of the story you really needed to know. So, it does affect your nature to be a CFO.

RADUCHEL'S VIEW ON WHAT BACKGROUND A FINANCIAL EXECUTIVE SHOULD HAVE

You have a degree in economics. Is that a better background than a business degree?

That's an interesting question. CFO is a very academic job, I believe. To be a CFO, your job is to discern truth from clutter—and academic training I think is very good for that. I think operational training is not necessarily good training. In a big public company, it's a very intellectual job. In a smaller company where you're doing a mix of things, it's a different story.

When I became CFO, I got lots of advice. One friend called me up and thought it was laughable that I was a CFO—he had always thought of me as the chief raider of the treasury. He said, "Listen, in the morning before you do anything else, go into your bathroom, close the door, look in the mirror, and practice saying 'No' until it's the first thing that rolls off your lips. Then you can go in and face the day." [Laughing] I think that was profoundly good advice!

On the other hand, that's what people have as the negative image of CFOs or the finance department in general, that they're, by profession, people whose job it is to say no.

Who does the CFO work for? Who is the customer of the CFO in practical terms? The number one customer is the CEO and the board. After that, are there any other customers?

This gets to the core of the issue, I think, which is that your job is to say no. And maybe, along the way, the CFOs I admired were people who understood how to play that role. You've got to live with it.

It wasn't personal. Their job was to push back. Their job was to question. Their job was to challenge. It was good and useful, and colleagues understood how to work around it; sometimes they didn't mind it, and their own organization performed.

FURTHERING A BUSINESS CAREER

Are there other things about the experience here at Sun that offer effective lessons for managers and leaders in other companies?

I think one of the hardest problems in business, especially in finance, is that what you're evaluated on in the early stages of your career may not be very relative to what you're evaluated on in the later stages.

Treasury is much more important to being a CFO than you would realize early in your life, yet most CFOs end up in accounting, because that's where most of the people go.

But aren't those the ones who are looking back over the stern of the ship?

Maybe. It depends on the business. It depends on what the president wants—the CFO has to be partnered with the CEO. Depending on who the CEO is, the CFO can play very different roles and be very complementary. I think again that there's no "one size fits all" in the world in general, and I don't think there's any one role model. I think who you are depends on the company, its history, its culture, and the role you choose to play at the time.

WHAT DO YOU WISH YOU HAD KNOWN EARLIER IN YOUR CAREER?

Are there one or two things you wish you had known earlier in your financial career?

I wish I had had more appreciation for the organization as a whole. Again, I think that's a problem with accounting training—that it doesn't necessarily let you see the organism as a whole. You can get lost in the process.

Accounting for a university or a nonprofit is about the same as accounting for corporations, but there's something mystical about a product business. You've got to go create products.

The Sharks [the San Jose, California, ice hockey team] have been having an ugly season so far, and my diagnosis matches that of the sportswriters in San Jose, which is that the Sharks' management fails to understand something.

There's a story—I believe it's true, I can't personally verify it—about a U.S. Olympic hockey team. The captain was a good but not great player, and the coaches had basically decided he was a wonderful guy but he'd have to leave the team. It was true he had less ice time than any of the other players, but he knew how to make that group of people into a team. So, when the players, who were smarter than the coaches, selected a captain, they selected him, forcing the coaches to change their minds and keep him.

The Sharks' management doesn't understand that. They keep looking for individual skills, and they don't understand that, at the end of the day, it's chemistry. Once you get to a certain level of ability, chemistry swamps the individual skills of the players.

In the same way, I think, to be a great CFO, you've got to understand chemistry. You've got to be able to go generate that chemistry and you've got to understand that you're part of that mix. If you don't generate it, nobody else is going to. I think that if you really aspire to the top jobs in the big companies, that's something you've got to understand.

CHAPTER 10

TACTICS FOR THE FAST-GROWING COMPANY: SILICON GRAPHICS

An Interview with Stanley Meresman, CFO, Silicon Graphics Inc.

Silicon Graphics is one of those prototypical high-tech companies that, in the process of creating its first product, launches an entirely new category, in this case, 3D computing—one of the hottest parts of the industry, hot enough to produce $3 billion in annual revenues for the company.

SGI products are grabbed up by toy designers, game creators, commercial illustrators, and anybody who wants to work in the captivating realm called "virtual reality." SGI is also used as Internet/Intranet servers and for big-time design jobs like creating the Boeing 777 transport aircraft. But the company's greatest claim to fame is that Silicon Graphics computers were used to create the breathtakingly realistic dinosaurs in the feature film Jurassic Park.

Meresman has an engineering degree from the University of California, Berkeley, and an M.B.A. from the Stanford Business School.

We met in his office on the ground floor of the executive building, looking out on a serene, parklike setting. On the day of this interview, he was wearing a dress shirt with white and blue stripes but, in the style of Silicon Valley, no tie, creating an informal air for the conversation.

BACKGROUND

What were you doing before you came here?

STAN MERESMAN:
Seven years ago I was the vice president of finance and administration, and chief financial officer, at Cypress Semiconductor. When I joined Cypress it was at about $2 million in revenue. We took it public and, by the time I left four years later, revenue had increased to over $150 million.

I left Cypress to come to Silicon Graphics which, at that time, had revenue of about $250 million.

THE CHANGING ROLE OF FINANCE

A lot of organizations today are beginning to expect their finance departments to serve a different kind of function than they did in the past. How do you see this change?

The finance function is changing from one that's mostly an accountant role, a scorekeeper role, to that of a partner in the business, a partner that's involved in strategic thinking.

I think it's very important for finance to be able to provide long-term financing strategies, that is, to be able to create methods to build, exploit, and leverage the corporate advantage over time, and also to identify and carry out strategic acquisitions and mergers.

Do you have a set of financial metrics that are different from the ones you used when you started?

Yes, but it's a bit more complicated than that. You have what I view as three different stages of company growth, with different emphasis for each.

MEASURES FOR A YOUNG COMPANY AND A COMPANY WITH REVENUE STREAM

You have the young or early-stage company, which is the survival stage; you're concentrated on a single focus: getting your product developed and launched. Financial management is managing cash flow. Cash is king.

In the second phase, as a company grows larger, it needs to broaden that product line so as to become more diversified, and then start to focus on profitability. A target business model or P&L model is really key. That's something we implemented here seven years ago.

MEASURES FOR A MATURE COMPANY: FREE CASH FLOW, DISCOUNTED CASH FLOW

And, in the third stage, in addition to your profitability model, you start focusing as well on the balance sheet and on asset management. You need to look at return on equity and return on assets and at your capital equipment and working capital requirements. These become more important as you grow into a larger, more mature company.

There are some interesting things that we're starting to look at, as we now enter this third stage. We're thinking about linking asset management, along with the profitability model, to stock price and shareholder value. As you become a larger company, still growing rapidly, you want to be in a position where you're not consuming a lot of cash, even with a significant growth rate.

Warren Buffett defines the intrinsic value of a company as the discounted value of the cash that can be taken out of a business during its remaining life. As you get into this third phase, that's an interesting way of looking at shareholder value. Shareholders make a return on their investment when their stock price increases, and the market rewards revenue growth only when you exceed your cost of capital over time.

So fundamentally it comes down to this: The stock's intrinsic value at a given time stems from the expectations of its free cash flow. When you're in the third phase, understanding the cash flow and at what level it can be sustainable over time becomes very important.

I look at free cash flow as the cash over and above what's required to finance the day-to-day operating cash needs of the company. That would include, for example, increases in working capital—primarily accounts receivable plus inventories, less accounts payable.

It also includes increases in fixed capital, such as property, plant and equipment, or capitalized software, as well as acquisition and technology licenses. It's the cash that can be freely distributed to the suppliers of capital—the people who provide debt and equity.

Discounted cash flow involves estimating what the cash flow will be in the future and then discounting it back to the present, recognizing that there's a time value of money. So, considering the value of it today, what would you pay now, to have that stream of cash flow coming in.

ASSETS INFLUENCE PROFITS

Once you're able to comprehend cash flow and communicate it inside your company, you can get people to understand how the assets that are used by the company are just as important as the profits that drop to the bottom line. It relates over time to your stock price in the future and to building long-term shareholder value.

So these are things we're beginning to do now—dealing with valuation and the impact that asset management has on shareholder value in a way that can be understood by our key managers.

NON-FINANCIAL METRICS: REVENUE PER EMPLOYEE

Another key measure we track very closely is revenue per employee, which will vary in different companies depending on, among other things, their distribution strategy.

For example, if you're at Compaq, where you have no direct sales people and the selling is all through distribution, you have very high revenue per employee. In the case of Silicon Graphics, where we have an extensive number of direct sales people, the revenue per employee is going to be lower.

So you compare yourself to companies that have similar distribution, which helps you focus on improving your revenue per employee and improving your productivity. Both are very important; we set as a goal improving revenue per employee about 15% per year, and we've now accomplished that over five years.

That's just a way of making sure that we find techniques that make us more productive. I certainly would rather have fewer, better, and better-paid employees that are leveraged with technology, where each person is adding more value and has greater job satisfaction. That's the strategy that really works.

You hear a lot today, of course, about the Internet, but the real opportunity is the Intranet—within a company or providing a company's link to its trading partners, customers, vendors, and so on.

Silicon Graphics has one of the most popular sites on the Internet today; we tend to be in the top 25 in the world in terms of people coming to our home page. We have five of our large servers supporting all those hits from the outside.

But, to support the Intranet, inside the company throughout the world, we're using about 500 servers. The Intranet has fundamentally changed the way we do business, giving tremendous leverage to having information available, instantly, to all employees inside the company. It's a great way to communicate and to give employees instant access to information for decision making and execution.

PHASE THREE AT SGI

How far along into the third phase are you?

Over the last year or so, we have been moving into this next phase. We've grown very rapidly in the year that ended in June of '95—we grew 45% in that year. Let's just take the last few years for a moment by way of comparison.

I came here in May of '89—about seven years ago—and, at that time, the company's revenue was $250 million. For the year that ended in June, it was $2.2 billion, so our revenue has grown eight times, our net income has grown 21 times, our cash has grown eight times, equity nine times, and stock prices have grown nine times over that period.

So, we've moved rapidly from being a child company to being a young adult company, having soared through adolescence. Now that we're a young adult company, in this third phase, we're starting to focus on these other measures in terms of being able to operate using less working capital and utilizing cash more efficiently.

NEW FINANCIAL METRICS AT SGI

And beside cash flow, there are probably some other new metrics coming into play as well.

We're starting to focus on additional items such as return on equity; we're in the middle of the pack there, compared to the rest of our industry, even though we have the highest profitability.

So what can we do to improve ROE? We can be more efficient in our cash utilization, in terms of our inventory, and receivables management. And we have more recently been focusing on these, and I would expect ROE improvement over time.

I believe that, when you have a good management team, anything you target and graph, and assign accountability for, will get better—even if you did nothing else.

In addition, on the asset side, we look at non-cash asset turns, receivable days, inventory turns—standard measures.

THE IMPORTANCE OF FOCUSING ON ASSET MANAGEMENT

Those are familiar metrics—but do people generally understand their value and when to focus on them?

Especially when you're beyond what I call phase one, it's very important to be focusing on asset management. What finance needs to communicate is that how efficiently you manage your assets determines the company's maximum cash-neutral growth rate.

For any company, that means that, from your operating profit percentage, tax rate, consumption of working capital, and fixed assets requirements, you can calculate the maximum revenue growth rate that can be accomplished on a cash flow breakeven basis. If you exceed that rate, then the company will need to borrow or to dilute its shareholders by selling equity.

And the revenue growth rate that relates to operating at cash flow break-even will obviously be higher if you're more efficient in your cash management. So, clearly, as you're growing rapidly, cash management is very important to keep you from diluting the stock by having to sell shares to raise cash, therefore diluting returns to investors over time.

This focus on asset management once you're out of the survival stage and into the expansion stage is crucial but is far less understood and gets far less emphasis than the income statement.

Many corporate managers and executives understand the income statement but don't understand the balance sheet and don't concern themselves with those asset-management issues. They don't give the same priorities to asset-management efficiencies as they do to revenue growth. But they should.

Tight control of the company's assets also provides a lever for managing the business. Lower profitability may be acceptable when it's accompanied by lower asset usage, as the free cash flow generated may be the same. And management can usually have more of an effect on assets than on the income statement.

For example, management can decide to outsource many activities that tie up capital or to run double shifts at factories instead of building new ones and consuming capital. Management determines payment terms for receivables and sometimes payables, both of which affect the capital tied up. The income statement, on the other hand, is more likely to be affected by competitors' pricing decisions or by the strength of the economy—things that management has no influence on.

And you're saying that these asset-management measures are important in the second phase and beyond?

We've been doing these straightforward asset-management things from the second phase forward.

RETURN ON NON-CASH ASSETS (RONCA)

Besides the metrics I already mentioned, once we reached the second phase, we've also been measuring, for example, RONCABIT, which is a return on assets measurement.

More specifically, RONCABIT is the profit before interest and taxes—which is your operating profit—divided by average total assets less cash.

Taking the cash balance out of the efficiency measure helps because some companies like to keep large war chests of cash. With cash removed, you can gauge the efficiency of the non-cash assets and the level of return you're getting.

That's a very good way, an operational way, of being able to have the company focus on more efficient balance sheet measures of cash utilization.

So, that's something we measure and track every quarter. We use a four-quarter rolling average, and benchmark how we do against companies in our industry.

ON USING A BUSINESS MODEL

You spoke earlier about a P&L model. Were you talking about traditional P&L or about some more sophisticated measures that go beyond that?

The traditional P&L model is all you need. What you're looking at is operating profit, that is, profit before interest and taxes. Because whether you have interest income or interest expense is a result of your decision on how to finance the business—through equity or debt.

Operating profit is the fundamental measure of how healthy your business is. The business model incorporates who you are and where you're likely to be going in the future. It helps define the culture of the company and how you manage your business, and what opportunities you take advantage of, and what opportunities you choose not to take advantage of.

Do you find that, by and large, companies understand the concept of using models for the business?

It's surprising to me that the business model is not as well understood and communicated inside a company as one would think. For example, we publish our target business model in our SEC documents—in our 10K and 10Q reports. I'm sure there are a few other companies that do that, though I've not seen it.

And, yet, it's very helpful. By having the business model widely known, then, as you operate above or below it, you can talk to the target model as a reference point of where your objectives are—where the target is that you're trying to achieve.

That makes it an excellent way of communicating outside the company, and inside the company as well. When we operate outside our business model, what actions we're going to take to get back into the model are very predictable.

Inside your company as well, having the business model available is a way of setting a framework for your managers when they're thinking about new products and new projects—they can think about how these things are going to fit into the business model and then make choices.

SELECTING A BUSINESS MODEL

What are the elements you use in the SGI model?

In the P&L model, or profitability target model, our target has been to have gross margins in the range of 50.5% to 52.5% of revenue, R&D at 11% to 13%, and SG&A [sales, general and administrative] at 26% to 28% [see Fig. 10-1]. We have operating margin at 11.5% to 13.5%, which is the highest in our industry.

We've chosen to be a highly profitable company. The gross margin percent is really an indicator of how much value we're adding. So, if you have value-added products that are really differentiated from the products of others, such that customers are willing to pay more for them, we'll be able to achieve a high gross margin.

We have in our industry the highest R&D investment as a percentage

SGI BUSINESS PROFITABILITY TARGET MODEL	
	% of revenue
Revenue	100
Gross margin	50.5–52.5
R&D expense	11–13
SG&A expense	26–28
Operating margin	11.5–13.5

Figure 10-1 SGI uses their profitability target model for making business decisions, budgeting, forecasting, and discussing expectations with the investment community.

of revenue. And those two are linked—so, if we invest a lot for the future and if we've done that efficiently and wisely in terms of our vision of the marketplace, then we should end up with high gross margins, which will help us to invest more in R&D.

In choosing a high gross margin target, aren't you at the same time giving up growth rate?

The model is the result of a definition of who you are and what you're doing. So, if you take a company like ours that's going after very high value-added products to differentiate from other products in the marketplace, you need to attain the higher gross margins that should result from this strategy . . . and use the results of those higher margins to support a high level of R&D. You're focused on good profitability and providing lots of value-added, and then trying to maximize the growth rate consistent with that.

Not that every product has to meet the requirements in the business model, but the overall portfolio of the business, the portfolio of products collectively, does have to. So, there are certain things we're not going to do

TARGET MODEL VS. ACTUAL RESULTS				
Values expressed as % of revenue				
	Model	FY93	FY94	FY95
Gross margin	50.5–52.5	53.0	52.2	53.7
R&D expense	11–13	12.7	12.4	11.1
SG&A expense	26–28	29.7	27.2	28.8
Operating margin	11.5–13.5	10.6	12.6	13.8

Figure 10-2 SGI financial target model vs. actual results.

123

if they have, say, low margins; even though it may be a very large, high-growth market, if it doesn't conform to our business model and who we are, we don't do it.

You would give up a recognized, demonstrable profit opportunity because it doesn't fit your business model.

That's the whole point of the model—to help you make valid business decisions that are in line with the kind of organization you've said you want to be.

So it's a very good means of communicating. Sometimes you have people say that, in a creative company, you can't have a tight business model because it puts you in a box. You have to be creative with the different things that you can do. But that's not good business, in my view.

Michael Eisner, the CEO of Walt Disney—clearly a very creative company, with a lot of creative artists and creative professionals—once said, "I have always believed that the creative process must be contained in what we call the 'financial box'—financial parameters that creative people can work in. But the box is tight, controlled and responsible." He also said that the key to this box at Disney was held by the CFO.

So here's a very creative company that views it the same way that we at Silicon Graphics view it—there's plenty of room for creativity, yet within structured guidelines. You can empower people because they know the environment and they know the structure, so just let them go for it.

Eisner got a lot of flack in Hollywood for sounding as if he was putting rigid structures and financial controls on creative people, but he went on to prove that the company could become very successful while putting people "in the box."

Absolutely, and one of the things that's interesting is that, if you compare our model to the models of other companies—these other companies don't publish their models, but you can look at the last four quarters of results and assume that they're executing against their models—you would find that they're very different.

Silicon Graphics, as I described, had the highest gross margin, a high investment in R&D, and high operating profit. If you take another company in our industry, Sun Microsystems, for the four quarters ending in December of 1995, its gross margin was about ten points less than ours, its operating margin two or three points less. Sun has lower operating expenses because it does more distribution as opposed to a direct sales force. And it delivers an operating profit of 8% to 9%.

DIFFERENT MODELS FOR
DIFFERENT SITUATIONS

And companies don't necessarily have comparable models just because they're in the same industry.

Right. A strategy that another company in our industry has used is to look for very high growth by going after mass markets. That means lower prices, which afford them less gross margin. They have less value added, but they're going after a much larger market, and they do that very well.

So, there's not a single right model; there are different models that work, even within a particular industry.

Still, your first example seems to apply to companies in high tech or to those that are able to market distinctive products. The second example, where there's less value added, sounds as if it's more applicable to the mainstream company, where the product is soap flakes or breakfast cereals or auto tires . . . although I suppose companies in those industries would be quick to claim differentiation and value-added for their products.

I've never worked in the cereal or the tire industry, but I think a model based on lower value added would be a more common model.

But the first model can work just as well. Take an example that's not quite in our industry but in the PC industry, Compaq Computer. Its gross margin is probably half of ours; its R&D investment as a percent of revenue is probably one-sixth of ours. And yet it still generates good operating profit, perhaps in the 8% range or so—which means that it has very, very low overhead costs. And so it has a model that works, even though it's very different from ours.

Compaq has accepted trade-offs to make that model work; we've accepted trade-offs to make our model work. We believe that, for us, this model is the right trade-off, the right balance, among all the factors, and is sustainable over time. The model reflects who we are and what we can add in terms of value.

So it's very important to have that framework because it helps you in making decisions about what opportunities to take advantage of and what opportunities to pass up.

If you look at the market as a pyramid, you could chose to operate in the larger, base part of the market or more toward the higher value-added kind of market. And the position you choose would depend on the competitive landscape. It would also depend on where the greatest talent lies in your company—whether you have innovative product designers, low-cost manufacturing, or great distribution capability. You have to look at all the different factors to see where you could be truly outstanding.

Just to complete the thought, using a business model is also a self-regulating process—if you have this model and it's truly well communicated and internalized within your company, then, when you find you're not performing to the model, you know you need to make adjustments, and everyone understands and is supportive of this change.

For example, if you become too profitable, then you need to be investing more back into your business. If you drop below the profitability number, then you need to be tighter on expenses to get into the range that you defined as the optimum trade-off.

The final thought is that the model can't be static. It's the financial embodiment of a business strategy and, as the strategy changes, the model must also. The model doesn't tell you *not* to lower your prices, or to increase R&D, or to change your distribution channels; it simply tells you the consequences if you do. The model needs to be used in conjunction with business strategy and is not a substitute for it.

SCORECARDS

You're beginning to look into different measures as the company moves into the third phase; how do you go about that process? And what governs whether you bring in a major outside company like Stern Stewart or Boston Consulting?

We're doing a number of things in terms of metrics for managing the balance sheet and cash flow that we have been doing for some time. And then there are some additional things that we consider more innovative that we're beginning to implement. So, certainly, we use what I would call two scorecards.

One scorecard is inside our company, dealing with what we committed to do versus what we have executed and ensuring that we have clear accountability for executing what we plan to do. So we look at that scorecard, including accountability, every quarter.

Secondly, we have a scorecard that compares what we were planning to do and what we've done, benchmarked against the rest of our industry, to be sure we set up goals that would put us in the lead in our industry.

Those areas that we have targeted for some time are the ones in which we've already become the leader. In those that we've targeted more recently, we're more or less in the middle of the pack; we would expect, over time, to lead the industry in those, as has been the case with the ones targeted earlier.

As your company enters a new phase, it's important that you get top management to agree on the concept, internalize the goal, and articulate how it relates to enhancing shareholder value. Then key operating managers must buy in to why it will make a difference. They should then participate in the goal setting and feel accountable for their piece of it. Oftentimes, a consulting firm can be helpful in this process.

STRATEGIES FOR STRATEGIC ALLIANCES

One of the things you're known for is what appears to be a very special talent for setting up partnerships and strategic alliances. What are some of the ground rules for getting into bed with another company?

I think it's very important to have a clear understanding of why you're partnering—what each partner brings. The value or advantage that the partner brings should be different from what you have to offer. The partners should be complementary, not duplicative.

One partner might bring technology; another might bring understanding of a new high-growth market. Or they might bring special capabilities for distribution or low-cost manufacturing. The value that each partner brings to the party should be clearly understood.

That would seem to be obvious; what is it that people sometimes miss here?

Sometimes, people think bigger is better. But when each partner brings a unique value add, you have something together, you have advantages that you didn't have before—things that go beyond just bigness.

A second area would be to have really well-defined long-term objectives, with both partners flexible enough to modify them as the competitive landscape changes; and to be able to identify what success is and how to measure progress toward that success.

A third area would be to have a win/win deal, where both sides have carefully thought through what the incentives are, such that both companies can win and meet their clearly defined business objectives. It's obviously important that both parties make money.

A fourth area would be to develop these relationships over time so that you have trust in the intent and motivations of the partners. That gives you the opportunity to build multiple relationships between each partner, which is very important.

These four things can give you a strategic alliance or partnership that will endure over time.

In addition to the formal relationship in communications, you need some informal ones, so that you always know when something is starting to get off track—when the unexpected happens, when things change in the marketplace, when things have to be tweaked and adjusted to make sure they're still meeting the needs of both partners.

Are you talking about the process of arranging to have a strategic alliance with a company, or once the partnership is under way?

I think that, initially, when you're considering a relationship and seeing whether it makes sense, it's important to have a champion within each company.

A champion has to have some clout, has to be able to have influence, to have the ear of the senior people, to be able to get teams to work on it and to get the necessary resources. You need to have a champion who is going to make this happen.

Once the deal is done, you need to have an executive who owns the relationship. If you don't, the relationship is going to get lost. People are busy, people are focused on their own objectives, and the partnership is something that can get in the way, take their time and energy from other things they consider important and for which they're accountable. So, you need to have an executive who's clearly responsible for that relationship.

Then, in addition, you need to have these multiple relationships at various levels in the two organizations so that, if things are getting off track or dissatisfactions are arising, you're going to hear about it informally and can address early the issues that inevitably arise. These relationships *always* need to be tweaked over time because the world is not static.

And if there's intellectual property involved, you need to define how it's going to be handled: What party is contributing what specific intellectual property? If you're developing intellectual property together, just how are the rights going to be addressed? Does each party own the jointly developed intellectual property? Can either party license it to a third party?

There are many other issues, but those are a few that typically need to be addressed.

One of the issues that has come up, especially when people talk about Silicon Graphics, is the question of what constitutes too many strategic alliances. How do you know when you get to the point when any more will distract attention and focus from what your own core company is trying to do?

Simple answer: When you can't get a champion to raise their hand, when you can't get an executive to say, "Okay, I'll take ownership of that."

At that point, you've run out of bandwidth to do any more partnerships. You certainly don't want to enter into a relationship where you don't believe you're going to be successful, and if you don't have an owner, if you don't have a champion, then you can't generate any excitement about making it happen.

That's actually a very interesting answer and one I wouldn't have anticipated—that some executive has to want this enough to be willing to take on the added responsibility.

You have to have ownership and accountability. If you don't have that, the project will wither and die and waste a lot of effort and resources.

From the perspective of finance, what are the implications of these partnership arrangements? Does there need to be financial oversight over what the partner is doing?

A strategic alliance or partnership is like any other part of your business. In order to be sure what it takes to win and be successful, finance needs to be helpful and supportive.

The CFO must be involved enough to know if the effort is not getting the resources it needs, so that he or she can focus on that and force a decision whether to put more resources in or to stop trying to achieve objectives that are not realistic and therefore change the objectives.

Clearly, in the future, there will be more consolidation in most industries. That makes it increasingly important to be able to value strategic combinations. How do you do that accurately and appropriately, how do you recognize the real value added and the strategic advantage, and how do you provide synergies and opportunities? In the process, it also means not squelching the very thing in the partner company that you found most valuable.

We've done three mergers in the last three years. We're in the process of a fourth merger, with Cray Research, a company with about $800 million in revenue and about 3000 employees throughout the world. These are real opportunities.

STAN MERESMAN

Personal Perspectives

AIMING TO BE A CFO

When did you first think of being a CFO?

Actually, my goal as a senior in high school was to be CFO of a Fortune 500, billion dollar, highly respected, profitable company.

Most high schoolers have never heard of a CFO. How did you know about it?

I'm not quite sure how I knew, but that was my goal. And I decided then that I'd do whatever would be the best preparation for that. I decided that having an engineering degree would be good preparation before getting a master's degree in business.

How did you figure that?

I believed at the time that technology was going to explode and be an important area, and so therefore, that industry would be where I wanted to spend my career.

To go into a high-tech company having an engineering degree would be the best starting point. So I set off to do that, and then I got my M.B.A. The combination of the engineering degree and M.B.A. was well suited to a career in the technology sector.

SHAPING A CORPORATE CAREER

For anyone with an eye to becoming the general manager of a business unit, or reaching the executive suite, what kind of advice would you offer about career preparation?

First, I think, get all the education you can; having an M.B.A. is very helpful. It's not that you can use a lot of the tools of the M.B.A. education early in your career but, later on, it will help you to have that broad perspective.

Secondly, always be sure you're on the steep part of the learning curve—be sure you take the jobs that are the toughest. So, for example, if you're in the finance department of a manufacturing company, find your way into cost accounting early in your career: that's the hardest part of accounting. It's part of the guts of what the company does, and it's very difficult experience to add later in your career.

Go into the bowels of the company and understand what makes it tick, what's mission-critical, what is its distinctive competence. Understand not only the accounting but how finance makes a difference in the business. Understand and participate not only in helping to explicitly define and communicate a business model but in setting goals and measuring the results.

And find out what the business structure needs to be in a changing industry. What might it need to be three years from now? What are the trends in technology, in the market, and with your competitors? Read all the Wall Street and industry research reports on your company and the industry—go on to understand that aspect as well. I think it's good to get a variety of different experiences inside the company so you can consider all the factors that should be taken into account in making decisions.

You said that, in manufacturing, cost accounting was the hardest area; for other kinds of companies, what would the hardest areas be?

Well, if your company is in retail distribution, make sure you get involved in the distribution part. Look at the core competencies that the company has—the things that differentiate it from others in the industry, the heart of the company—and be at the heart of the company.

Don't go into something just because you enjoy it; go into the hard stuff. Be close to the heartbeat of the company.

CHAPTER 11

PURCHASING AS A
PROFIT CENTER AT AETNA

An Interview with Tom Brown, Vice President,
Purchasing, Aetna Life and
Casualty Company

*Tom Brown is an informal man with a quick mind—so it's little surprise that
the operation he ran for Aetna out of their corporate headquarters, in Hartford,
Connecticut, broke ground in a number of areas.*

*Aetna is a $12 billion financial services company with assets of $100
billion that offers health and life insurance and retirement services.*

*Since the interview, Tom has moved to Pfizer, where as vice president for
corporate purchasing, he is applying the same principles described here.*

BUSINESS RESOURCES AS A
STAND-ALONE OPERATION

**The organization you head is called Aetna Business Resources. Would
you explain what that is?**

TOM BROWN:
It's all the services for the corporation, under Kathy Murray, who is the chief
operating officer and who has sponsored this whole project. She's the key
player. If there's a support mechanism, Kathy's been it.

Business Resources is all the services for the corporation—purchasing,
accounting, the cafeterias, the stores, security, the facilities, the rent—she's
the "mayor," and she reports to Aetna's chief financial officer, Dick Huber.

It's really unusual, isn't it, to have a separate, almost stand-alone company, running those things?

It's unusual, but Kathy Murray pulled us together as a group about two and a half years ago. She started by asking how would we like to take the talent we have and break loose from the corporation, and then sell services back to it, and see if we couldn't successfully compete with the outside world?

And the more we worked on this, the more this group evolved and the more cost-competitive it became.

What activities is your organization responsible for?

We do purchasing, accounts payable, and asset management. I run the whole acquisition team—from the time somebody decides to buy something to the time the bill is paid and the assets are booked and it goes into the general ledger—the whole concept.

Usually there's a separation of church and state—the accounts payable and purchasing are different organizations. It's fairly new to have somebody run both of them together.

The CFOs in the different businesses that agree to this are people who want the behavior changed so that the cost of acquiring goods and services will go down. This was the original mission: Simplify the process, reduce the cost by half, and improve the quality.

The 1996 mission just says: We're going to be the best when we acquire goods and services. Very simple.

We're outsourcing the maintenance of our facilities, and it's one of my people who's leading that. Security, the information center for the corporation, the leasing of all our buildings and real estate, all these are things that purchasing is involved in now that we were never involved in before—we were just buying pencils.

And we have critical success factors that say that we have to be cost-effective, we have to have a skill-diverse team, and we have to have effective marketing—because you can have the greatest thing in the world, but if you can't get it out to your customers so they know what you have, you're in trouble.

And your customers are . . . ?

The 42,000 people in Aetna and in any new companies that we acquire.

MAKING PURCHASES WITHOUT A BUYER

So you do all the purchasing for the whole company?

We do all the purchasing. There's no other purchasing in Aetna or its companies.

But your purchasing operation doesn't work the way it does at most other places?

Our customers do most of the purchasing themselves. You know you want ball-point pens, you know the color you want, and you know the tip—fine, medium, or broad. What value do we add if we act as your buyer on an item like that?

So, instead, we put it into a catalog; we've negotiated all the prices in that catalog, and it's electronic. You find your item, click a button, and it's done. We've made it so that you can do your job easier, and we've taken away that tactical type of operation from purchasing.

This June, we're going to have a point-and-click graphical interface and interactive voice menus—it's similar to the way you do your banking by phone. The system is going to be set up so that people can order by phone.

When we acquire or merge with a company, as we just did, we can put a catalog onto a person's phone over the weekend. That following Monday morning, they can start using our system with this interactive voice.

KEEPING CONTROL OF SELF-PURCHASING

What's the limit on what people can buy in a routine way?

There are some assumptions that you have to make to go forward with this. The number one assumption is that the people you hire in the corporation are basically honest.

But you still have to have safeguards so people aren't tempted to be dishonest.

Sure. We allow people to go up to $750. Somebody who wants to rip off our corporation could place an order for $750, but they'd have to do a lot of them to get any real money and, of course, there are audits looking for problems.

Suppose somebody needs a modem for his computer. With nobody looking over his shoulder, he might select a top-of-the-line with a lot of bells and whistles he doesn't really need. Aren't you stuck with a lot of those decisions?

People do that, but understand that the bill for that would be charged against that person's cost center, and then that cost center budget goes monthly to a budget coordinator, who reviews all the bills. The coordinator will want to know, How come we're buying modems like this?

Or, it could get through and nobody catches it. If a few of these get through, how much does that cost us? The answer is, it costs altogether a lot less than the old way did. You've got to take a look and say, What are the big problems? The big problem was that everybody and his brother was handling paper—too much processing.

And we didn't even have part numbers for the goods we bought. That pen would have a different part number every time we bought it. We now know what we're buying; we know the volume we're buying and how much we paid last time.

How do you make purchasing a simple process in-house? In bigger companies, the ability to buy goods and services sometimes can be so damn complicated, people just say "Why bother!?" and they go around it. You've got to lead them right into that corral, make it so simple that they just march.

A NEW APPROACH TO
PURCHASING AND PAYABLES

How did all this come about?

Back in November 1991, the Aetna chief information officer, the chief financial officer, the controller, and Kathy Murray decided that they had to pull this thing together. I was brought in at about that time to run purchasing, and we developed a process document, the "Company Acquisition and Payment Process."

And what was the goal of the new process?

The motivation was that only $200 million worth of the $1.2 billion purchasing total was going through any system. There were six systems being run at that time. How were the other ones being paid? People would send an invoice in; we'd attach a purchase order to it and then pay the bill. And there were hordes of people doing this all over the company; it was totally out of control.

It's like the guy with the broom at the end of the circus parade, and when I came in, it was, "Here's your broom, here's your dustpan, either get up in the front and lead this thing or you're gonna be stuck back here cleaning up."

So, that was the analogy I used with the people: Let's get to the front of the parade.

A NEW RELATIONSHIP WITH VENDORS

So the employee's end of purchasing has changed. How about your relationship with the vendors—I assume that's undergone some big changes, as well.

As far as buying is concerned, we're not bidding everything, the way we used to. Those days are gone. Maybe the government still does it but, for us, my marching orders are: Select the right suppliers, build relationships with them just as if they were part of your department, review the goods and services they provide on a monthly basis with their management, and then move on to the next project.

And, about once every 18 months, go out and get some quotes or pick a few items and benchmark them.

When we started, the material acquisition cost was seven cents on the dollar; we're down to a penny and a half, going to a penny, which is our goal—to be at a penny. But you can see what happens when you start cutting costs and improving service.

And, if something goes wrong, when you have that strong relationship, you pick up the phone and say, "Bill, what's going on here? The price on this item has been dropping for the last six months—we're seeing one price reduction from you, and from the rest of the world we're seeing 16. Will you go take a look at it for me." And then you hang up—just like you're managing another department.

Ninety-nine percent of the time, you get a response: "Oh, Tom, there's a mistake. We'll take care of it." It's how you *manage* your relationship.

A NEW TYPE OF PURCHASING EMPLOYEE

And how is your employee turnover through all of this?

We have a number of new people, and the employees that we've hired are not purchasing people. There's an electrical engineer, an M.B.A. in marketing, a manager of a major department store, and a helicopter pilot. That's the sort of people that we've hired.

Why? Because we want that diverse base. If we had all purchasing people, they'd be thinking purchasing. I can teach purchasing to people, but broad-based business skills—I can't teach those—that's something people acquire in different worlds.

What kind of business skills does the helicopter pilot have, for example?

He's got a degree in information technology, and he supports our information technology end of the business. So he understands the methodologies and where we're going with our systems, and so forth.

A BONUS PROGRAM DEVELOPED
BY THE EMPLOYEES

Have you always had a bonus program in purchasing? How did that come about?

If you go from tactical to strategic and you're getting rid of a lot of the manual processes, then you're going to have to change the skills and competencies of the people. In 1992, eight people in this department plus one HR person put together what they call "Pay for Performance in Purchasing," which set up bonuses.

There are now 42,000 people who are on this Pay for Performance in the company. It wasn't me who did this; it was the people in the department who said: Here's what we want to do. And because they put it together, they believe in it, and it works.

If I had put it together, or upper management had, we would have had to force it down people's throats, and it probably wouldn't have worked.

They designed it themselves. That's a fascinating concept. I've never encountered that anywhere.

We also have our own degree program in purchasing that we offer. There's an associate's degree, and there's also an advanced degree, designed by the people in the purchasing organization. It's different from the C.P.M., the Certified Purchasing Manager's degree, which deals a lot with inventory, M.R.P., with manufacturing, and so forth, and we're not in that business.

COMPENSATION AS A CARROT
FOR INDUCING CHANGE

You see compensation as a motivator for change.

Change how you pay people and you'll see how things get changed. If you tell people you're changing the process, changing the environment, and you're still paying them the same way they've been paid for 25 years, it doesn't go down very well.

But say to them, "You've got to do something different, but you're going to get paid differently," all of a sudden they wake up.

WHEN PURCHASING BECOMES STRATEGIC

You've used the phrase "from tactical to strategic." How do you explain what that really comes down to?

Tactical is different day, same tasks. Same stuff, different year. Buying the same items over and over again, a processing of paperwork every time—that's tactical.

When you get rid of this and start adding value to what you do, now you're moving in the strategic direction. For instance, you can send in a request and ask me to buy that ballpoint pen, or I can put that on the system and you can go in and select from a bunch of pens, push a button, and it's done automatically—and I didn't touch it.

You didn't have to come through me, I didn't have to do all the tactical paperwork tasks, so now I have time to be strategic. I'm out working other issues, I'm thinking about other things: Should we outsource our facilities? How do we do our commissions? What's the best way, when we acquire a new company, to integrate our systems?

When purchasing is working those broader-based business things and not working the routine—the requisition for your pen—then it has become strategic.

PURCHASING AGENTS BECOME STRATEGIC (AND EARN BONUSES!)

Something tells me that your employees were probably happy about these changes.

It's like the cloudy day when, all of a sudden, the sun comes out. Once people see the change, you can see in their eyes that they understand. Once they see it, it's almost like a religion.

They say, "Yes!, that's what I want to do—I don't want to sit here and do this paperwork—I want to go out and do contract negotiations. I want to work with my customers. I want to travel out to my customers in the field and help them understand the system we're using. I want to go out and consult at Warner Brothers."

When you tell them that's the job that they can have, they look at it and say, "Yes!—that's an exciting job. I never thought I'd have a job like that."

And they can earn a bonus, above and beyond their base salary—in some cases, up to 30% of their salary. That's big money for some.

Especially at a level in a corporation where people aren't used to getting bonuses—except the sales people.

Not everyone here is getting a bonus. Some are making good salaries and doing their job but not qualifying for the extra.

FEWER PEOPLE, LOWER COSTS, INCREASED PERFORMANCE

And you believe you've seen real improvements with this new approach?

In '91, for purchasing alone, we had 213 people, and the operation was costing the company $19 million. Today, it's at 80 people and costing $10.5 million. For 1997, we think we'll be at 70 people and spending $8 million to run it all, including a lot of things we now do that we didn't do before.

So the operating cost is less than half; and the services are not twice as good, they're 100 times better than they ever were before.

GETTING RID OF THE "PSEUDOBUYERS"

You got rid of an enormous number of people.

There were extra people all over doing purchasing—in every part of the country. People filling out blue requisitions, administrative assistants, pseudo-buyers all over the company.

What's a "pseudobuyer"?

It's somebody in Paducah, Kentucky, who says, "Give me all your requisitions—I'll do all the buying for our group."

They weren't authorized to buy, but they start doing it. It was by default that these people sprang up. And it happens all over—I tell the story to any company, I can watch all the people going, "Yep, yep, yep, I know just what you're talking about." And then you have all these invoices coming in without purchase orders.

Today, if an invoice comes in without a purchase order, not only do we charge back to process it, but we charge them a $10 fee just to handle the paper. And, next year, we'll take it up to $50, and the year after that, we'll take it up to $100 to handle paper. So, if groups in the company want to continue to use paper instead of the system we've created, they can do it, but it will cost them.

A VENDOR SHOULDN'T BE A PARTNER

Another change is that suppliers aren't our enemies anymore. It used to be us against them—"They're going to screw us around." Instead, you've got to pick suppliers—I'm not going to use the word "partner," because you can have good business relationships with a company without being a partner; I think "partnership" is overused.

What is it about the way people use the term "partnership" that you reject?

Partners is like being married. I don't think you end up marrying a supplier. I think you end up in a good business relationship. You don't have to be partners, you just need to have a good business relationship. Sometimes we forget this.

There's one company we did business with in the information technology area that ran this place for a while. I said, "Wait a minute, what's this company doing? They have 23 people running around here." I was told, "Yes, but they'll get mad if we do thus and so." I said, "Would you do this at home—would you let a plumber take over like this?" "Yeah, but they're the best." Even if your supplier is the best there is, you still have to be in charge of running your own business.

OPERATING AS A PROFIT CENTER

Is Aetna Business Resources looked on as a profit center—does it need to show a profit?

Right now, it's operating at breakeven internally and as a profit center externally. If we do our business internally, it's at a zero base so that we don't end up with taxes, since we're doing profits between different parts of the corporation. But if it's external, it's for profit and that's the way it's set up as an organization.

When you say "external," do you mean you're doing the accounting as if it were an external organization, or do you mean you're doing some business outside the company?

We're being hired to tell other companies how to set up their purchasing acquisition organizations. We sell services to Warner Brothers, and I have one of my people going out there to consult. Arthur Anderson is Warner Brothers' accounting firm, but this isn't an area where Arthur Anderson really understands how to work it. Warners called us and said, "Will you come in and consult for us?"

Aetna sold The Travelers a piece of our business, the $4 billion of property and casualty business. With it, the Travelers wanted the purchasing services. We charge the Travelers for that. These services we make profit from because they're external to the corporation.

PROVING THAT COSTS ARE COMPETITIVE

The crux seems to be that somebody in purchasing has to be looking at what the organization is doing to make sure you're doing it well enough to compete. And that's the problem in a lot of places, isn't it? People take the operation for granted and don't really look at the numbers to see what it's costing.

The business plan each year has got to say that in-house purchasing will be competitive with the outside world and that it measures that. There's a financial item called cost of goods sold; we're working on one that's cost of goods *acquired*. What's it cost to acquire goods?

United Technologies is working on it, too; this goes back to that penny and a half on the dollar. If people start using that target, then they'll understand whether they're competitive or not. I think the measurement has got to become strategic, not this overhead mush that you spread like peanut butter, but something representing the real cost.

People are afraid to look at the facts. But they have to start sooner or later. This interview will appear in your book, and sooner or later there'll be an article in *Harvard Business Review*—"Purchasing: Moving from Tactical to Strategic." And as soon as that hits, the CFOs are going to think, "Wait a minute, here's an area I can save money in."

Then the CFOs come to the people that are running these acquisition units and say, "What's it costing?" And, in most cases, the answer they'll get back is, "I don't know." That's that broad-based business idea—that you should be watching, scanning the environment, and understanding what's going on.

BENCHMARKING

What kind of benchmarking are you doing?

We usually benchmark against other corporations and know where they are—and they're higher than we are.

Who are you benchmarking against, for example?

Coca-Cola, United Technologies, Fanny Mae, Pepsi-Cola, GE, NBC, Johnson & Johnson, Westinghouse, IBM, Nynex, Xerox.

That's a very impressive list. And how do you get the numbers?

We talk to each other; we're a very close-knit network. A lot of the heads of those purchasing groups continue to share information with one another because we believe in what we're doing, we believe in this whole acquisition idea, we believe it's a profession, and we believe that it should move from the tactical to the strategic.

People come in and say, "You're charging me too much." I show them how much it's costing and lay it right out financially. I say, "If you can do this cheaper, be my guest; go outside and get it." But, to be able to say that, we as an organization have to work continually on the business and update it so that the outside competition can never catch us.

THE COMPETITION: OUTSIDE BUYING SERVICES

You've talked about being better than the competition. Who is the competition for a purchasing organization?

There are services that are slowly coming up now that will do purchasing for you. IBM will do some of it, and American Express will do it with its card. There are people who've said they can do it inexpensively. EDS, out of Plano, Texas, is peddling a purchasing service that says it can take 10% out of your cost just by walking in the door.

There are a lot of people out there now who are saying: We'll do your purchasing for you and we'll do it cheaper than you could ever do it. Outsource it to us and we'll take care of you.

Those people are going to our CFO, Dick Huber, and saying, "Dick, we can do it cheaper than your in-house organization." And Huber says, "Okay, show me." And, that's when we say, "Come on, show us your proposal, and we'll see who's more cost-effective."

We've got to know what the people out there who are selling purchasing services are selling them for. We had to do market research on that. The nice thing about selling inside, the hidden thing, is that you don't charge any tax for your service and there's no profit margin. So, if you do it well, you'll always beat the outside competitor.

NEW REVENUE SOURCE: SELLING THE TOOLS OF PURCHASING

Are other companies using the idea of an on-line catalog so that employees can buy without the purchase-order-paperwork hassle?

They will be. Now that we've developed the software that operates the on-line catalog, we're going to sell it for commercial use; our software company didn't think it was a business application, but we showed them it was, and now they're going to buy it and market it.

We believe the Internet is key in where we're going. We'll expand the catalog with pictures and sell our services.

Also, other companies are calling us and saying: Will you help us with outsourcing? Will you help us take a look at how we do our compensation for commissions? They never called purchasing for that before.

CAN THE SMALLER COMPANY DO STRATEGIC PURCHASING?

What size does a company have to be before it can have the kind of operation you're describing?

It can be a small company. What we're doing, companies from small to large can do.

How small?

Probably as small as $20 million. Companies of that size ought to take a look at it; if they can do it well and they're good at it, they should do it; if they don't do it well, then they can get it outside and manage it.

SERVICE COMPANY VS. MANUFACTURING

How different is it running this kind of organization for a service or financial company rather than for a manufacturing company?

In a manufacturing company, the products that you buy are all defined by engineering; there are usually specifications, there are usually two or three suppliers, and there's a price that's pretty well established out in the marketplace, whether it be for a DRAM chip or a metal casting.

And, for the non-traditional purchasing, as they call it, the world's the catalog. It can be helicopters; it can be a consultant; it can be a fire extinguisher in Paducah, Kentucky; it can be window glass for all the cars that are insured by the corporation; it can be temporary help—anything.

It's very difficult to manage that. And that's partly what brings us to our employee concept—we have only one job title in purchasing: everybody is a purchasing consultant.

That's a novel idea. What was your thinking?

I just wanted broad-based business people; I wanted to make it a small, entrepreneurial type of organization.

In our business plan, it says that our strategy is that we'll be a stand-alone organization, not an overhead allocation.

INFORMATION SYSTEMS FOR PURCHASING

Do the information systems have to change a lot to support the changes you're making?

We're working with our software developer on the West Coast, Walker Interactive. We went with a single software manufacturer for the whole acquisition chain. It covers purchasing, accounts payable, asset management, and general ledger. As a matter of fact, we have people who live out there to make sure that where they're going and where we're going is the same direction.

Kathy and I were out there two weeks ago to sit with them and our team. Are we going to stay mainframe-based? Are we going to go distributed? If we're going to go distributed, how do we make that transition?

What's the product going to look like? You have got to work with a software supplier as a part of your department.

As a matter of fact, we're doing a joint venture with the software people. As they go out to sell systems and implement systems, we'll do the business applications and they'll do the technology. So, this purchasing group will be picking up money consulting in that area. They're a major software manufacturer, and that's how we keep up-to-date with what the software can be made to do—by driving the product. It was either that or sit back and take whatever came over the wall. And, if you put this much time and effort into something, you want a say in it.

THE BRIGHT WORLD OF ELECTRONIC
DATA INTERCHANGE (EDI)

Aetna sounds like a company that I might expect to be a leader in taking advantage of EDI—electronic data interchange [a rapidly growing approach for companies to exchange purchase orders, invoices, and shipping notices and, sometimes, to make payments, by means of direct electronic exchange of data, computer to computer, which does away with the need for manual data entry].

The more data we get moved electronically, the less paper we have, and the more tactical work goes out the door. Eighty-nine percent of our transactions are now electronic, headed for 95%. Reynolds and Reynolds said they were going to do that a few years back, and we picked up on it and set that goal for ourselves as well.

But when we take a look at our invoice activity, where's our dollar spent? Eighty-one percent of the invoices we have are 6% of our dollars, so a lot of our invoices are little dollars. How are we going to do that?

Do you recognize value in an approach to EDI that lets a small vendor, for example, communicate with your in-house system?

That's our next step. We want vendors to be able to process their own inquiries into our system—to be able to come in and check their invoices. We spend a lot of time answering the phone: Where's my check? Did you receive my invoice? I definitely think that the vendor should be able to come into our system.

We take all the billing in from the vendors now EDI-wise. They feed in the vendor invoice; if it matches the data in the database in our computer, if it matches the purchase order in the way it's supposed to, we'll take it in and pay the bill.

NEW APPROACHES TO EDI

Are you looking into the new solutions coming along—Sterling has a low-priced translator, and there's an inexpensive all-in-one package from BridgeWorks that can get even one of your smaller vendors up and doing EDI with you in a matter of hours.

I think it's something that we'll use. Today, we're going to print a prospectus for the new company we just bought, U.S. Healthcare, and I've had 40 phone calls from printers. I want to be able to put the specs out there and say: We're looking at printing this. If you're interested, here's what we need from you.

GE is doing this; it's got a program that sends out a message, "Here's what we need; please reply." Then the winning vendor is fed a purchase order electronically over EDI.

They're probably using a program like BridgeWorks. And it sounds like your catalog system is basically a form of EDI.

When a customer goes into the system and clicks to make a purchase, it goes right out to the vendor. And 59% of our orders are being handled like that. The contract's in place, the vendor has been selected, and so the order goes directly to the vendor, and we're out of the loop.

You haven't said much about accounts payable. That's another area where EDI is starting to cut costs dramatically for some companies.

We pay some of our bills once a month—Express Mail; we have 650,000 envelopes going out. We used to pay every day.

We now track these costs. Same thing with our air travel. And we measure the dollars that are under contract to minority-owned, women-owned, and Americans With Disabilities–owned companies. What does it cost us to process paper? Are we doing well at that?

LOOKING AHEAD

The things going on in finance today are, it seems to me, very much along the lines of something you expressed earlier about the shift from tactical to strategic—being able to tell the company what it needs to do to make the future better, to improve shareholder value. From your experience, what do you see happening in that way, and what do you think the hot buttons are?

I believe that we the buyers, we the people who are going to the suppliers, are demanding quality performance. We're saying, "Don't tell me what you've done—that's history—we can't live on history. What are you going to do for me?"

As we go into a contract, there are three pieces of the process. One is, "What does it cost you to manufacture and what are your margins? If I'm going to do business with you, I want you to open your books up." Before, that was a secret.

Two is, "Now that we have a base, what are you going to do for me next year, and the year after that, and the year after that? How are you going to reduce it by 15%? What will you put in place to make sure you stay competitive?"

Number three is, "We want to manage this on a monthly or quarterly basis. We want you to measure it and tell us where you are." This wasn't done in the past. In most cases in the past, it was just, "Give us your best price and make sure we get the product." Now we're getting into your business and saying, "That wasn't good enough; we can get that from anybody. We want to be with you to know how you're going to make these improvements, so that we can guarantee ourselves that we're going to improve, too."

It used to be that the vendor would have to justify his numbers. That he does very quickly now. What we're looking for today is, "How are you going to make them better?"

All of this suggests a very different role than people usually associate with the finance, purchasing, and accounting operations.

I believe in this profession, and I just think it's got to be moved from the days of policeman types out shuffling papers around, to where purchasing people can really help the corporation save money.

I know we can save millions and millions of dollars. I think people know that—it's just a question of the willingness to go through the change. It's not easy, but it's necessary.

147

TOM BROWN

Personal Perspectives

BACKGROUND

Tell me about your own background and what you've done at Aetna.

I got a degree in mathematics and education and then, in the late 1980s and early '90s, I went back and got an M.B.A. in international business. I wanted to teach, so I went back to school. That was an interesting approach to life—going back to school in my late 40s.

You worked at other places before Aetna?

Yes, I did. I taught high school for three years in Northern New Jersey and coached football, basketball, and track. And then I went to Vermont and ran a ski lodge. Then I worked for a tool company, for Black & Decker, and then for Digital Equipment, where I did purchasing, materials management, and transportation, both in the United States and offshore.

Timex in Connecticut was looking for somebody to do its Sinclair computer, somebody who understood the Far East and manufacturing. I've done a lot of traveling from Puerto Rico to the Far East and Europe, and so I took the job and was with Timex for four years, when it closed down the Sinclair. That was the first time I had ever gone through deselection, reengineering, whatever you want to call it.

I was 39 years old. It's tough, you know, when you think you're a hot ticket and somebody asks you to leave.

It doesn't feel quite so bad if they ask you to leave because they're closing their doors.

After that, I kept moving through a lot of companies in the electronics industry.

Four and a half years ago, Aetna called me and said, "Are you interested in running a worldwide purchasing operation for an insurance company?" After seven interviews, I realized that they bought $1.2 billion worth of goods and services. They were living in the '60s and they wanted to take the purchasing organization into the year 2000. It was an opportunity I couldn't turn down.

Are there any experiences in your career that you look on as a kind of turning point or watershed?

When I was at Black & Decker, there was a man named Don Marchese, who was a few years older than I was. My job there wasn't in purchasing; I was doing new products and systems work. The job kept me running in and out of Don's purchasing department. One day he said, "You come in here again, I'm going to make you a buyer." And I just said, "Don't give me any lip, Don, just get me the product. Your people aren't cutting it."

The next day, I was back for something else and he said, "Don't leave the department. You don't have a job back where you came from."

I said, "What are you talking about?" He said, "I straightened it out with human resources; you're in purchasing now." He told me, "You've got this big mouth—you're here."

He had really done that. I sat down and started buying wire and cable, and he was a helluva teacher. He was the guy who really inspired me to just keep going after what I believe in.

IF YOU HAD IT TO DO OVER . . . ?

If you had to do your whole everything all over again, are there things you'd do very differently about your career or about the way you've learned?

You've got to pick a company that's comfortable to work in. There are a lot of companies where it's a tooth-and-nail environment. They pay you a lot of money but degrade you—fortunately, none of the ones I've worked for were that way, but I've talked to people in companies like that. You've got to enjoy going to work in the morning.

I've always had this theory that the corporate environment comes down from the top—however the top guy treats his people, that attitude gets handed down. Do you find that?

There's a lot of truth in that, absolutely. Maybe not the top, but upper management. Kathy Murray runs an organization that she's strict and stern with, but she always says that you've got to have fun. If you screw up, you're in trouble but, if you do your job, it's a great place to work. That's the way it should be.

We're in business to make money for the shareholders; that's the number one reason. When you start to forget that, you're in trouble. If you can blend in community and diversity and fun and learning and all that with it, then you're really successful.

CHAPTER 12

THE BALANCED
SCORECARD AT NSC

An Interview with Richard Sessions,
Director, Strategic Planning and
Market Development, National Semiconductor

Rick Sessions is not quite what you might expect from his job title, which conjures up the image of someone staid and focused on details. From the moment you meet Rick, you get the feeling that he approaches life, and probably work as well, with spirit and irreverence. It's the necktie that gives him away: It's colorful and wildly patterned.

A graduate of Cornell University with a B.S. in engineering, Richard has over 25 years' experience in sales, marketing, and business management. His background includes launching an engineering start-up that specialized in advanced UNIX computer designs for government research. After selling his company in 1984, Richard joined National, where he has led the drive to adopt best practices in global, fast-cycle new product development. He is also an international lecturer and teaches marketing at the graduate school level.

In this interview, Sessions describes National Semiconductor's adaptation of the balanced scorecard concept, which NSC calls balanced metrics.

A BALANCED METRICS PROGRAM
FOR NATIONAL

What led up to the development of National's balanced metrics program?

RICK SESSIONS:
National wanted the various divisions and manufacturing sites to begin using the Malcolm Baldrige National Quality Award application as a means to surface

business process gaps and to drive continuous improvement. I was asked to attend a meeting of the implementation team because they were having difficulty getting Baldrige accepted as an analysis tool—people just wouldn't do it. The reason seemed pretty obvious: Who wants to do an 80-page application? The team wanted some inputs from a strategic view.

It's not the application that's important—it's the process you go through and the realizations you get out of the process. So we came up with something called *assessment light*. It's a questionnaire that reorganizes the Baldrige principles around what we call our CBIs, or critical business issues. We leveraged the culture and nomenclature in the company—same objective but in a form that people could deal with on a reasonable and timely basis. This then led to the idea that we might be able to design a real-time continuous improvement process.

What were you trying to achieve with this?

Most importantly, we wanted to look at the company in non-financial terms. Financial metrics are not in themselves indicators of the capability of a company to deliver value to its customers and shareholders. Research has shown that great companies are healthy on several key dimensions, striking a balance between financial performance and other critical metrics. Most of a company's measures are financial in nature, but financial measures are after the fact: By the time a problem surfaces, the horse is already out of the barn—the horse left three to six months ago.

In any company, there are people issues, organizational issues, operational issues, R&D issues, customer issues—all of which you have to be looking at on a regular basis. And we were doing that, to some degree, but not in an organized way. Our meetings tended to be dominated by the financials. When you stop to think about it, that's the common language we've all had since the Industrial Revolution. It's the one thing that finance, manufacturing, marketing, and HR all have in common.

But financials don't tell you about how you're doing vis-à-vis the marketplace and your competitors. Even a market-share analysis can tell you only *if* you have been gaining or losing share, but not *why*. The balanced metrics program, which we've adapted and modified for our use at National, begins to get at the why.

BALDRIGE VS. BALANCED METRICS

What is it that's *balanced* in balanced metrics—financial or non-financial?

Both. The balanced metrics program is based on our six CBIs, and a seventh we recently added—leadership, which guides the pursuit of excellence.[1] The two things that you can definitely measure on the results side are customer delight and financial performance. The other CBIs are what drive results.

As part of developing the balanced metrics, we did a Malcolm Baldrige map versus our CBIs, and there was almost an exact reflection. The only one missing was leadership—the measure of "walk the talk"—the issue most crucial to a corporate transformation.

To me, the match was amazing; it demonstrated that Baldrige is a natural set of criteria to work with. All we did was to put it into National's language, which helped gain an acceptance that Baldrige would otherwise never have within the company.

How are the key leading business metrics chosen for each CBI?

Each CBI has two to four metrics that encompass many subcomponents that we call *value drivers*. Profit before tax, for example, isn't just a number, it's the end representation of many financial subcomponents. Every functional entity of a corporation has different value drivers, so that each needs to choose the key leading indicators that are most relevant to its business.

We found that four basic principles govern the choice of leading business metrics: First, is the metric at a high enough level to encompass many value drivers yet low enough to be meaningful and sensitive to changes external to the business? Second, does the choice of metrics and their measurement help you compete—that is, satisfy customer needs better? Third, does what you measure as a metric add value to the company? And fourth, does the chosen metric lead or help predict future performance, and can it be benchmarked?

Many of the financial measures being used today have evolved over the past hundred years. Identifying proactive metrics in the other CBIs was more problematic.

Is there any proof that a "balanced" approach works?

A recent study by the National Institute for Standards and Technology shows that quality management can result in impressive returns. As a group, the 14 Baldrige National Quality Award winners outperformed the S&P 500 by greater than four to one, achieving about a 250% return on investment compared to 59% for the S&P 500 over the same period. This kind of data might make you want to reevaluate your stock portfolio.

HOW BALANCED METRICS
WORK IN PRACTICE

In the real-world daily life of the company, how does the balanced metrics approach actually get put into practice?

Many corporate review meetings kill entire forests. People spend hours creating a foil-fest of visuals.

We ask people to come into a quarterly business review with no more than ten foils—a one-foil overview, one foil of financials, and then they get into whatever CBI the executive committee has chosen as the key topic for the quarter. It might be operational excellence—that's really hot just now—yield or scrap or one of the others. Or it might be R&D ROI, which is another hot topic right at the moment.

Then each general manager addresses the CBI areas for critical improvement, and one shared learning—a "boast" foil, something they're doing that's working well enough to interest other GMs in trying it.

All the items discussed must be benchmarked against external criteria. We're trying to get away from inward-looking self-evaluation because it tends to be biased. But, when you have to go out and benchmark it externally and score yourself that way, you can surface the gaps. You can clearly see where you've got critical issues that need immediate attention.

CBIs that are on target are shown in green, borderline in yellow, and items falling short in red. Anything red, you must talk about in the QBR meeting.

When you get a red, the process is to ask "Why" five times, and that will get down through the tree to the root cause rather quickly.

An example: Customer delight is red. You find out it's red because you missed the goal on customer request date, CRD. Why did you miss the CRD? You find out it's because of scrap rate. So then you ask: Why is the scrap rate so high? "The operator put the wrong recipe in."

You go down one more level: Why did the operator put the wrong recipe in? And the answer, you find out, is, "Because the automated system was off-line."

You keep drilling all the way down until you find the root cause, and you fix the root cause.

It's surprisingly hard to implement this kind of methodology. We still see examples of no follow-through. Teams keep encountering the same problems and repeating the same fixes.

How does that Einstein quote go, about the definition of insanity being to repeat the same behavior and expect a different result?

Exactly.

At the quarterly meetings, a GM could be in the red on most items; that's very embarrassing to come into a room and admit; it announces, "I've got some serious problems."

Peer group and management behavior is very important under these conditions. Senior management should cheer the GM for having the guts to admit that he has some problems. But the group also expects him to say, "Here's my plan for making things better." With this kind of approach, another GM might say, "We did this very successful thing in R&D ROI, and it may be just what you're looking for here." The peer group and executive management become coaches and mentors.

Which financials do the GMs report in these sessions?

There are only four: revenue, gross operating profit, bookings, and profit before taxes, PBT.

THE "PERFORMANCE CONTRACT"

And these are reported on a benchmarked basis?

Yes, in the sense that we've built that into the strategic planning process. We use something we call a *performance contract*. It's a contract that I as a GM have with you as the CEO of the company, based on the CBIs and strategic imperatives, to improve my business relative to what the rest of the industry is doing.

Part of the performance contract is the financials related to the financial performance CBI. A series of financial benchmarks are set that all the GMs have agreed to and have divided up among themselves.

The financial part of the performance contract is based on a success model, which is an external measure based on what a top-quartile company should be doing.[2] The other performance contract elements are also taken from the CBIs and strategic imperatives.

THREE MODES: HARVEST, FOUNDATION, AND GROWTH

Because we know that all businesses are not alike, we've also created a 3-by-3 matrix for looking at how a business is performing versus the performance of the leading industry competitors in each cell of the matrix. The matrix is pretty straightforward. Across the top are the market segment types and down the side the three business modes. On the bottom is the harvest category. A *harvest* business is throwing off cash—what's often called a "cash cow."

On the other extreme are the growth businesses. *Growth* businesses are your future. But a growth business generally consumes a lot of cash, so you have to watch it very carefully. Benchmarking against competitors can be very important here.

In the middle is foundation. It's the *foundation* businesses that keep a company operating. They grow a little, and they throw off some cash. They're the older, established groups in the company that provide the cash needed to keep the growth businesses funded and growing.

BALANCED METRICS FOR SMALLER COMPANIES

How small a company can successfully use the balanced metrics approach?

I was at a Baldrige Best Practices conference to give a talk on balanced metrics. An individual spoke to me afterward who was with a company of 22 people. He said they do Baldrige; they try to live it, to make it a daily part of their business. That's what balanced metrics does—it takes Baldrige from an 80-page application to a daily process for running a business, a daily yardstick. That small company was a Baldrige winner and didn't mind doing applications just for the learning, but thought that balanced metrics might offer an even better approach to continuous improvement.

In a much larger environment, where senior executives are much further removed, like Varian Associates, Baldrige is done on a six-month cycle. When they go out to a far-flung division, they ask questions around Baldrige—"What are you doing about customer delight?" They don't ask financial questions—they can get that off their computer reports.

How far along is National with this?

We're still working on getting the balanced metrics process accepted and deployed. It's been a bumpy course at times.

Our version of the balanced scorecard has been recognized as a world-class approach to metrics deployment by the same people who administer the Malcolm Baldrige National Quality Award. I think it's a really hot process and will continue to press the deployment.

RICHARD SESSIONS

Personal Perspectives

The talk today is about the change in the role of finance. What changes do you see at National?

Traditionally, finance people have been the keepers of "the metrics." Today, however, the role of the finance function has gone beyond financial spreadsheets. Most of the finance staff I know realize that managing a business by the financials alone is about where you've been instead of where you're going. We need better tools to assess the capability of an enterprise to deliver shareholder value.

Finance at the corporate level is becoming more strategic. When a modern semiconductor fabrication plant costs over $1 billion to build, corporate finance must be very strategic. In fact, a major contributor to the design and execution of our new success model–based planning process was the VP of corporate finance, and the corporate finance staff provided much of our external benchmark data. From a balanced metrics perspective, two people—the CEO and the CFO—must champion the effort to facilitate a durable, successful implementation.

At the division level, the controllers often fill the role of assistant general manager, which requires them to take a much broader view of the business. They're beginning to think along the lines, "What's going to make for a successful new product?" rather than just asking, "How much is this going to make?" and "What's the net present value?" They're increasingly asking marketing questions: "Why is anyone going to want to buy this new product? Why will it be a success? Do we have the competencies required?" and so forth.

Again, from a balanced metrics perspective, because our traditional monetary measures are held by the finance staff, it only makes sense that they become the keepers of a broader set of "health of the company" measures.

CHAPTER 13

FINANCIALS AT MGM/UA

An Interview with Sid Sapsowitz,
Former CFO and Director,
Metro-Goldwyn-Mayer/United Artists

As a young man, Sid Sapsowitz joined the bookkeeping staff of MGM at its Manhattan offices at a time when he had no college degree and a single course in accounting. He rose to become the company's CFO, senior executive vice president, and a member of the board of directors. His friends say he achieved all this on the basis of very high native intelligence and a willingness to call the shots as he sees them.

During his career, Sid worked for MGM/UA[3] on two different occasions for a total of about 20 years; in the intervening years, he held a variety of jobs in aspects of motion picture distribution and exhibition, as well as in other industries.

AN ACCOUNTING SYSTEM FOR
A CREATIVE COMPANY

A movie studio deals with a lot of projects in quick succession, most of which have a budget large enough to launch a business or build a factory. Are the business and financial fundamentals very different from a mainline industrial firm?

SID SAPSOWITZ:
It's only been in recent years that the motion picture industry has started to operate as a business as opposed to a creatively generated enterprise.

At one time in my accounting career with MGM/UA, I was in charge of reporting to participants [the actors, director, producers and any others whose contracts on the film granted them royalties]. It was the end of the line, so to speak—the accounting statement to participants was the culmination of everything else that happens in the business.

It made no sense to automate this late part of the accounting process when all the pieces at the beginning weren't automated. So our recommendation was that we go to the sources and collect data, and then make the accounting of the participant statement the offshoot of a system for the company, rather than the other way around.

So we developed a film distribution system that started with the use of the 1401/1410 accounting machines. The problem was that they were so new on the market, nobody had them and you couldn't get them. But we found out that they had some at the Pentagon, and we worked out an arrangement to use the Pentagon's system at night on a rental basis.

We developed a regional system; six regional offices transmitted their information via high-speed tape to New York. This was actually the first commercial application of data transmission via telex.

ACCOUNTING PRINCIPLES FOR THE ENTERTAINMENT INDUSTRY

There appear to be a lot of, shall we say, "peculiarities" about the way accounting is done in the motion picture business.

Until the 1960s, every studio did its accounting and reported its financials in its own individual way, so nobody really knew, Is this studio a better investment than that one? Is it more profitable?

At that time, a board was formed by the Financial Accounting Standards Board, the FASB, made up of certified public accountants representing each studio, to attempt to establish a set of industry-wide criteria. There were, I think, nine official voting members, and they had the job of settling and agreeing on what would become the accepted accounting practices for the motion picture industry.

I still remember that each of the various platforms, if you will, in this program passed by a five to four vote—and yet today they are the gospel of reporting and accounting in the industry. There was no single plank that passed by a wider margin than that. And it wasn't always the same five to four. They voted like Congress—"I don't like your idea on this very much, but I'll vote for it if you support me on this other item."

158

What was the motivation for creating this set of accounting standards?

What was going on in accounting in the industry was so diverse. There had to be a series of criteria so that everybody would report film numbers that could be compared and the analysts could understand how they were arrived at.

The primary tenet of the new rules with regard to motion picture accounting was that you had to forecast out to infinity, which we call "the life of the film." For a theatrical film [as opposed to a television movie], it's considered to be 15 years. This has come to be known as the income forecast method.

FORECASTING INCOME FOR THE LIFE OF A MOTION PICTURE

I think that would border on the absurd most of the time. Nobody ever seems to have a clue which movies are going to be big hits and which are going to be giant bombs, and every producer in the business seems to have stories about pictures he turned down that became the hit of the decade. Unless you've presold a lot of the foreign rights and cable TV rights and so on, how can you possibly establish a forecast for accounting purposes that means anything?

We were wrong on every picture we forecast. But in the aggregate over an extended period, we were off by 1%!

You have to forecast how much revenue you think the picture's going to do theatrically, and what it's going to do in television and in cable, market by market. Of course, in the '60s, we didn't have a home video market.

We'd go to each department—for example, the sales department—and say, "Theatrically, what do you think this picture's going to earn?" Every quarter, you go back and redo it, revising it up or down.

If a film is forecast to be in profit, you record income on what they call a flow of income basis. It's based on how much income you have in the current period on this picture compared to the total income you've projected. Suppose that, in the current quarter, you received $10 of income, and you have projected $100 over the life of the picture. If your projection said that you'll have a profit of 5%, you're going to record 10% of that 5% in real numbers in each period going forward.

This is going to change based on how much income you receive in each period. The ratio of numerator to denominator is also going to change based on changes in the estimates. Adjustments are made on a cumulative basis.

But here's the catch: If the picture is projected to be a loss in your estimates, then, under the accounting rules, you must book the loss immediately.

So, if you've projected income to be $100 and the cost is $110, you must book a $10 loss, on the theory that you can't hold inventory at a greater value than what the market tells you it's worth—it's got to be booked at the lower of cost or market.

So I can have two pictures—number one, which is forecast to lose $50 million over its life span, and number two, which is forecast to have $200 million of profit over its life span. And for the first period of the accounting on these two films, I've got to show a loss, no matter how much money is coming in. Under the accounting rules, there's no way I can show a profit.

That's the income forecast method. As you can see, it makes it very difficult for a motion picture company to show profit when it has to book 100% of its losses and, on the successes, it picks up the profits only on a flow of income percentage.

And therein lies the reason why the small companies with limited production and distribution that try to get into this business show a loss from a P&L standpoint.

It's one of the reasons why it's taken many years for Wall Street to really understand the inner workings of the film company: you have a P&L that goes on the forecast method, and you have a cash flow that deals with the real world. The cash is working with the grocery store concept: What comes in is a plus; what goes out is a minus.

What's most interesting is that these tenets are 35 years old and remain the gospel for the industry, relatively unchanged to this day.

EXECUTIVES IN THE MOVIE INDUSTRY

Altogether, you had quite a lengthy career at MGM, when you consider that most of the creative executives don't last very long.

Up until the corporate conglomerates started getting into the motion picture business, the longevity of the top studio executives was 3 to 5 years, if that long. Because of the nature of the beast, most of these people focused on making a hit picture. They worried about how many pictures they could come to the table to make, regardless of whether the projects were sound from a corporate standpoint.

They were ready to put another $15, $20, or $30 million into production costs of a picture because they wanted it on their curriculum vitae, so that the next place they went, they could point to the 3 or 4 hits they had, not to the 17 or 18 failures.

They weren't interested in a studio improvement or an investment that would pay off in 7 years—they wouldn't hear of it. Even if it paid off in 4 years, that was too long because they figured they would be long gone when the payoff came, so why let the next guy reap the rewards of it?

ACCEPTING MONEY FROM OUTSIDE INVESTORS

The idea of an individual investing in movies is a little like investing in racehorses—it seems very glamorous, but the odds of doing well aren't very good. There have been a number of high-profile syndicates for the individual investor to put money into movies, but they don't have a very proud history, do they? I'm thinking, for example, of groups like Silver Screen Partners.

Silver Screen Partners is probably the most successful of these from an investor's standpoint. It's an interesting concept marketed by Disney that did make some money for its investors—but, over the long haul, they probably got their money back and only a small amount of profit, when you consider the time cost of money.

The concept on many film company board's was that, if you were going to make a picture, that meant you had confidence in it, so why would you want to share the profits with outside investors? It's a hard thing intellectually to explain to a board of directors that the more pictures you make, the greater the chance for a runaway hit, which is really the name of the game.

The fact of the matter is that winners happen when you least expect them, losers happen all the time, and, over a period of time, hopefully, if you manage your assets and your company properly, you wind up with a profit from the aftermarkets and runaway hits.

I could tell you stories of producers bringing two pictures to us; we pick one and he takes the other to MCA, or wherever. And, in one case when we did that, we took *Poltergeist*; the other one was *ET*!

So there was the board saying, "Why do you want to take in partners if you think the picture's going to be a success?" The answer, of course, is that, over time, you're better off to have help funding them because most pictures aren't going to make much profit, if any, and so taking in a partner is sharing the risk.

We made one partnership deal back in the early '80s, a seven- or eight-picture deal. It's probably the only deal ever designed within the industry where the investors were in the same position as the film company—they were exactly in the same position as MGM/UA, with the exception of a small distribution fee.

Seven or eight pictures—that should be enough to have a fair chance of making money.

It was probably the biggest failure of all the film investment packages. Unfortunately, MGM/UA lost a fortune and the participants lost a fortune—in the same percentages.

Had it worked, it might have been the pattern of the future because it helps the studio beat the accounting rules: If you sell receivables and they generate revenue, for profitable films, it enables you to book income immediately.

So all this is really to say that accounting in the motion picture industry is unlike accounting in any other industry.

NEARLY BANKRUPT? BUY A COMPETITOR!

The entertainment industry seems to go through a continual churning of companies being bought and sold, spun off, and reacquired.

[Laughs] In 1981, MGM was practically bankrupt. So what did we do? We acquired United Artists—another near-bankrupt film company!

We did a number of things, spinning off various companies, including the music company. Years earlier, when we needed cash, we had gotten rid of the music company—we sold it to Fox. And when we bought Fox, we got it back again. So we sold it again!

WHEN PROFIT CENTERS DON'T WORK

Has the role of the finance person changed in recent years in the motion picture industry?

The concept these days is to use the title of chief administrative officer as opposed to chief financial officer, which brings a whole different connotation. It's important that your financial people understand operations because, otherwise, it becomes a pure numbers game and your financial people can't sit down and explain to the operations people what's happening and what would help the overall company from a stockmarket standpoint.

I'll give you an example. At one point in time, MGM/UA turned to this very popular "profit center" concept. And every individual business unit chose to start its own profit center.

We had one company that I was chairman of, which dealt with commercial exploitation of the properties. At the time, we were producing a picture called *2010*, a sequel to *2001*.

The people in advertising had their theatrical advertising business, and our commercial end of the business, a different division, made a wonderful tie-in with one of the pizza companies. They were going to have a "*2010* Pizza," and we were going to print these posters with big pictorials about the movie and about the pizza.

The pizza people were going to pay us for each poster, and we were going to profit since each poster that we sold cost marginally less money. If we could sell several million, we would generate $100,000 worth of income, which was a sizable amount of money for this division.

We had a roundtable discussion group with representatives from every division, and we talked about what they were doing for each film. Well, the man from the commercial division got up at one meeting and made a big speech about how this was such a huge profit for "the company"—meaning his division.

I said, "Let me ask you a question. If we gave away the posters, could we get the pizza company to increase their expenditure for national advertising and international advertising for their pizzas and our film?"

And he said, "That company spends $6 million a year in advertising."

"Could we get them to increase that over the next year to $11 million, which they're going to benefit from, and so are we. And we'll give the posters away. I don't care how many posters we print, we'll give them away."

The answer was, "We could probably do that. But that's terrible—our division is going to lose $100,000 worth of income. Do you know what $100,000 of income is to this division? How can you, as chairman, even propose that?"

[Laughing] But I said, "Do you know what $1 million worth of advertising is worth to the studio in revenue from ticket sales? It's probably worth millions of dollars."

The final result was that I gave the commercial division $150,000 credit as intercompany profit from the motion picture company to make up for its "loss" of revenue, and the division's people were happy with that. We hit a home run all the way around.

This is a case in point. When you get to this profit center concept, you can start to lose the overview of what's happening. And it can be costly.

The profit center direction creates a lot of pluses, but you have to be careful that you don't throw away the baby with the bathwater.

SID SAPSOWITZ

Personal Perspectives

Are you originally from New York?

Yes—born and raised in Queens.

I started in the entertainment business in 1957, in the accounting department of MGM. I had taken one accounting course in my life and had no undergraduate degree. And I spent the next ten and a half years at MGM in various phases of accounting and operations and systems and data processing in days when we had no computers.

There was a long period in the middle of my career when I left MGM/UA to do other things before I landed back there again. Later, I decided that I wanted to go back to school and get my undergraduate degree and maybe get my master's in accounting. I thought that, at some point, I might want to teach, and I needed some credentials. Plus, my oldest daughter was about to graduate from Simmons College, and I said, "I might as well get my degree before she does." So I got my undergraduate degree in 1980, six months before she did.

In 1981, MGM/UA rehired me and brought me out from New York, and I was very fortunate to be again in the right place at the right time. I started in a director's job and became vice president of budgets and forecasts.

I then became chief financial officer and then I was on the board of directors.

At that time, we were MGM Entertainment Company, MGM Incorporated, MGM/UA Entertainment Company, and on and on. And I was chairman and on boards of various subsidiary companies, up until my leaving them in October of '89, when I was senior executive vice president, member of the board, and member of the executive committee of the board.

This is a difficult industry to deal with. Up until, I'd say, the late '80s, there was no longevity in the senior management of the company. I think I worked for 11 chairmen and heads of production during my tenure at MGM/UA.

Sometimes, I'd address memos, "To the office of the chairman, to whom it may concern."

I used to go to lunch and jokingly say to my secretary, "If my boss calls, get his name."

CHAPTER 14

SHORT TAKES: THE U.S. SUBSIDIARY OF A FOREIGN CORPORATION AND OTHER TOPICS

An Interview with John Staedke, Former CEO,
Hitachi Data Systems Corporation

Hitachi Data Systems is a $1.7 billion sales and service company offering mainframe CPUs and storage devices, 80% owned by a Japanese firm, Hitachi, Ltd., and 20% by EDS.

John has a B.S. degree, and an M.B.A. from the University of Dallas. He has held executive positions in sales, marketing, and consulting.

Since this interview, John has moved to Stamford, Connecticut, as president of the EDS global strategic business unit that provides services to Xerox under a $3.2 billion contract, making Xerox the second-largest EDS customer (after General Motors).

The conversation, however, deals with Staedke's perspective as CEO of Hitachi Data Systems.

DECISION MAKING: A GREATER ROLE FOR FINANCE

In a Japanese-based company, is the vision of the CEO limited in any way by the CFO?

166

<u>JOHN STAEDKE:</u>
Based on my experience, I would say that the CFO's role is definitely stronger in a Japanese company than in a typical American company. CFOs are definitely the gatekeepers and the auditors.

Further, in the Japanese approach—at least at Hitachi—the financial people are not only responsible for the development of financial plans but are held responsible for the organization meeting those plans to a significantly greater degree than in an American company.

In a U.S. company, the financial people would definitely be involved in putting the plans together, but execution of those plans would be mostly the responsibility of the operational executives.

So the CEO is somewhat limited in ways that he wouldn't be in an American-based company. Can you share an example in which the decision made was not the one you wanted, because of the stronger role of the CFO?

The introduction of new business initiatives has been more difficult. At issue is the front-end investment and inherent risk of the new business versus the CFO's drive to minimize those factors that might jeopardize attainment of the current-period financial plan. In an American company, the CEO would take counsel from the marketing people, the operations people, and the financial people, and if he was convinced that the opportunities warranted the risk, they'd go for it.

In the Japanese model, the influence given to the chief financial officer in a decision like this is greater.

For example, we've been actively working to augment our traditional business with new lines of both products and services. We've presented a variety of plans, and we've viewed them from a variety of perspectives over the past several years. We're only now getting to the point where we're making any reasonable progress, mostly because we've had to reassure the financial side of the house about the risk involved in expanding into new areas.

REPORTING TO A CORPORATE
OFFICE IN JAPAN

Do you maintain financial records in any different ways because the parent company is Japanese?

What we report is standard in terms of financial format. We complain about the detail, but what we provide is very similar to what any subsidiary company anywhere is doing. I'm sure every subsidiary complains about what it has to do in support of the parent's interests and concerns.

The Japanese are said to take a long-term view compared to the U.S., where a company is judged by its most recent quarterly earnings. Do you see a difference in what's expected of Hitachi Data Systems?

I'll be facetious and say that we've improved on the U.S. model by 100%—we work on a six-month plan, not a quarterly plan. Hitachi works on what we call an annual operating plan, but we do it every six months.

Hitachi clearly plans a number of years ahead but, from an operational perspective, it's only recently that we've begun working together on longer-term plans—in this case, three years. Part of the maturation of our relationship with Hitachi is the intent on both sides to clarify the role that HDS is supposed to play.

My belief is that many of the Hitachi executives who were involved when HDS was formed expected that HDS would function as the sales arm of Hitachi's Information Systems Group. As an independent company, however, we've operated with Hitachi on an arm's-length basis.

But, in relation, for example, to market strategies, approaching markets, and product planning, we have constant discussion about Hitachi's approach versus ours and what the differences mean to the plans of both companies.

How about Hitachi's thinking on market requirements relative to production capacity, the use of their patent and technology capabilities, and those kinds of things?

In the plug-compatible manufacturer market (PCM) that we've been in, IBM has been the architect of the overall environment, architecture, software, machine specifications, scheduling of availability of products, pricing, and so forth, of the defined mainframe marketplace.

We've then relied on Hitachi's consummate technology and quality design and manufacturing processes to create competitive, functionally compatible products. Hitachi's huge R&D capabilities make this possible. It's a constant struggle to assess potential market share and needed production capacity.

The normal tension between a market of accelerated product life cycles and the engineering and manufacturing time frames of highly expensive, complex capital equipment is made all the more difficult in our case by the cultural and distance differences.

The commonly accepted notion about the Japanese willingness to take the long view and not demand immediate results doesn't sound as if it's confirmed by your experience.

I think it may be true in markets not as competitive as ours where the margins aren't as slim. In our market, it's increasingly difficult for all manufacturers to reduce their manufacturing costs at anywhere near the rate at which market-price erosion is occurring. I guarantee you that Japanese companies are absolutely, month by month, quarter by quarter, half by half, concerned about profitability.

And, like any other American company, we've made many decisions over the last three years that are definitely, absolutely short-term, and not in the context of "We're in this for the long term, so we'll suffer a little here and make it up in the long run."

What specific numbers, charts, or graphs do you ask for in making decisions?

I pay a lot of attention to our P&Ls, but I don't think there's anything we look at that would be unique.

LOOKING AHEAD

Other executives I've interviewed for this book have talked about a change in what's expected from a finance department today. As a subsidiary of a foreign corporation, are you shielded from that, or are you also seeing, and being affected by, these changes?

Many companies today, foreign as well as domestic, still have too great a tendency to steer by the wake instead of trying to anticipate the future. The rate of change in product life cycles, technology, and customer requirements demands that every company get better at sensing the future if it expects to remain competitive.

The data that we have had access to have been largely spin-offs of systems that are more measures of transactions or signifiers of activity than predictors of the future. This is particularly true of financial information.

Now that things like data warehousing and related kinds of capabilities are being introduced, decision assistance is becoming much more available. This is something that a lot of companies are attracted to in terms of trying to figure out what the data say and, more importantly, what they don't say to enable them to better address the future.

Are there some specific things you'd like to be able to do?

We've been working to access information that we can use to get a better sense of where our customers are going and what that might mean to us in terms of products or services that we could offer them.

If we can get that information out of the data in our databases, we can shape products that our customers want to buy from us rather than buying from somebody else.

One difficulty we find is that many of our customers don't really have a good sense themselves of what the future looks like. We're trying to help them achieve clarity, which will then help provide direction for us.

What are some of the newer or more powerful approaches you're using?

We're just beginning to approach our customers on a total profitability basis, so that we can address what they've acquired, what we think their potential appetite is, and what it is that we're spending in selling to them. From that, we want to get a sense of whether this is a profitable relationship for us. If so, we want to invest more in it and, if not, we want to change our approach.

CHALLENGES FOR THE SPIN-OFF COMPANY

An Interview with Michael Steep,
General Manager, Worldwide Business Development,
Lexmark International, Inc., and President of
Lexmark International, KK (Japan)

Lexmark started life as a computer printer operation at IBM and was spun off in 1991.

Mike Steep has an M.B.A. from the University of Virginia. After 16 years in Silicon Valley working for companies including HP and Xerox, he joined Lexmark as the executive in charge of worldwide OEM [original equipment manufacturing] *business, and high-growth market development and has since been given added responsibilities as president of Lexmark Japan.*

FINANCIALS FOR THE SPIN-OFF

When we think of a spin-off, we think of a company that starts at the run because it already has all the people, all the procedures and, usually,

all the resources it needs to be successful. But I suppose it's not all sunshine and light.

MIKE STEEP:
When a company comes into life as a spin-off, it's natural for people to rely on a lot of the metrics and procedures they've been accustomed to using in the old organization.

Five years ago, many of the measurements that Lexmark used at the geography level—meaning out at the sales level in each region—reflected the legacy inherited from the parent company, which was based in part on looking for an absolute increase in revenue year to year without a lot of focus on market share. Although the corporation might decide to target a given market share in key countries, the metrics would reward managers based on an absolute revenue increase, with little emphasis on which countries would be pursued or how the manager would execute strategy.

Suppose you were a geography manager under this arrangement. You'd be given a revenue target of, let's say, $100 million of revenue in year one. Your plan the next year would call for a 15% increase, to $115, and you wouldn't have much motivation to link or coordinate your sales plan with the corporate umbrella strategy. So, for example, instead of trying to penetrate a larger and more sophisticated key country targeting a 10% market share, you'd go out to many countries and attempt to target $1 or $2 million in revenue apiece, which would give you the absolute increase in revenue.

A popular phrase used to describe this tactic is "picking the low-hanging fruit." But, from a market share point of view, it would give you one or two points in each country market which, for a technology-based company, can be insignificant.

What happens with this approach is that you never get deep enough in your penetration rate, and so the gains are not sustainable. The competition comes in and can kill you because you don't have enough market share to weather the storm.

My personal view is that, when we were part of a larger company, the printer division seldom focused on market share because it was part of a connect-rate business driven by placement of personal computers [that is, sales of printers were "connected" to sales of computers, so that the printer group pinned its expectations for market share growth on the growth of PC system sales].

When the spin-off took place, the newly formed printer company could no longer depend on IBM-PC sales to drive printer revenue growth. The situation had changed, but the inherited metrics remained the same.

Today, Lexmark has adapted and changed its metrics system to focus on the new market situation; the new focus is on market share in addition to absolute increases in revenue. We've changed the system to break out share targets by country, with emphasis on understanding how each country strategy will play out as part of the total region strategy, and to reward based on our performance against the industry growth and competition penetration rates.

ALLOCATING CREDIT FOR OEM REVENUES

One of your responsibilities is for Lexmark's sales to OEMs. From a financial perspective, have you made any changes in the way the OEM business is conducted?

Once again, we had to adapt the metrics system to market realities. The OEM business at Lexmark is a worldwide business, but we had to consider carefully how our metrics would motivate and drive behavior all the way down to the country level.

Let's say that there's a Japanese firm that I'll call the ABC Company. It comes to Lexmark and says, "We want to buy your ink-jet printer technology equipment and sell it as our own product, with our own logo on it, and using our own channels of distribution."

Lexmark negotiates a contract with ABC. We give it access to our technology, which allows it to sell the products as ABC Company printers—but, of course, it's actually Lexmark technology underneath the hood.

When we first started our OEM business some years ago, the Pacific sales region would receive credit for all the sales of this ABC Company product because ABC was headquartered within the Pacific region. The rule was to credit the sales region where the OEM customer was located rather than where the resulting product was sold.

Now, who actually generated this business, and why is it important to know where it gets sold? In my example of the ABC Company, Lexmark's Pacific personnel won't spend the resources, or significant time or energy, to support ABC Company. In fact, under the old system, they didn't even participate in the final contract negotiations—all the effort was put out by Lexmark corporate. Yet the region received credit for the revenue as part of its sales plan.

Does that create any problems? Yes. The region took that revenue stream and used it to support the overhead structure. So we at corporate really never understood how well they were developing the other priority markets outlined by the company's strategic plan, nor did we understand whether our OEM's sales forecast in a given country was realistic since we never tracked where they sold their products.

Region managers were being compensated for revenue that had been developed by HQ. Region budgets were receiving budget credits that went along with the revenue. And we had little understanding of the risk to our forecast for a given OEM's product line.

Now, let me stress that this was the situation five years ago, when we were spun off. We changed the metrics system to reflect the realities of the marketplace, to focus on where the equipment is sold, and to compare sales to the competition and channel situation in each country. That has resulted in a change in behavior. Our region managers now consciously assess risk down to the country level.

We've already seen positive results. Region managers are refocusing resources on the critical countries and tracking themselves against industry growth. In Japan, we grew revenue 100% from 1995 to 1996, and substantially increased overall market share—all within the framework of a lower-overhead organization structure. So now we track what the industry is doing, with a plan to stay ahead of competitor growth.

SURVIVABILITY

How do you determine survivability factors? How do you know what factors are key?

That's a really good question. Success is based on understanding the price/performance dynamics of your products, as well as the industry's financial model.

For example, in an industry where the performance doubles every 12 months while product prices remain the same or decline, you have tremendous change going on, which managers find very difficult to keep up with. It's not just a market change, it's an economic change, *and* a financial change.

Each year, you have to sell many, many more units just to be able to maintain your current share position and revenue because the prices keep declining—so the financial model is always undergoing major change. One of the first things you have to recognize is that your financial models have to be as flexible as the market is—and, in most companies, it's a difficult task to stay this fleet of foot.

REEMPHASIZING MARKET SHARE

When you say *financial model,* what you're talking about is tracking things like market share as your guide in decision making?

Yes, one of the guides. But many financial people don't see market share as linked directly to any of the financial metrics.

Market share is taught in just about every business school class; how could people not be focusing on it?

Businesses are on the cutting edge, and even they have a hard time keeping up with the pace of change. Business schools are removed from the front lines. Market share is always taught as being important but, in my view, it's seldom integrated and linked to a financial model driving the success of a company.

Although people often don't see it this way, market share becomes a driving factor of financial metrics—in the sense that market share can be correlated to how quickly you come down on the price/performance curve. The price component of price/performance is your margin, and the performance is the feature set you build. So they're directly related.

DIFFERENT METRICS FOR DIFFERENT LINES

What's the general rule from this? What would you say to people in other companies as the take-away?

The major take-away is that you must truly understand your industry's model and how well your own company can compete to take advantage of that model. What are the few key critical success factors? Is your company positioned to deliver these factors better than the competition? How do the company's distinctive competencies link to a success strategy? Have you linked your metrics system to reward behavior that optimizes achieving your plan?

In our business, we use a razor-blade model—which is to say that we want to sell as many printers as we can in order to get the cartridge revenue, which is very profitable. So I would argue that the main metric has to be market share–driven on the printers, with margin delivery on the cartridges and supplies.

Every company has to decide what the critical aspects of survivability are, for the long term, in its particular industry so that it can decide what metrics to put in place.

A STUDY IN CONTRASTS

An Interview with Robert Selvi, CFO, Cooper and Chyan Technology, Inc.

Cooper and Chyan develops products called routers—*software tools that help designers create the complex interconnections for the printed-circuit boards and integrated circuits that are today the heart of everything from computers and television sets to washing machines and factory assembly lines. The company completed its initial public offering (IPO) in October 1995.*

Rob Selvi joined the company about six months before the IPO. Prior to that, he was CFO and senior vice president of finance and operations for Claris Corporation, the software company. He holds an undergraduate degree in science, and an M.B.A., both from Santa Clara University in California.

BACKGROUND ON COOPER AND CHYAN

How large a company is Cooper and Chyan, and how would you define the finance role for a company of this size?

ROB SELVI:
We're a public company; we've been shipping product for six years.

Measures like cash flow ROI and RONABIT and EVA, which the Fortune 500 companies are using, don't really have much of a role here. I'm making decisions like (laughing) how long we can live with these chairs before we can get some decent ones.

Okay, that's exaggerated, but you get the point.

The first thing finance has to deliver is functional excellence. The financial function itself has to be run well, but the other half of the job is the business side. How do you act as a change agent in the company? What things do you look at? Large companies are focused on profitability metrics, efficiency metrics, shareholder value added, and so forth; in a company like ours, what you're mostly focused on are ways to accelerate revenue and improve resource allocation.

THE FINANCE ROLE IN REDEFINING
STRATEGY AT CLARIS

As CFO at the software company Claris, you saw a quite different level of finance operations.

Yes. Claris was a $160 million *[revenue]* software company with 600 people. We're in the $30 million range, with 120 people. At Claris I had 25 people in finance and 20 people in IS [information services]. My finance department here has recently grown by one: the U.S. organization has a controller, an assistant controller, and two accountants. My HR department has two people, who also do facilities. A lot of people wear several hats.

Claris was a wonderful experience. The founding management team had just left—they lost the whole executive staff and 50% of the directors in something like four months. We had to implement a completely different strategy—which is not to denigrate the strategy they had had in place, because it had been the right one for the time, when they were trying to reach a critical mass quickly. But we had to engineer a whole turnaround.

As CFO, did you have a role in the new strategy?

I think I played a fairly key role in helping to develop the strategy and then implementing it.

We began with a very McKinsey-esque strategy session. It was my first day at Claris, and we went over to Il Fornaio [a restaurant with locations in San Jose and Palo Alto that are favorite gathering places for the high-tech community]. They had arranged for a consultant who was, in fact, an ex-McKinsey person.

We started looking at all the businesses we were in and weighing each software category against two factors: Do we have a position of dominance in terms of existing market share? And what's the growth potential of the category?

We had thirteen different products and, ultimately, we exited all but three.

That's very drastic. But apparently it worked—Claris is still in business and still successful.

The strategy change on the meta-level was to determine whether or not this could be a growth business. We concluded that it was possible, but not if we remained so completely fragmented—we were a micron deep and a mile wide: we had very broad coverage in all these categories, none of which we had a dominant position in. So, yes, it was drastic, but successful.

MOVING BEYOND START-UP

Clearly the role of finance has to change as a young company moves into different phases. What are some of the most significant changes you see in that change of roles?

When a company is moving from start-up to a growing revenue stream, with a good product that's been well received, and there's a good story to tell, I think the CFO really needs to start making sure the investments being made are the right ones, because you can really optimize investments—by which I mean how much you're spending within operating expense categories by function.

How much are you spending in R&D versus sales and marketing, and what's the model for that? Are you using indirect channels or direct channels? What's the cost of each, and are you really using the right ones? In G&A [general and administrative expenses], how much are you going to spend on systems and how much on people?

All those things end up being really critical because you're not dealing with a large resource pool. Mistakes in suboptimizing your resource pool expenditures can really cripple you.

The CFO needs to highlight these things for the management team. As an example, I look at how much we're spending on publications. I don't know how many people it takes to write a manual, but a lot of companies outsource this, and we have four writers on payroll. We could hire three engineers for the cost of these four people. So I present the challenge: "Tell me why this is sensible."

The CFO is a combination of change agent, ombudsman, information provider, strategic thinker, and implementer. Ombudsman, because conflict resolution and building consensus are really important parts of the job.

And teaching people the business proposition as you go—teaching people not to be afraid of the numbers.

Yes, giving people the information so they can make informed decisions and agree with the decisions that are made, as opposed to just reacting viscerally.

Certainly, you want people to be well rounded in the business proposition, but which background would you pick for a CEO—technology, law, or finance—for the end of the '90s into the 21st century?

Of those three, I think I'd take sales and marketing! Because the most critical thing is sales revenue.

SPECIAL
PERSPECTIVES

CHAPTER 15

WHEN THE RED INK FLOWS—STAVING OFF BANKRUPTCY

An Interview with Charles Berger, CEO, Radius, Inc.

The Radius building features a jazzy lobby with abstract neon artwork set into the walls. In a style originated by Apple Computer, the conference rooms have frivolous names like "Charlie Chaplin," and "Clark Gable."

That tradition came to Radius along with its current CEO. Chuck Berger spent six years in banking and a prior finance position, and then joined Apple Computer, first as treasurer, then as VP of marketing, and finally as a senior vice president at Claris, Apple's software subsidiary. He later worked at Sun Microsystems as head of the desktop products division and then in charge of the government products organization.

Bergen joined Radius as CEO in 1993.

Despite some 20 years in the business world, Chuck looks so young you might almost mistake him for a summer intern. He seems to have kept up his good spirits despite his recent tribulations at Radius.

THE FIRST RECOVERY

What condition did you find Radius in when you arrived?

When I joined Radius, we were about a $130 million company in need of a turnaround. We transitioned over a couple of quarters and got ourselves back to profitability and back to growth.

In only a couple of quarters? That's very impressive.

Then we merged with our biggest competitor, SuperMac, virtually doubling the size of the company; and we finished the last fiscal year *[1995]* at about $310 million. Since then, we've unfortunately been beset by a lot of the same issues that are beleaguering Apple Computer: since we are 100% Mac-focused, when Apple's revenues come down by a third, we come down by at least that much.

METRICS FOR THE TRANSITION

In that first transition your team did when you arrived here, what were the financial numbers you were looking at to manage the return to profitability?

The most important thing was that we focused more on our gross margin and how we would get that to be a bigger number; it had shrunk prior to our getting here, through a lot of what, after the fact, looked like mismanagement of the inventory asset base.

In managing the gross margin, we spent a lot of time shrinking our inventory. This is a business where product life cycles are anywhere from three to nine months, and so we had to make sure that we had very fast turns in the inventory base and that we minimized our cost of components and cost of manufacture.

The revenue line as part of the gross margin equation, at that point in particular, was largely out of our control. Our pricing was determined by competition and how fast we wanted to get market share back.

The other area we focused on in the early part of the transition was operating expenses, which we brought down by 30% or 40%—all aimed at getting back to positive cash flow and profitability.

NONFINANCIAL METRICS

In terms both of the inventory and of reducing operating expenses, what kind of measures were you using—what was it you were focusing on there?

One of the most important measures was a nonfinancial one: In terms of the inventory, we were focusing on the number of months' sales we had in inventory. Our goal was to get down to one month in inventory—an inventory turn once a month. We actually got to a rate slightly better than that.

Did you aim to do that by slowing the rate of production to match the rate of sale, or what?

Actually, what we had was a lot of old inventory that we had to get rid of. We quickly identified it, measured what we thought its value was, and sold it off as quickly as we could. And then, at the same time, we made very sure—and we did this through a greatly enhanced forecasting process—that what we built was exactly what we sold. That's somewhat easier to do when you're in a business where there are indirect channels of distribution and your distributors will carry inventory, so that you can buffer your own inventory a little bit against their inventory. You have to be careful not to do that too much or you end up with a stuffed channel [*i.e., forcing distributors or dealers to stock and pay for excess inventory; this allows the manufacturer to book the sales and receivables, but for obvious reasons, can create ill will among the company's distributors or dealers, and ultimately create financial exposure for the company. In an industry with short product cycles, it also leaves obsolete and higher-priced product in the channel, which vendors must deal with.*].

ALLOCATING OPERATING EXPENSES

On the expense side, we looked at a couple of measures. We looked at just an absolute dollar amount versus what we thought our gross margin would be—so we knew how much we could spend in operating expenses and still achieve our target profit margin.

Second, within that number, we tried to look at really successful peer companies and how they spread that number across sales, marketing, R&D, G&A, and fit ourselves into that allocation of the expense dollars.

What was the hardest part of that?

The hardest part of the expense allocation was the question of needing to increase sales and marketing, which had been under-invested in the past, and decrease R&D—which is counter-intuitive for a technology company to do. But we were well over 10% in R&D and that was just way too much. Even so, to cut back on product development in a company whose heritage has been excellent products was a fairly tough challenge.

Was that a culture change or was it temporary—how did you handle that?

It required something of a culture change. In particular, there had been a major development project for a product that, in my belief, was never going to get done, and if it did get done, we wouldn't have the right sales and marketing structure for that type of product. So it required mostly just canceling that one massive project that had tied up about 50% to 60% of our engineering resources. And that was one of those cases of "You gotta finally step up to the line and make a decision." That's what a CEO gets paid for.

MANAGING THE RED INK

You've been through an experience that is unique among the people I've been talking to, in that you've been to the brink of bankruptcy and peered into the chasm. I'd like to explore that since it's something that every executive might face at some point, and there aren't a lot of places to go to get guidance on what to do. So I'd like to ask you to talk through that experience: What happened, what were the signals, and what steps did you take?

I will say it has been and is one of the hardest things I've ever done. It's incredibly draining emotionally, and it's hard seeing what it does to the people around you. But whatever I do in the future will be 10 times better for having gone through it.

I had an experience like that once in flying. I was letting down to a little airport in Georgia. I was probably at a couple of thousand feet or so, and it suddenly got very, very quiet. But I did all the right things—I trimmed for a glide, and I reached down and switched fuel tanks—and the engine started running again. And I thought: Well, I found out something that you never know about yourself until it actually happens: I didn't freeze up, I just did the right things, and now I know that, in an emergency, I'm not going to freeze.

That's great. Fortunately, I haven't had that happen in an airplane yet, but I know what it feels like when your *company's* engine quits!

I have to go back a little bit. Radius is in the color display business; that was half our revenues. We're also in the Macintosh graphics-art business and in the digital-video business.

Prior to the merger, we spent an inordinate amount of time examining inventory, which was valued in the financial statements at $60 million. How-

184

ever, we didn't spend enough time on it because we ended up getting about $10 million of value out of that. We examined the inventory very closely, but unfortunately it took almost nine months to really get to the hard realization that we weren't missing something—the value just wasn't there. We got to that realization late last summer, when the management team went to an off-site to look at where we were, because the strategic direction of our business was being heavily challenged.

We were starting to see the first signs that Apple was about to hit a downturn. I think we were one of the first leading indicators of that fact. We've made products that increased the functionality of a Mac. But Apple continues to put more of that functionality into the base computer. Four years ago you needed a graphics card just to turn on a monitor; today you don't need a graphics card on any Mac—you just plug in the monitor and you get good, fast graphics and color.

So, our graphics-card market had shrunk to only high-end professionals.

We had pegged our hopes for significant growth on digital video. The industry had been forecast to grow 10 times in four years. It's now clear that it will not even double in that time frame.

We were also caught up in being the first Apple clone maker, which tied up a huge amount of capital and a huge amount of management band-width.

Put all this together and it boils down to two things. First, the fundamental strategy of the company for the last eight years was putting it on a course to fail, some of which could have been foreseen, some of which couldn't. Second, our primary partner, Apple, was about to drastically alter our available market—in the wrong direction.

With Apple's fate and the impact of the merger, we got to the end of the September quarter in '95 and realized that we were out of cash. We were just out of cash. And we were about to break through our covenants on our loan arrangements with our primary lender.

When you realize that you don't have any more cash and that your bank isn't going to give you any more, you start this process that we've been through—in a very rapid way, surgically removing things that aren't creating value and restructuring in a way that best enhances the parts of the business that can create value.

With the benefit of hindsight, should you have seen that cash problem coming a lot earlier?

With the benefit of hindsight, we made a very big bet on the Apple clone business, and that didn't pay off. We should have thought through the what-if better. And the what-if in this situation would have made us face this question: If it didn't pay off, where did it leave the company? Where it left the company was technically insolvent.

On the other hand, if you don't take risks in business, you never grow. Dennis Dammerman of GE, in my interview with him for this book [Chapter 5], told me of the meeting in which he and Jack Welch decided to spend a billion and a half dollars on developing an aircraft engine that won't start producing cash flow for more than 20 years from now. On a grandly different scale, sure, but yours was the same kind of thing—you were betting on something that you thought was important to the future of the company.

Yes. In hindsight, we knew we had to do something or the business would just slowly erode underneath us. This industry doesn't reward negative-growth companies, and it doesn't reward companies whose markets are dying out from under them. We had no choice but to take some risks to try and find other markets.

It was an educated risk. At the time—this was the winter of '95—Apple had a billion dollar backlog, their revenues were growing at 25% plus per year, and a lot of that growth was in the high end, where Apple was making greater than 50% gross margins.

The systems that we were cloning at the time were a big part of that billion-dollar backlog and were selling for in excess of $6,000 street price. We believed that, if the market grew by 5% or less, which seemed achievable, given our brand, our presence in the channel, and our connection with the customers over nine years, it would be a phenomenal success for Radius.

What we didn't foresee was that, in June, the price of an Apple 8100 PowerMac was $6,000 and, that by September, it would be $1,500.

In 20 years, I've never seen a 75% reduction in price on anything in three months. Over three years, maybe, but not in three months. We've all beat ourselves up over this, but no one could have foretold that.

A CALL FROM THE BANK

What signal tells you this isn't just a little downturn, this is a disaster?

You get a call from your bank saying, "No more money."

Did you literally get a call like that?

Yes. This was the stuff of great drama. Our CFO and I flew out to visit our lenders and had a wonderful meeting for about two hours. We went over the results of the business—what had happened and where we were. We reported that this wasn't going to be a great quarter but it wasn't going to be a complete disaster, and we covered some things that we had learned we needed from them and from our manufacturing partner—who happened to be another part of the same company.

Two-thirds of the way through a three-hour meeting, they looked up and said, "You know, we thought we only lent you $30 million; we've actually lent you $50 million, and no one approved that." And suddenly we became bystanders at an argument among our lenders, including the senior credit officer. About four different functions were trying to cover their tails.

And we're up there trying to tell them, "Things aren't great, but give us a few things here and there"—one of which would increase their credit exposure—"and it will all be better again."

Were you aware that they thought they were lending $30 million and it had really gotten to $50 million?

No—no clue. The total credit was $30 million of bank-type debt and $20 million of trade debt through the manufacturing subsidiary. The manufacturing subsidiary had gone to the lenders and gotten them to guarantee the trade-debt risk.

Again, we didn't realize that transition was happening, although we knew we owed $50 million to somebody. But, at that meeting, it became clear that the senior executive at our lenders didn't know that they had just bailed out their sister company from the credit risk on Radius.

Nonetheless, we left the meeting with everybody calmed down and happy. We got on the plane, and my CFO and I had a nice ride back from New York and enjoyed dinner on the plane and a couple of glasses of wine.

In the morning, the call came. They said, "We're locking up your accounts. We're taking your cash. So, figure out how you're going to run the company under those circumstances," which you can imagine came as a complete shock. In fact, they had already notified the deposit bank that they were exercising their right as a lender to basically take control of that account.

What does a company do at that point?

A whole bunch of things that I didn't know at the time. First of all, you should panic. You *should* panic. I didn't even appreciate the gravity of the situation. We just had this nice meeting. I was thinking, "Well, okay, that must be some procedural thing. I don't know why they didn't warn us."

It was like having the engine go out at 50,000 feet. You have a long time to think about it and, all of a sudden, time goes by and now your engine's still off and you're not at the runway yet, and you're down to 1000 feet and, all of a sudden, your priorities get real clear again.

What I didn't appreciate was that, in taking control of the account, the lenders were withdrawing all the money to pay themselves down, and they had little interest in helping Radius continue operating.

We had to learn how you deal with lenders in that situation to get them to give us our money back, or at least enough of it to run the company. We were just fortunate that, while we were still at 40,000 feet, there were accounts around the world that they didn't control. They didn't have access to our Japanese or our European accounts, and we happened to have a fair amount of cash flow there.

So we ran for almost 90 days off our international cash flow. And we learned how to push the right buttons with the lender to regain a portion of our domestic collections.

What were the buttons?

The biggest thing that had to happen was that I had to go meet with them face to face and get them to understand that the business couldn't run without cash; it seems obvious, but they didn't appreciate that. And I had to make them understand that their recovery would be greater if Radius was an on-going business.

I really got face to face with them, to get them to see that, if they forced Radius to liquidate, their payback would be drastically less. We were spinning off parts of the company but hadn't realized the value of those spin-offs yet; and we had an ongoing business that could produce cash and retire debt.

Since then, we've paid them down from $50 to $25 million. We paid about $20 million of trade debt down as well. We've done everything I said that we'd do at that meeting.

A financial metric nobody ever wants to learn about is your bank calling you to say your creditor has taken over your account.

RONA AT RADIUS

Through all of that, I wonder if you were looking at numbers like return on net assets—RONA.

It's very easy to lose track of your balance sheet. The stock market and the industry focus on revenue growth and profit margins and rarely ever comment on the balance sheet. But now we are very heavily focused on our return on net assets.

In fact, at that off-site I mentioned, we brought in a management consultant to teach about return on net assets so that everybody could understand why it's important to keep inventory down and to keep receivables down.

We were at a juncture where we really had to decide what businesses we could afford to be in. Where RONA became very important to us was in determining what the true financial impact of each business was. We began using RONA as the principal measure of value creation.

Take our monitor business, for example. If you looked at it just on a P&L basis, it had barely adequate gross margins but would look like a business that was all right to be in—until you realized that it was tying up almost $60 million worth of hard assets and, therefore, the return on net assets calculation was abysmal.

More importantly, it ended up being more capital than we could afford to tie up in a marginally profitable business. Beginning about a year ago, we started to focus very, very hard on RONA and what it meant to the business, particularly in evaluating strategically which directions we were going to take.

So we attempted to sell off the monitor business, but no one would buy it, for the same reason we wanted to get out of it.

We just shut that business down over a period of one quarter, which meant that, in three months, we halved the size of the company. It really took us two quarters to bleed off some of the purchase business we had. We should have done that a lot sooner. We knew that the monitor business was going to become a commodity business but, until we looked at the RONA calculation of it, we continued to think that we could still make a small profit.

The idea of using RONA wasn't new to you.

No. It came from the experience I had at Sun, which had gotten into problems back in 1989 [see Chapter 9]: It lost money for the first time, was in the midst of a system conversion, and had gone from the Motorola architecture to the Sparc architecture. When I started at Sun, I couldn't figure out why the company had no cash. In fact, it was borrowing heavily.

Sun put in a new forecasting system, started to manage inventories and receivables and, about a year later, went from a heavy debt position to a substantial positive cash position. Today, I think, Sun has a couple billion dollars in cash. Since the problems in 1989, RONA has been where Sun put its executive compensation focus.

And, you think that the concentration on RONA was partly responsible for the success?

I think it was heavily responsible for it. And, when people's bonuses were tied to it, they took to heart the message, "Okay, I better make sure I only buy as much inventory as I'm going to sell" or "If I'm going to extend trade credit to somebody, I better make sure it gets paid as fast as possible."

We're not a capital-intensive company. Our capital is intellectual capital, and that doesn't show on your balance sheet. Unfortunately!

Was RONA being reported on your internal financials?

We started to a year ago, after that summer off-site.

So you were now out of the monitor business. How were the rest of the businesses doing at that point?

Our RIPs business was doing very well. We looked at it from a market capitalization standpoint and did some theoreticals—If this was a stand-alone company, what would the stock market value it at.

It turned out that this business was going to be valued very highly. Its market valuation was higher than the valuation the market was giving to the whole of Radius.

So we found an investment group that bought an 80% interest in that business and will soon take it public. Radius itself will realize, in cash, twice the market cap of Radius at the time we did that spin-out.

And that whole thing started when you began looking at the numbers that told you how the market would value that part of the business?

Right. But it's a hard decision to break up your company and sell it off in pieces, no matter how rational the metrics are.

We next looked at the systems business and really came to two conclusions. One, it has better margins and better structural aspects than the display business, but it's a capital-intensive business that probably requires captive manufacturing and definitely requires fairly deep pockets. Unfortunately, it's largely a commodity business, and that's the way people look at it. So we spun that off as well.

We didn't get a large up-front financial return. However, we own 20%

of the joint venture, and it will probably go public—if the Mac market holds up—in a year and a half or two years. We should realize again about the equivalent of the market cap Radius had at the time we spun it off.

After we had gone through this exercise of closing down nonprofitable and asset-consuming businesses, the result was a much more focused company, a company that had the right margin structure to get back to a positive cash flow and, someday, hopefully, to significant revenue growth—though, right now, that is a very distant second or third priority.

What are the other key metrics besides RONA that you're looking at?

We don't look at return on capital expense [ROCE] very much because, right now, we're not spending that much capital. In addition to RONA, we look at our inventory turns and our receivables days outstanding, and I look pretty closely at almost every individual item on the receivables.

And then, going back to the P&L, we're looking at our revenue achievement against goal, our gross margin percentages, and our operating expense targets. It's reasonably simple.

NONFINANCIAL METRICS

Are there any nonfinancial metrics in particular that you're relying on?

Sometimes you have to keep special watch on things that don't show up on the financials. We have to order parts in February for products we're going to be building in August. We have to make noncancelable purchases, and they're with people like Texas Instruments and LSI.

It's very difficult in this industry to have perfect information six months ahead of time. The lead time on components is huge and, again, something that a lot of companies in this industry forget to monitor because it's not a balance sheet exposure—but it's definitely an exposure.

What's the size of the commitment you have to make?

When you're about to take on a growth opportunity, like the one the clone business appeared to be a year ago, the commitment can be substantial. For Radius, it was nearly double the level of our existing commitments.

After all that, what are the businesses you're now focusing on?

We're now focused on graphics cards, which have leveled out and may experience renewed growth with our recently announced 3D products; digital video,

191

which is starting to show some growth although not what had been previously thought possible; and a very high-end display business, which consumes a fair amount of assets, but the margins are 40% and 45%—so that the RONA is actually very positive. Those three businesses, after a lot of pain, are all doing pretty well.

What was the process for getting all these things done?

We more or less did this in two steps. The first was to get the business focused, as I just described. The second was to bring our expenses down dramatically because the company was now much smaller; we cut operating expenses from $25 million to about $5 million this quarter, and did that over a nine-month period.

Are you laying people off?

We were a little over 500 people nine months ago, and we are now at about 130 people.

What were the other elements of the "salvage program"?

A lot of things. It used to cost us $250,000 a month for this facility; we sublet two-thirds of the building that we didn't need anymore and actually cut our costs to about $40,000; that was a huge component. We shut down our field offices and had our salespeople work out of their homes or move into shared office suites, where the cost was about half that of maintaining our own sales offices. We greatly curtailed marketing activities—to a point that we couldn't sustain and, in fact, we had to get back into PR and advertising, which we hadn't done for a while.

LOOKING FORWARD

With regard to the financials, what steps will Radius take to continue rebuilding?

As a $300 million company, we created a fair amount of debt, trade debt as well as bank debt. We're in the process of restructuring that, converting the debt into equity. As soon as that's done, we'll get back to positive net worth and a sound balance sheet.

The steps going forward from there are to take these three core businesses and continue to solve problems for customers. We've been fortunate to retain key engineers who are capable of doing that, which will get us back on the high road—which, unfortunately, is hard to travel on when you get into a life-threatening mode.

You said that, as a result of this painful experience, you'll be much better able to make decisions in the future. What are the things you think are the principal lessons from this?

I will definitely evaluate more thoroughly the downside risk of any decision we make. In fact, when some of our key executives ask me the same question you just asked, that's the first thing I tell them. We had a great management team and some of them, because of our downsizing, are no longer here—in particular, Dan Shaver, who was our head of sales and marketing, and Matt Maderos, who ran operations.

Their attitude was: It can be done, it can be done—which is a great attitude to a point, but you always have to make sure at what cost and at what risk it can be done. So I think that any of us, particularly myself, will make sure we temper this notion that it's always possible to work through something to a positive result and, in future, will look harder at the cost and risk associated with that result.

What numbers should you have been looking at that might have raised the red flag earlier?

Probably three things. The biggest one in our situation was really to evaluate how much capital we were going to use and how fast it would come back under some what-if scenarios, from the most optimistic to the worst possible. I'm not sure we could ever have imagined the 75% price reduction in three months; we probably wouldn't have gotten far enough down the layers to the worst possible.

Probably the right way to look at it is to take it down to where you can't afford the pain; at least then you know where that mark is, so that when it comes, it doesn't hit you from left field.

To finish answering your question, there are three things that I would do differently. One is really to appreciate the downside of the decisions matter. Two, I've become a much harder manager on expense control. There are a lot of people, including myself, with backgrounds in companies that had very plush cash flow. We were plusher than we had a right to expect for our size company, and that made us overconfident.

And the third is exactly what you said about your flying experience. We learned, when the engine turns off, not to start writing our wills or doing the rosaries; instead, start figuring out what you're going to do to make sure you're going to get through it.

And that was actually the hardest part—when you finally do see that ground coming up underneath you, to say: Nope, don't let go of the controls yet; just hang in there. And it turns out it's pretty hard to kill a company, even a little one like ours.

The crucial question would seem to be: Can you convince the bank that they're better off extending you more credit and letting you keep operating than closing you down?

The liquidation value of a company like ours is believed to be very low. If you have the balance sheet of a National Semiconductor, which has billions of dollars in capital equipment, it's a different story. We don't have that; we have $2 million of fixed assets; a company like Apple probably has $100 million for a $12 billion company. With us, the bank can't liquidate railroad cars or container ships or trucks or tanks—there just aren't those kinds of assets in our business.

And then, if you look at the inventory and the receivables in the high-tech business, people don't buy products from companies that aren't going to be around to service them, support them, and upgrade them. There are hundreds of companies in bankruptcy today. Home Express is in bankruptcy. We go there every weekend and the lines to the cashier are as long as they've ever been. If Radius were in bankruptcy, our product sales would go to zero, probably instantly, as would Compaq's, or Apple's, or almost anyone else's in this industry. When sales stop, inventory builds in the channel, and distributors want to return it for credit. Inventory stops selling and collections stop happening. So, no liquidation value.

What's the take-away from the whole experience?

I heard Lee Iacocca speak back in the mid-'80s after he had pretty much put Chrysler on its feet again. He said, "It's amazing when your back is against the wall, your priorities become instantly clear and you get focused on what's called survival."

Because in the middle of the crisis, for a couple of quarters, all that mattered was getting cash in from wherever you could and spending it only on the things that you absolutely had to and getting through the restructure. There are some people who will have to learn that lesson but haven't learned it yet.

We've now gotten through the crisis mode and back to a normal business operation, back to forecast meetings, and back to checking the financials every month and measuring against the important metrics.

How is Radius managing today?

We returned for the second time to profitability last quarter and should be profitable again going forward.

CHUCK BERGER

Personal Perspectives

You started on the numbers side of the house?

On the finance side; more in the deal making, in the treasury function—setting up financing, handling the cash management, doing foreign exchange. Earlier in my career, I put in place the first private-label credit-card program and the first floor-planning programs for the computer industry.

The credit-card and floor-planning projects turned out to be how my career segued into sales and marketing.

Do you view a finance background as important for people who want to rise to an executive position?

I think that, no matter what function you're in, functional experience in other areas is helpful. I certainly think that, if you're going to be a CFO or CEO or general manager of a large P&L function, to have had more than one functional executive-level experience is very important. I think it would be hard to try to manage the sales organization, the engineering organization, the operations organization, if you'd had only one view for 20 years.

As for finance, specifically, you have to have the experience by actually having been a treasurer or a controller, or you really need to gain the experience some other way so you can understand the numbers.

What we're all here for at the end of the day is to create value for the shareholders, and that value is measured by numbers. If you don't understand how that value equation works, then I don't think you can be successful as a senior executive.

CHAPTER 16

DESIGNING A COMPENSATION PLAN THAT DRIVES SUCCESS

One goal today in leading companies is to redefine compensation plans so that they promote the behavior and decision making in managers and executives that leads to increasing shareholder value. Several of the participants spoke about this key issue.

BILL RADUCHEL, SUN MICROSYSTEMS:

Before going to RONABIT as an incentive factor, what had Sun been basing incentives on?

Basically, we were on revenue—people were paid on *revenue,* believe it or not, not even profits! In contrast, RONABIT is a combination of asset usage and a cash metric but basically cash.

John Doerr [a key partner in the venture capital firm Kleiner Perkins Caufield & Byers], who is a director of Sun, had been urging RONABIT, but it just hadn't happened. When I first became CFO, when the company was in trouble, we had a tough three or four months but, in that time, we made a lot of changes.

It's hard to change a company but, in a period like that, you can make a lot of change. What's amazing is how many of those changes are still here today and are basically unaltered.

What you have to do is take advantage of the situation and turn liabilities into assets. I think Scott [McNealy, Sun CEO] was willing to use that time to make a lot of culture changes that would have been hard to do any other way.

You're not using RONABIT now for compensation. What have you replaced it with?

We pay on revenue growth and cash growth.

There's a cash factor as well?

There are some other bonus points on cash, but they're relatively minor—you know, EPS and revenue. We've talked about putting RONABIT back in, but we haven't. We have a goal that's tied to RONABIT accomplishment, and we have to grow RONABIT this year, but it's a relatively minor part of compensation compared to revenue growth and EPS growth.

The new metrics approaches—even the very complicated Boston Consulting Group approach—all have as their bottom line the goal of determining whether you're increasing shareholder value. From the sound of it, you're getting close to it in a more direct and simple way.

What we pay our top management is very heavily based on stock options. We have experimented with complex incentives. Let me tell you—they've never worked. Very bright, talented executives have not taken the trouble to figure them out.

We've tried a variety of things, and I'm prone to trying them. We put together one plan that paid out a year ago, and people got these very nice checks. They all came by and thanked me . . . but they had never read the plan.

We have another one that most people haven't cashed out, that people aren't focusing on either. I realize that many of my colleagues have a payment of $100,000 plus waiting for them, and they don't even know it's there, much less what they did to earn it.

People do not understand this stuff. If the incentive comp plan is not something that somebody easily understands, what good is it? We put out a vastly improved plan over what was there the year before—the expected value was much higher—and we took nothing but grief over it. The VPs hated it. So what did we do? We killed it. We went back to what we had before, and everybody said, "Great!" But we had actually taken money away from them!

Obviously, a compensation plan doesn't do much good if people don't understand what it is they're being compensated for.

We didn't think it was that hard. But we've learned that it can take years for people to figure out a comp plan.

DON MACLEOD, NATIONAL SEMICONDUCTOR:

Up until a few years ago, we had incentive programs that were based on six-monthly P&L performance. We wanted a longer-term perspective, so we introduced first—for about the top 700 people in the company—a one-year incentive plan called KEIP, the Key Executive Incentive Program, which was based on RONA, return on net assets. For the executive management team—probably 12 or 13 people—we introduced the long-term incentive plan, which was based on blocks of three years.

The first of these plans covered fiscal years '93, '94, and '95. It paid out in July of this year [1996]. That plan was based on improving return on equity—if we achieved the specified return on equity goals, growing the equity over time, we'd get paid out in shares.

The second version of that plan covered '94, '95, and '96. It will pay out this year, and was also based on return on equity.

The third version, covering '95 through '97, is based on a combination of ROE and the compound annual growth rate of sales as a percentage. We're trying to drive growth, but we're also trying to make sure we don't throw our profitability away. So it's a trade-off between the two.

The big question is: How do you develop the trade-off between these two? The shareholder, according to our model, would be indifferent between certain levels of growth and certain levels of ROE. Obviously, the trade-off will be skewed because, if you've got less growth, stockholders will be happier with higher profitability; for greater levels of revenue growth, they'll be happier to accept lower levels of ROE, on the basis of the view that the earnings and the revenue growth are sustainable over time.

The long-term payouts for the executives are based on a model. Depending on the ROE and sales growth, we will get paid, let's say, 105% of target for the three-year plan, paid out in shares.

What we have, then, is shareholder value as the payout factor in this trade-off.

RICHARD SESSIONS,
NATIONAL SEMICONDUCTOR:

In your Baldrige work with other companies, what are you seeing in terms of compensation plans?

I find that compensation managers are still very locked into the traditional financial measurements of health of the company. I have, however, seen compensation schemes that are as on-the-edge as senior managers being rewarded only on their company's Baldrige score.

In theory, if you have a good Baldrige-based approach that's deployed throughout the organization, you're going to get the results. The financials will happen. There's also a fiduciary responsibility that the senior executives have to have. And, especially in a highly capital-intensive business like semiconductors, the financial metrics can be quite severe.

A compensation scheme we're working on now is around normalized growth vis-à-vis the industry, Baldrige score, and gross operating profit (GOP) or cash flow for "harvest" businesses—because it's cash that allows you to afford the R&D investment you need to generate the lifeblood of the company—new products.

There isn't one of these measures that can be sandbagged. They're all indexed to external criteria. For example: 30% growth year-on-year sounds pretty good but, if your industry is growing at 50%, your business is losing share—not good. Should you pay senior executives a bonus on 30% growth under these conditions? Probably not.

However, if the business is growing faster than the industry, that's a different story.

TOM ZUSI, ALLIEDSIGNAL AEROSPACE:

Today, we're more outward-looking and we're getting better at it. If you look at the financial rewards that the senior people get, they're based on the stock price. That's where their big payday comes. That has created a lot more alignment.

In Hennessey's day [the previous corporate CEO], we gave lots of options but the stock price didn't move—it stayed at 30.

Today, on an equivalent basis, the price has moved to 120 in four years. It doesn't take very much math to figure out that, if the stock price is moving 15% per year because that's what you're growing the company, then those stock options over five years have a very attractive compounded rate of return.

The compensation package hasn't changed one iota. What happens is that what was supposed to be the long-term incentive element of it really didn't provide any incentive push. And the reason they didn't get that message before is because the stock price didn't move.

It took a Larry Bossidy to establish credibility in the marketplace and to be able to demonstrate for the management team that, in fact, they had

200

the capability to affect the stock price. The price has gone up as a result of his leadership.

What that has meant to the managers is something I found interesting. Some say, "You know, the reality now is that my incentive is to see Allied successful. If we continue to make our quarterly numbers, I'll be rewarded. I see that it's not a question of whether I succeed. If I succeed and the company fails, I lose."

They tell me, "I've got to make sure Allied wins because that's ultimately where I will get the biggest reward. Not because my business unit succeeded—even though that may give me a slightly bigger bonus—but because Allied succeeded."

DENNIS DAMMERMAN, GENERAL ELECTRIC:

It's never perfect, but there's been a dramatic change in how the leadership of our company is compensated. And in many cases, it goes far beyond the leadership. Our wealth creation device today is the value of GE stock. That's how I accumulate my net worth.

My annual compensation, the pay I get for how I do in the short term—my base salary plus my bonus—for me is important, but the way that I *really* get rewarded is in terms of the value of GE stock.

It's not just true for me, it's true for every one of our business leaders, and the management teams in every one of our businesses. So there's this *huge* incentive, in the long-term view, for all of us to want the whole company to do well.

That's a dramatic change. Partially because the stock market was not performing well in the '70s and the early part of the '80s, annual bonuses and a good pension plan were for many, many years the way you would think about providing for your future.

Everybody assumes that the pension plan is going to be there, but the annual bonus becomes a short-term orientation. So we have greatly increased the number of stock options granted. And not just to the fat cats, by the way, who hold less than 10% of our outstanding options—we've got 22,000 people in our company who hold options, down to the lowest level of salaried employee. They don't necessarily get them every year, but 22,000 is a lot of employees.

At today's stock prices, there's over $2.5 billion of gain in unexercised options.

This approach works for middle-sized companies, as well. And, of course, the leaders in the whole option game are the Silicon Valley start-ups. But the only way they get people to come is to give them a big piece of the action. Often it's the only way you can convince a supplier or consultant or accountant, or whatever—"Come on in and help me, and I'll give you some options."

But in terms of our own behavior and how people act, in terms of their well-being and how they think, we've found that stock is a wonderful incentive.

START-UPS AND THE "VIRTUAL CORPORATION"

CHAPTER 17

THE VENTURE CAPITALIST'S VIEW

An Interview with Yogen Dalal, Ph.D.,
Partner, Mayfield Fund

Mayfield Fund is one of the brightest lights of venture capital in Silicon Valley. In early 1996, when this interview was conducted, the firm had over $700 million under management and had, in the previous 12 months, taken 15 companies to initial public offering.

Mayfield's offices are on the gold brick road of venture capital—Sand Hill Road in Menlo Park, California. The suite is framed by an imposing entry that bespeaks money and success. Inside, the atmosphere is high-pressure but low-key; walk past a glassed-in conference room, and you realize that the intensely focused presenters in discrete, conservative clothes are making a case for several million investment dollars. On a typical day, two or three such meetings may take place. Few of the groups will get funded by Mayfield, but even getting this far is some measure of success: in most cases; they got in the door only because someone in the start-up group had established a strong enough reputation to become known to a Mayfield partner.

Yogen Dalal, who is known in Silicon Valley as "the elegant gentleman of venture capital," holds a doctorate in electrical engineering and computer science from Stanford University, did R&D work at Xerox PARC, and was a codeveloper of the Ethernet and TCP/IP protocols. He was a founding member of two successful start-ups—Claris Corporation and Metaphor Computer Systems. In conversation, you are struck by the precision of his intellect and the warmth projected by his slow smile. You're left with a clear impression of true balance—the too rare fusion of brains and humanity.

P/E'S AND MULTIPLES FOR
HIGH-TECH COMPANIES

Some of the standard measures that the stock market has used since time immemorial don't seem to apply very well to companies that are the stars of high-tech today. Not just the high-flying start-ups like Netscape but even some of the well-established companies have unreal numbers. What's going on?

YOGEN DALAL:
I think the relative numbers are changing because people ascribe new meaning to them. For example, if you look at today's IPO [initial public offering] market—once upon a time, people would talk about P/Es of 25 or revenue multiples of 2 or 3. In a fast-moving industry like high-tech, all the numbers are meaningless because they don't capture growth, or dominance in a market.

So people are now talking about even 100 P/Es because we're using old metrics to capture new properties of high-growth companies.

Does this apply just to start-ups, or to mature companies with a revenue stream as well?

I think numbers like P/E are still very useful to the operating company with revenues. Within a company, you have to keep track of these numbers because they do have meaning.

But I think that, in the high-tech world, they are less useful and they are used less in determining the value of companies.

Some of these new measures help the operating executives and the CFO justify the value of the shares. How do you talk about performance so that Wall Street can think about things like intellectual property and human capital? People are talking more and more about these as important ingredients in determining the value of a company, and not just the traditional smokestack ways of measuring.

OWNERSHIP BY THE FOUNDERS

Does Wall Street have a problem when a new company issues shares for the first time and the founders get rich overnight—at least on paper?

We're big believers that a large portion of a company should be owned by the employees. In a funny way, that's what start-ups are all about. And, indirectly, that's how you preserve intellectual capital in a company—by allowing the people to own a large piece of the company. Even after it goes public, we ensure that there are big stock options for all senior employees in the company.

It's amazing—we often meet private financiers who invest in nontechnology businesses, who operate completely differently. We just made a new investment alongside a private investor, who sat in our offices and literally turned white when we told him that we were going to reserve 8% of the company for the CEO and another 10% to 15% for other executives and employees.

He came out shaking. He looked at us and said, "We have a lot of confidence in you, but maybe we were not meant to be partners because this is not the way we operate." He felt we were giving away a large gift to these people.

But he calmed down. We met for breakfast the next morning, and he said, "We don't do things the way you do, but you're right." It's like culture shock the moment people come into Silicon Valley.

I don't think that the government in Washington really understands what makes the whole West Coast click. They don't understand how to measure intellectual property and human capital, and they don't understand the incredible ethnic diversity of the people making it all happen. People forget that the reason Microsoft is where it is and Apple isn't has to do with human capital. [Bill] Gates still owns a large percentage of the company that he created. The pride of ownership boils down to the fundamentals of what is America.

VENTURE CAPITAL'S THREE YARDSTICKS

It sounds like you put a lot of emphasis on the people in a start-up. What are the other leading factors you look at when you're considering an investment?

There are three things venture capitalists look at. One is what we've just been talking about—people; the second is market momentum; the third is the product. For us at Mayfield, we look at the items in that order.

When we make an investment, we want two out of the three: If you have the people plus an incredible technology, you may be ahead of your time, but the market momentum will hopefully get there. If you have market momentum and you have people who can reasonably be expected to create a good product, then probably they will succeed.

207

That sounds like, "Any two out of the three, as long as one of them is the people."

Absolutely. The right people, plus either of the other two requirements. Part of our assistance to them is to help them work on whatever the third piece is that they're weakest in.

How does the list differ for other vc [*venture capital*] firms?

Some venture capitalists invest only in market momentum. They figure that, if the company isn't working, we'll just put someone else in to run it—and, as long as there's market momentum, it will attract good people.

THE PEOPLE TO RUN THE COMPANY

But the attitude at Mayfield is different?

We want to find the best people we can who have the hunger to be entrepreneurs. Today, we see a lot of "wanna-bes"—people who think they should be entrepreneurs because they see everybody else making a lot of wealth. What we really want to find is the next Marc Andreessen [founder of Netscape], the next Reed Hastings [founder of Pure] and, yes, even the next Bill Gates—people who are young and have a lot of energy.

You want to get them and have them come sit in your offices. [Mayfield and some of the other Silicon Valley venture capital firms provide office space for what might be called "entrepreneurs in residence"—people they have identified as worthy of receiving financial backing as CEO of a start-up; these people read the proposals that come through, select the few that they believe have the potential and market momentum and, ultimately, choose an operation they would like to lead. If the company agrees and the package receives the vc firm's approval, the company gets its new CEO and its initial or next phase of funding.]

Our history has shown that it really is the people. If you have people, and the wind in their sails from market momentum, then those people will be able to complete a product that will satisfy the needs of the market.

On the people side of the equation, what are some of the guidelines, what are some of the things you're looking for?

In the high-tech world, a venture capital firm has to pair a businessperson with a technologist. You cannot build a company without both anymore. I think that, now, in addition to a CFO, you really need a CTO—a chief technology officer—who isn't just a founder who's been promoted up and given this title to keep him out of the way but somebody who will have as much impact on the future of the company as the CEO does.

That's what went wrong at Apple. After Steve Jobs' departure, they were never able to fill that position.

MARKET MOMENTUM: PAINKILLER, NOT VITAMIN

You've been using the term *market momentum*. What do you mean by that?

By market momentum I mean a receptive market that's ready, through a variety of ways, to absorb the product—ready and perceiving a need.

I think of a product as being either a vitamin or a painkiller. A vitamin is something you *should* take; it's good for you, but not taking it won't do you any damage. Vitamins are available on every streetcorner. As a consequence, a vitamin company has to spend marketing megadollars to sell its products.

A painkiller is something you really need. You know exactly the names of the products. When you want it, you'll place an order for it, even if it's two o'clock in the morning. You don't mind paying the money.

Start-ups succeed when they have a painkiller. They succeed because they know how to find you, their customer. And, hopefully, nobody else has a solution as good as theirs.

But your product isn't a painkiller unless buyers have a big enough pain. Otherwise, the market is too small. Market momentum is the frenzy that says, "I've got to have it yesterday."

Sometimes, you create market momentum on your own, the way Netscape did. Or it happens because of a variety of phenomena, all of which you control. It often has to do with social and economic changes and with things happening elsewhere. It's what Geoffrey Moore, in *Inside the Tornado,* called "a big sucking sound"—people whisking the product off the shelves.

Moore talks about the tornado as this *momentum* happening—because, in the tornado, things are crazy. Apple went through a tornado, Cisco is going through a tornado, Netscape is going through a tornado. In a tornado, the basic premise is that if you don't ship the product, your competition will ship.

So, when you're in a tornado, there's only one premise: people can work all day, all night, but all that counts is whether you ship the product first because, if the competition gets it out first, they will get market share. He who goes into the tornado first, and obeys the rules of the tornado, will come out first, and will be king of the market.

Sometimes, you create a company in a world that already has market momentum—and you hope that you're carefully enough differentiated that you can get into the slipstream.

Or, sometimes, you anticipate market momentum—you're ahead of the market—when market momentum happens, you're ready. Today, people are rushing to invest in any company offering a new feature for the Internet because they think there's incredible market momentum, and so they say: There'll be three, four, more companies—but who cares if there's competition because the demand's going to be so great that we'll all be sucked right in.

EVALUATING A VC PROPOSAL AT MAYFIELD

When people come to you for venture capital, their income projections are, of course, always optimistic. What do you look at in the business plan to tell you whether the numbers seem believable and on target?

In addition to the classical items of top-line growth and bottom-line earnings growth and how the two change, we want to see when the company says it will turn cash flow–positive. With a start-up, which is what we're looking at, the most important thing is cash. Cash is king.

When we get a business plan, the number we start looking toward is cash flow analysis. How is cash projected to come in and go out? It's not just the P&L, which is what a large company would look at—a large company has so much cash that it has a buffer. But a small company has very little.

We also look at measures to show when revenues per employee will break over $200,000 a year; that's a very important metric for us. It's a rule of thumb. Once a company is doing this level of business, we figure it's crossing this line [from a start-up to a business with a positive cash flow].

Is that a Mayfield rule of thumb or is it more widely used?

I think it's a yardstick developed here in the Valley. Over time, distribution models have changed. And I think that Apple was one of the first companies to break this rule. It went from about $100,000 to $150,000 per employee to over $200,000.

Generally speaking, a company cannot break that $200,000 per employee unless it has market momentum because, otherwise, the cost of sales and marketing, or customization, gets too high.

So, again, we're looking for situations, whether a niche market or a specialized market, where a company can *own* the market. It means that it has to have momentum.

How do you tell whether the numbers you're looking at are trustworthy?

[Laughs] That's a very good point. Again, when they give us their pro forma, we will often ask them for more detail on a quarterly basis. But we'll also grill them—"Have you worked it out on a *monthly* basis?"

We'll go over the detailed pro forma to see if they've looked at all the assumptions. But, in the end, it comes down to rules of thumb based on the particular market segment: How fast can you grow? Can you really grow from $2 million one year to $15 the next? You can't build a sales organization that fast.

If people are suggesting more than 100% growth a year, it's suspect. There will be some years early on, of course, when 100% may be reasonable because the numbers are so small, and even a growth from one to five may be achievable—but not over the longer run.

P/Es are now being talked about almost as if they were indicators of market growth. If a company is growing at 50% or 70% a year, it's likely, in today's bull market [in 1996], that P/Es will reflect what the annual quarter-to-quarter growth rate looks like.

But there's another protection built in, and we make sure people understand this up front. Once we fund a company, the revenue projections in its plan become a commitment. If we see that it's not making the numbers the plan said, then it's a reflection on the way the company is managed. We might decide that some people need to be replaced.

The sales VP?

The sales VP or the technology team may need some beefing up, if they're not getting the product out. Or maybe a new CEO is called for. It depends on the situation.

In other words, if the company's management has exaggerated their revenue projections, those numbers may come back to haunt them.

There's a strong incentive to keep the numbers honest.

Missing revenue targets is the problem that Geoffrey Moore had in mind when he coined the term "crossing the chasm." His book describes what goes wrong in meeting revenues and how to create an effective strategy.

WHY SO MANY VC INVESTMENTS DON'T MAKE MONEY

What are your financial expectations when you fund a start-up?

We're investors who handle other people's money—we have university endowment funds, pension funds, and so on. For us to make money, and for our investors to make money, we have thresholds at which an investment doesn't make sense.

For example, we wouldn't invest in a company that came in and said, "Put $5 million in and you'll get 10% of the company." Thank you, no. Our goal is to have reasonable ownership so that, as the company raises more money, we can still make that home run—even though our percentage is being diluted each time the company raises additional investment capital.

When we look at our own business, we find that, with 10% or 15% of the companies, the money invested gets completely written off as zero return. Another 15%, after three or four years of effort, we get back more or less the original investment. So one-third of our money has made no money or has lost money.

About 20% of our investments give us over a 10-times return.

As a consequence, unlike a mutual fund investor or a mezzanine [second or later round] investor, we don't look for the two or three times return—because we can never judge that. Some venture capital firms can do that—they have hordes of people poring over every aspect, advising the company on how to restructure, how to maneuver the entity to succeed.

But we're what you might call "optimistic investors." When it clicks, it moves. The intuition we've developed over the years about people, about market momentum, is really the driving force. And then we make sure that it fits together—that *they* have enough ownership, and *we* have enough ownership.

You referred to an investment being "diluted." I'd like you to explain what that's about.

It's a standard part of the financing process. Take the case of Tom and Dick who form a business together around some new technology, and they split the stock 50/50. Then they get venture capital financing—let's say they get $4 million, and the vc firm takes 40% of the stock.

The stock of the two founders originally represented 100% of the company; now it represents 60%. So Tom and Dick now have $4 million to build an organization and get their product into the market, and the company has a much higher valuation than it did before. But each of the founders now owns 30% instead of 50%.

Typically, there may be three rounds of financing before the company is ready to go public, and all stockholders—founders, venture capitalists, executives, and employees who were given stock to come aboard—have their percentage diluted on each subsequent round of financing.

So it's quite common for the founders to have only half or a third of what they started with by the time of the IPO. But those few points have still made paper millionaires out of a great many people in the Valley.

SETTING THE VC PRICE AND VALUATION

To get to the specific numbers, the question that so many people wonder about is: If we get venture financing, how big a piece of our company do we have to give up?

There isn't a formula for this, unfortunately. When you're successful, it doesn't matter. With Netscape, Kleiner Perkins had 10% of the company; but, in a home run situation like that, 10% is enough to make them smile. With companies like Global Village and Yahoo, Kleiner Perkins had very large ownership—upwards of 30%.

What you're really looking for is a very large gain for the time, effort, energy, and work you put in.

Most of the A-class venture capitalists—that includes Mayfield, Kleiner Perkins, IVP, and Sequoia—at an early stage, which means that the team is coming together and there may be an "alpha" prototype of the product, all like to have at least 20% of the company for each of the investors. So, at the first round of financing, if two venture capital firms are sharing the investment, they would each want 20%.

We've been in situations where we've had as little as 10% and in others where we've had as much as 30%. It isn't so much the numbers themselves that are critical; it's the composition of ownership between investors, employees and management that makes for a good working balance.

There is a kind of benchmark for how much the investors should own and how much the employees should own. If employees have less than 20%

of the company, it often isn't attractive enough to motivate them. Usually, management and employees should have between 20% and 35% at the IPO.

The question is: What is the starting point to arrive at that level?

Let's say you're a vc firm in the top-tier category. A team walks in the door with a CEO, an engineering executive, and a couple of engineers; they've got a plan, they've got a pretty good idea of what they want to do and, if it's a software company, they may even have a prototype. And they say, "We think we need $4 million."

They would probably have to give up 40% to 45% of the company for that much investment. Each of two vc firms would put up half the money and take 20% or 20-plus% each.

If the company needs $6 million in the first round, the team is more likely to have to give up 50% of the company. And there would be a question about whether that $6 million would be put in by two venture funds, or three.

Generally, 50% of the ownership is given to the investors pretty early in the investment cycle unless the management has been able to get a lot further along on its own. That often happens if the people have done some consulting work or have gotten a contract from a corporation to build some part of the product, which has let them get down the road before seeking venture funding.

So the ideal situation from the company's perspective is to get some of the work done first.

I wouldn't say it was optimum, but it is a path.

What would the downside be?

The problem is that the corporate entities may be asking you to do development that's not in the best interests of your enterprise. They have you spending your time customizing the product in a way that isn't really getting you closer to having a version for the general marketplace.

METRICS AND PRACTICES WHEN THE CASH FLOW BECOMES POSITIVE

As a venture capital firm that's provided the financing for a company— once the company is up and running and has been in business for a couple of years—what different parameters would you start looking at to see if things are tracking the way you had expected they would?

Once things have gotten out of the incubation or development mode and are really moving into the marketing mode, companies tend to have a more typical P&L statement. I think what you're really looking for at that point—when the company is still prepublic—is basically cash flow. The nature of this business is that you manage your cash flow correctly and get as much growth as you can.

At this point, some of the *non*financial metrics become more important. Manufacturing people look at inventory turns—the number of times a year you replenish your inventory. You want to minimize tying up capital in inventory. And just-in-time says you should be able to do it 12 times a year or, in some cases, even 20 times.

In the same way, I think, from a financial point of view, you want equipment lease lines. And also, you want to try leveraging your cash—working with banks to get a receivables line.

As someone who isn't a financially oriented partner here, when I go to a board meeting or look at P&Ls, I'm really looking at the fuel tank and asking, "Do they have enough fuel?" Because I *know* they're going to hit turbulence.

So we encourage companies to have a little more cash than a sole proprietor would have. For somebody who has his or her own dry-cleaning store or consulting business, you can operate on much thinner margins.

But, after that, it's making a trade-off—how much of your margin dollars do you spread between the R&D function, sales and marketing, and G&A [*general and administrative expenses*]? Look at that ratio constantly.

If you look at a typical annual report, you might find that R&D is between 7% and 10% whereas, in our companies, R&D is always much greater. So, if R&D is greater, what's going to be less? It has to be G&A or sales and marketing. As a result, companies here in the Valley just run on thinner G&A. But, at times, you shift the trade-off between sales and marketing and R&D. Once you get out of the development mode, you really want to look at that—because whatever you can save in sales and marketing, you want to put back into R&D.

At this stage, you would be using two-year pro forma plans. This is something of a treadmill business in that, if you don't stay ahead, you're going to get trampled.

Also, small companies are very nimble in how they have to cut back. A couple of years ago, every time Apple said, "We're going to lay off some people," it would ricochet through the Valley. Now people don't talk about that so much. And Apple can trim 2% or 3% or 4% off the sales force, and you don't hear about it. The company will pare down, slow down a little, and then build back up.

There's one partner here who was an operating CFO himself who can look at a P&L or balance sheet and see things the rest of us can't. So we rely on him to keep us honest. Every time we do new financing—a second or third round—he pulls out his glasses and is able to tell us, for example, "There's a lot more capital in this particular bucket than there should be."

There's a reason why the Silicon Valley is such an incredible hotbed of activity. One of my partners often said that the Valley is the Venice of the 20th century, a place that attracts smart people. The cultural diversity is incredible.

With it comes the same intrigue and politics that Venice had, too.

And the beheadings and the spy networks?

I prefer to think about it, again, in the terms of Geoffrey Moore. He says that you go from the bowling alley, to the tornado, onto Main Street. Initially, in the bowling alley, the two important things are product leadership and customer intimacy. When you get into incredible market momentum, you have to give up customer intimacy and become operationally excellent.

That means you must have an organizational change.

When you go from the tornado to Main Street, you must start segmenting your market—as Hewlett-Packard has done with its cellular phones: You have to have operational excellence plus customer intimacy so that you can get your customers to buy the third phone and the fourth and the fifth. But, often, you don't need *product* leadership.

Organizational changes, which are sometimes perceived as beheadings, are part of the natural changes a company goes through as it grows. Very few people can be CEO for all three phases; Bill Gates is a noteworthy exception, and that's another reason Microsoft is as successful as it is.

THE "VIRTUAL CORPORATION"

Are the financial measures any different in what's being called the "virtual corporation"—when the company is contracting on the outside for most of what it needs, maybe forming strategic partnerships, and may not even have any offices of its own?

This is the part of finance that's actually getting more complex, and I don't think we've got our hands around it. The whole concept of the virtual corporation is, I think, critical.

In the old days, you had a vertically integrated company—General Motors, IBM, Campbell Soup. At least at our end of the business—and I think it's also true of the larger companies—the notion of a virtual corporation is basically that now people are focusing on what they're good at and outsourcing everything else.

As one example, you have new semiconductor companies that don't have their own fab [chip fabrication plant]. The fab lines and foundries are something they rent or lease or outsource since companies that own fabs are often not using them to full capacity.

New companies that have the brains to do the design work and the marketing and distribution to sell the chips can easily come into existence. So you can build semiconductor companies without ever having any capital equipment.

That concept has been taken further into a variety of other businesses. I look on every start-up as a virtual corporation, and Silicon Valley itself is the virtual corporation that enables a start-up to succeed—which means that the entrepreneur does what he or she is good at and outsources everything else. And what venture capitalists do is tell you how to find those outsource services.

You can create an interesting company where there are maybe 20 people onboard, and you have marketing consultants, manufacturing consultants—all these other people—selected from a kind of vast service organization, helping you out.

But a good CFO then has to figure out, as a company is growing, what you are going to do inside the company and what you are going to continue to outsource. That's where people like Geoff Darby and others have developed good business intuition as CFOs. Darby's company, Visioneer [see Chapter 20], makes products—it has an amazing little scanner that you connect to your PC or Macintosh—but it doesn't do *any* manufacturing. So here's a hardware/software company that's gone public on Wall Street, is doing $18 million a quarter, but has no manufacturing line.

And with distribution changing, you can build these companies and pump products out without a sales force. Again, look at Netscape, which is distributing its software electronically.

So, now once again, the economics of creating the corporation are changing *dramatically*. And I think that companies are learning that they need to become more "virtualized."

But I think that, in a small company, it's easy to manage the cash flow and the finances of a virtual corporation. As you get bigger and bigger, the stakes for outsourcing—the same as with just-in-time—get more complex; if you don't have somebody who really understands how money flows through this virtual corporation—then, one slip and you pay the biggest price. For leverage, you pay a high price. But if you can use leverage to your advantage, you're succeeding.

HOW THE WEST COAST IS CHANGING AMERICAN BUSINESS

How much of this description you've been giving applies all across the U.S., as opposed to just in Silicon Valley?

To some extent, I see a West Coast/East Coast difference. Many of today's high-tech leaders are products of West Coast business schools. A friend of mine at the Stanford Business School teaches finance, and he trains people to be Wall Street and corporate CFOs.

But he says that, if you really stand back and look at the graduates from the Harvard Business School, the University of Chicago, and Stanford—you can almost tell where they're going to land. Harvard will train its business school students to be executives of GE and places like that, whereas the Stanford people tend to be more mavericks; they're the entrepreneurs. And even as financial people, they will bounce around.

That's because the courses have guest lecturers like you!

[Laughs] Right!

But I see two ways in which the West Coast is influencing the rest of the country. One is the whole business of the virtual company, which I think is having a profound effect on the rest of the country. You're reading about people in Boulder or in Kansas City having ISDN lines at home, working out of their home.

The second is that because of that change, companies are using consultants more and more.

Those are both trends that started on the West Coast but have national implications for how companies will be structured, and how new companies will need to structure themselves. The very fact that the country is absorbing this technology that the West Coast is delivering—in terms of remote access or telecommuting, and so on—is causing the mainstream companies to reshuffle their own financial structures.

So now they're looking at their own P&L, and rethinking how much they'll spend on R&D, and sales and marketing. Managers and their financial people are looking at this and saying, "I can create an organization that's lighter, that has less overhead."

HOW CHANGES IN COMPUTING
ARE CHANGING FINANCE ATTITUDES

What people seem to do in the Valley is always go forward to new ways. In a lot of places, you see companies thinking they're moving forward because they have adopted new technology while their thinking in other areas, like financial, remains stagnant.

There is that fight, but I'll tell you why I see it winning on the side of going forward, and affecting some of the financial models.

The answer has to do with the computing systems that people use. In the '60s, everything was centralized on mainframes. The system was based on cranking out monthly reports, and management as a whole got geared up that once a month when they got a report; so, "What are the best metrics to use in managing our business on reports that come out month to month?"

That was the only time constant with which they could get information. Now, it's immediate. Because of personal computers and LAN-based departmental computing systems, and also the notion that you give every department its own finance person, people are not relying anymore on the centralized computing system for a monthly report, and you can get reports on almost any basis you want. As a consequence, the financial function, which was centralized, is becoming decentralized. And, in a funny way, organizations are becoming more autonomous. Of course, this is the way that most human beings really want to work.

So the mainframe computer forced you to work in a hierarchical structure; and even though the conservative desire to stick with the familiar may be there, the computing resources are moving forward at such a dramatic rate that, lower in the organization than anyone would have anticipated, people are controlling their own destinies.

As a consequence, when this new breed of aggressive financial mavericks or whatever you want to call them, this next generation, become managers or executives, they haven't been trained to become rigid in the way that mainframe computing once would have forced them to be. They grew up with the personal computer, so their attitude is, "I've got this whacko idea, and I want to see if it makes business sense. Give me the answer *now* so I can verify that it's any good."

So you think the West Coast start-up is a good paradigm for other companies.

I think there are definitely aspects that are good and that are already influencing "mainstream" companies.

ADVICE TO THE WOULD-BE INVESTOR

Do you have any advice to offer the successful real estate mogul or surgeon or attorney who has a few million he'd like to be earning more money with and is thinking of putting into some start-up companies?

Being a private investor—or "angel," as we say—can be fun and very rewarding. But, as with all things, you've got to do your homework on the people and the markets. You've also got to understand the life cycle of financing a company from start to IPO. So it's best to focus on the business arena you know, be prepared for some failures, and plan to fund 5 to 10 companies so that you have the odds of success on your side.

Finally, remember that the goal is to make the pie as big as possible: A small slice can still be very profitable!

YOGEN DALAL

Personal Perspectives

You've made a rather unusual transition from electrical engineering and software development to management to . . . whatever category of job venture capitalist belongs in. How did that come about?

When Bill Campbell was getting ready to start Claris [an Apple spin-off for software development, later brought back into Apple; at the time of the spin-off, Campbell was made CEO by John Sculley], he instinctively recognized that he didn't have a technologist, somebody that could, through his training, say whether this particular product was likely to work or not.

And Campbell picked you for the job. What made you think you'd be able to do it?

Why did I take that job? [Laughs] It was the *least* high-tech job I had had in my life. What I had missed through my Xerox years and my years at Metaphor was a true sales-oriented leader. I had had good technical leaders and mentors but not a person like Bill Campbell, who wanders through marketing, wanders through sales, and says, "We're going to take this hill." You just felt as if you would follow him. It's the human factor.

There's more to life than technology. [Laughs]

I miss some of the operational things now and then. I know this is going to sound trite, but I miss the everyday people—bumping into the people who provide customer support, the people who do the development and actually make the company grow. One thing I learned from Bill Campbell is that spanning the whole range is important—being able to excite somebody who is an average person and bring something greater out of them. For Campbell, I think it's love of people.

A NEW TYPE OF FINANCE PERSON

Do you think Campbell's choice of you for the job says anything about the type of finance people today's companies need?

This new electronic world has absolutely amazing implications for the CFO and finance. Distribution is changing, cash transfers happen electronically, you can place orders on-line—you can do so much on your own.

Before, you would have cash locked up in inventory, you would have cash locked up here and there. In this new world that we're moving into, the places where cash is locked up will be different. The CFO has to be somebody who understands the whole nature of the business in these new-age companies.

So, today, you need sophisticated CFOs who understand where cash is really important.

What happens on our side of the business equation today is that the CEO may be an outstanding leader, perhaps a maverick, but does not understand this flow of the money. The CFO has to really rise to the challenge of being a sage about handling budgets and money. On the high-tech side, this whole interrelationship between the CFO and the virtual corporation is, I think, critical right now.

The interesting thing to me is that not all people are going to make this transition. Traditionally, finance has been able to demand discipline. What's happening now is that the new breed of CFOs have to be more than financial people. In high-tech, they almost have to be technocrats themselves. They can't concern themselves solely with the control function or the cash flow or the treasury function—they've really got to be able to succeed in a situation where nothing remains the same for two weeks in a row.

CHAPTER 18

FINANCIALS FOR A START-UP

An Interview with Randy Komisar, CEO,
Crystal Dynamics, Inc.

*At age 42, Randy Komisar had a job that many young people would envy
and that, in some ways characterizes a leading edge of business in the 1990s:
he was first a CFO and then CEO in high tech, running a company that
creates interactive video games.*

*Randy has an infectious enthusiasm and vitality and, although he has an
amazingly diverse background, it is talking about business that brings the sparkle
to his eyes.*

*Our conversation took place on a park bench in the tree-shaded courtyard
of the small office complex in Menlo Park, California, that houses most of
Crystal Dynamics.*

FINANCE AS A POLICE DEPARTMENT

**In a lot of companies, people from finance are looked on as traffic
cops. Would I be right in assuming that that doesn't happen in a
start-up?**

RANDY KOMISAR:
When I became CEO of Crystal Dynamics, there were two cultures—and
two groups of people who had offices in buildings two blocks apart. One
culture was financially oriented, with international sales, domestic sales, and
operations; the other was oriented toward product and marketing. You would
have thought you were in two different companies. It was a war.

I could join hands on either side, but I couldn't pull them together. I
struggled to get them to understand each other's agendas and to appreciate
that they were really in this together.

223

I'm very proud, though, of what's been happening this week. We've been working through some very difficult budget issues as we look at the next year. Both camps are cooperating more and more because it's become apparent that there is no "us" without "them."

I've had the CFO and the controller and the head of production and executive producers in the room with me for the last two days, and they've been doing extremely well together. They've been making trade-offs, they've been communicating well, and there's an appreciation that they're really trying to help each other. I see this as one of the biggest victories in the last six months.

After our recent move, the two groups are now a two-minute walk from each other, much closer emotionally and physically, and things are improving.

What are some of the things you look for from your CFO and financial people?

Finance in a start-up needs to be in the hands of somebody who is very capable of raising money, building strategic plans, and creating a sense of operating discipline in the organization while, at the same time, being flexible.

In a way, companies immersed in today's rapid pace of change become start-ups over and over—they continually have to reinvent themselves and their business models. So, as these companies keep moving through each successive start-up phase, their people have to be able to adapt and lead. Flexibility is key. Some financial people you talk to are very rigid; it's something they've relied on—it's been their strength.

One of the things that I think qualifies someone for doing start-ups is a love of change. I believe change is healthy. It's creating processes to address change in a healthy, constructive way that allows you to build successful companies.

FINANCIAL NEEDS OF THE CREATIVE COMPANY

Crystal Dynamics is in a rather specialized field. Do the same business principles and financial principles that work elsewhere apply here as well?

I want people to think about the way they spend money and invest money as if it were their own. That's something you don't accomplish simply with a handbook on spending policies or a primer on financial planning; it's something you do by including individuals in the process and by demonstrating and emphasizing financial responsibility in each of the meetings you're in and with each of solutions that you implement. The CFO must lead this process, with sensitivity and purpose.

And I look to the CFO to create a sense of financial discipline inside the organization. I think that's different from the sort of financial discipline you need in a bigger organization—here we're much less rule-based and much more culture-based. So this restraint has to be part of the genetics, and I look to the CFO to build that into the genetics of the organization. Rule-based structures, especially in creatively driven organizations like this one, will just fail—there's simply no tolerance for them.

I'm not saying that our company is devoid of rules, but you cannot rely on policies alone to make the business work. Rules are touchstones. Here you're dealing with a very fast-moving, flexible environment, and you're in a situation where you don't have a lot of middle management. The people who actually have to carry the financial discipline forward are the people who you'd never think of as managers at all; they're actually implementers, executors.

We're in a situation where the rules, standing alone, won't lead to the right conclusions in the trenches. Because rules are not tolerated, there are too many opportunities to evade the rules if you don't truly internalize them.

What kinds of guidelines are there when you're developing a new game and, say, the production head wants to spend three times as much for music, or wants to hire a couple of expensive Writers Guild writers from Hollywood? Where do you get the guidelines for deciding whether that makes sense?

One way is the bigger-company approach where you have a set of rules. That's how many productions are put together: "This is the normal budget range for each item; you have authority to sign within that budget norm." Outside that range, you have to go get three levels of approval.

The way it works here is that you start with budget norms, but a producer who's looking at the overall budget and believes that better sound or better writing is going to lead to a better game has to justify that in terms of the competitive environment and the sales they expect from that game.

So, rather than looking at it strictly in terms of expense, we focus our people on the product and the success of the product in the marketplace. If they can justify their belief that a $10,000 increase in the sound or writing budget line is going to improve the gross profit margin by more than the added expense, if they are willing to stand up for that, then they do it. That becomes an individual decision, not a policy decision or a rule-based decision.

The individual is accountable, and especially accountable outside the norms. We're still small enough to afford this level of autonomy.

When Michael Eisner came to Disney, people were horrified because they said he was going to kill the creativity. For example, an outside special-effects unit would be brought in and told, "This is what we want." They'd come back with a budget and be told, "No, that's too much; you'll have to do it for this amount."

But it didn't stifle the creative. A few years later, people were looking at Disney as the studio that was proving you could hold creative people to a budget and still get great, creative, best-in-the-world work.

That's a good story. It's hard to teach that to young people in our business today. They often think that more money will build them a better product.

I just had that discussion with my head of production. I said, "What's the biggest risk in the business plan you're putting together?" She said, "I don't believe we can deliver the innovation and quality we need with the product budgets in the plan." I told her I believed we could, that we had to in order to be competitive, and that if we couldn't, there was something wrong with the way we were developing our products.

She said the industry-standard production budgets were rising rapidly. I pointed out numerous dark-horse products that became hits without large budgets. We also talked about leveraging our successes better to reduce both risk and expense.

The debate about budgets, risk, and hits is continuous in a creatively driven company. It's a healthy one; the line shifts, depending on the stubbornness of the parties. In a hit-based business, a single hit excuses many misses. Finding the right balance will require a few product cycles—and time, if we have it.

So you're saying that you don't have to be a "bean counter," to use the old pejorative; you can demand very careful financial controls without raining on the parade of the R&D people, the creative people, and the innovators.

Absolutely. One of the things that George Lucas is fond of saying with regard to creativity—and I learned many things about leading a creative business from him—is that it's actually much easier to "create" when somebody is imposing limits than when there aren't any. He told me, "You can look at a blank canvas for a long time . . . but if you put four dots on it and then work with those given elements, you can start being creative more quickly."

And that probably applies just as well to engineers as it does to people who are making movies or creating interactive video games.

Yes—the reason HP is so successful is not because it built some rigid structure that got it from 1937 to now but because it built up organizations that are led by great people. And these people were presented with real-world business constraints and then empowered to go off and build printers and build video-on-demand servers and do things that are not necessarily tied together in a way that a good CFO/strategic planner would have designed them.

METRICS FOR THE START-UP

Are the metrics you use any different from those in more traditional companies? Does "creative" bring with it the need for different measures?

When I look out my windshield, I'm looking at gross margin as one of the signs on the side of the road that tells me whether I'm moving at the right speed and in the right direction. At this stage of our company, gross margin is not something I set as an objective in and of itself; rather, it's something that allows me to judge the success and viability of our current strategies against those of our competition.

What would happen to a company that had high gross margin as its objective?

I think the problem, when your company is at an early stage of evolution, is that you begin to make very short-term decisions to optimize gross margins, which may deter you from building the right company for the longer term.

We've seen major companies in Silicon Valley that had the objective of growing and maintaining high margins early on. In doing so, they failed to adapt to a market that was changing. And that's what happened—while these companies were focused on preserving humongous gross margins, their competition moved more strategically and left them isolated, eventually starving them out of their gross margin fortress.

That was so obvious in the middle years at Apple; we desperately needed market share but we focused on gross margin. And, by the way, Silicon Graphics may be doing the same thing right now. They're in a gross margin fortress—a bad place to be if it works to the exclusion of taking risks and building market share. The question is: Will Ed McCracken [CEO of SGI] see that before the

227

company has to pay the price for its high-margin, proprietary strategy? I'd much rather fight from the open fields of a high market share position.

THE MEASUREMENTS USED BY VENTURE CAPITAL PEOPLE

Everyone in high tech seems to have his own venture capital stories. You, too?

Venture capitalists—when I first started dealing with them, I thought they were the devil. Clearly, these were people who were usuriously taking advantage of all the creativity and hard work of others.

I realize now that that's not the case. These are people who take long odds to do things that more conservative people won't. And they have rate-of-return models they live by in order to justify undertaking such risks. While any single success story may paint the vc's as greedy, one must take into account all the failures and marginal successes that balance out the big hits.

Without vc's taking chances on Intel, Apple, Sun, Netscape, and the like, the Silicon Valley phenomenon and the technological revolution it has launched on the world would probably never have happened.

What they generally want is to build value—ultimately, shareholder value. Take Netscape, for instance. Do you think John Doerr [a partner at Kleiner Perkins Caufield & Byers, a leading high-tech venture capital firm that financed Sun, Compaq, and Netscape, among others] worries about what Netscape's traditional metrics are—gross margins and ROI and the like? Absolutely not. He knows that Netscape is in a market share battle with Microsoft and that maximizing gross margins and ROI is not important yet.

PICKING A CFO FOR A START-UP

Are there some special talents needed in the CFO for a start-up company?

What I've looked for in my CFO is somebody who can do deals, plan strategy, and track results against an operating budget and an operating plan.

Another important talent: somebody who's capable of raising money, which is a continuous effort in a start-up operation. Also, somebody who's capable of building management discipline throughout the organization—to allow people to function in what is essentially a state of loosely managed anarchy.

Start-up companies can't perform the sort of financial and business planning that larger companies with more mature businesses and professionally experienced staffs can. You're in a situation where your planning—at least at an operating level—can extend out no more than six months with any credibility.

And so you have to have a finance organization capable of constantly looking out six months, to help steer the company but, at the same time, loosely managing within certain control parameters. You want to stay within budget, and you want to hit your tactical objectives, but you also know that these can change quickly in response to market circumstances and other things outside your control. A start-up's plans and strategies are always evolving.

Today, most industries in the long term are not capital-based; they're not even product-based. They're talent-based—because only talent can adjust to the marketplace quickly enough to make companies successful in the long term. Hewlett-Packard is a talent-based business; it may not see itself that way, but that's what it is and why it's so excellent at whatever it does.

The world of the start-up is built on ever-shifting sands. A change took place in Randy Komisar's status after our original conversation, making an update appropriate.

You recently reorganized Crystal Dynamics and transitioned out of the company. What's the story behind that?

Crystal Dynamics was founded almost four years ago to lead the market in video games for what were termed "next-generation" game systems—the successors to the overwhelmingly successful Nintendo and Sega 16-bit consoles. The first next-generation system was the 3DO Real Machine, launched with much fanfare in 1993. Since then, Sony has launched the PlayStation, and Sega has released the Saturn. Nintendo is due to release its next-generation system, the Ultra 64, later in 1996. *[It reached the stores in November, referred to by the press as "long awaited."]*

Like all start-ups, Crystal began with a "Big Idea" and a great amount of urgency. To take the lead from established winners like Electronic Arts, it needed to master the next-generation technology and develop great products as well as establish its own publishing arm. It was staffed and funded to do that, bringing in a well-known CEO who epitomized the much ballyhooed convergence of Silicon Valley and Hollywood. Its investors had high expectations, and a lot of money was raised on the promise of its becoming the next great game publisher.

Unfortunately, the 3DO machine was stillborn, as was what somebody called the "Silly-wood" convergence, and Crystal's time-to-market advantage was largely lost. By the time Crystal shifted its development strategy to the Sony and Sega machines, the competition was close on its heels. More importantly, the business infrastructure of the publishing organization was a financial drag on the production group and was proving difficult to sustain in a lagging market.

Rather than reduce the size of the company, Crystal chose to roll the dice again, raise additional cash, and hire me to redirect the business toward Sony and Sega. The company hung unto the vision of being a publisher, in large part because the greatest returns have consistently gone to those game companies that managed their own products into the channel and subsequently built brands.

But the market disappointed once again. Sony and Sega were unable to create a big enough market for a full-service publisher like Crystal to survive. We were unable to meet our plan, and losses mounted.

We took all the tactical financial measures you would expect—froze growth on the publishing side, cut all expenses unrelated to production, signed deals with publishers on other platforms to leverage our development costs, and reined in production budgets. But the market was still inadequate to support Crystal's infrastructure.

Finally, we had to acknowledge that, though we had nearly $20 million, we were going to use it up as working capital in the publishing operation by year-end if we didn't move decisively. Since neither I nor my management team believed that the game market would progress sufficiently by Christmas to give us a return on that investment, we bit the bullet and decided to jettison the publishing business.

That was a difficult pill for many of the team and our investors. The "Big Idea" was lost or at least postponed. Crystal was going to regroup as a production house and stretch out its cash to wait for the market. With the new plan, it could hold out for almost two years if it had to.

Nevertheless, for me and the key members of my team, the fit with the company no longer made sense. I came to Crystal to lead a fast-growing, fully dimensional developer/publisher in a dynamic industry. In a production company, I saw myself largely as overhead. So the plan that we presented to the board excluded me and my direct team.

I'm proud that we acted decisively to position Crystal for a future market, if it materializes. I'm very disappointed that we couldn't find traction in the market to make a go of the Big Idea. It's probably one of the hardest decisions a CEO ever has to make. Many people were affected—half the staff lost their jobs and not because they had failed personally.

Start-ups are a high-stakes game but, win or lose, they can be addictive.

RANDY KOMISAR

Personal Perspectives

For a man who's been a CFO and is now a CEO, you have quite a varied background.

I started out, after graduating from Brown University, doing a number of different things. I worked with a group promoting rock concerts, still one of the coolest, most fun things I've ever done.

And, in a fundamental way, that experience has had a lasting impact on me. It was my first time dealing with talent in a business context. And the fun, satisfaction, and unique challenges of working with talent have been an underlying theme throughout my various careers—through the PC craze in the early '80s, where the garage technologists replaced the garage bands of the '70s, to the digital entertainment craze of the '90s, where the talent is composed mostly of twenty-something creative artists, designers, writers, and musicians.

Immediately following graduation I also managed a community development program for the city of Providence and taught economics at a small four-year college—all at the same time.

After that, I attended Harvard Law School, with no intention of ever practicing law. But then, lo and behold, I enjoyed trial practice, so I pursued that for a while, joined a Boston law firm and hated it, persuaded the firm to transfer me out to a branch office in Silicon Valley in the early '80s, and established a high-tech practice. That's where I got involved with the next generation of talent, the PC software engineers.

I worked with these highly creative people to help build businesses, do deals, and so forth. Then I was invited to work in the legal group at Apple. At the time, Apple had just launched the Macintosh, and it was an opportunity for me to join a newly charged Apple, to do deals—basically to be a business development guy.

I did that for only about a year before management decided to transform the group into an "inside" law firm, which was the right thing for Apple and the wrong thing for me. At the same time, they were about to spin off Claris, and I became a cofounder of Claris with Bill Campbell. That was a blast. It was probably the most exciting time of my life—great people, a great mission, and great success.

It was my first opportunity to take a company from a seed and grow it into something very real. I started there as general counsel and VP of business development and later assumed an administrative role and became more of a general manager.

When Bill Campbell moved from Claris to the startup company with whimsical name, GO, it was evolving from an R&D company into an operating company. The first person he hired was me, as CFO and VP business operations.

It was an unusual job for me at the time because, while I had managed business development, had been general counsel, and had run many aspects of business operations, I had never served in a financial role.

The reason Bill Campbell chose me was that, while I had always been strong financially when we were at Claris—even though I had no accounting background and no formal financial planning background—Bill was looking for a "business man" as CFO, someone who could establish good internal processes while driving deals, building relationships, and raising money. Thank goodness the Claris CFO, Dan McCammon, turned out to be an excellent model and teacher for the financial experience I lacked.

GO eventually was sold to AT&T, through a strategy that Bill Campbell and I devised. After that I was contacted by a headhunter for the CEO/ president spot at LucasArts, which was a small, fledgling, but well-respected game company owned by movie producer George Lucas of Star Wars fame. I don't think the Lucas people knew what they were really looking for, but they wanted a leader, someone to build a company around all that talent in a supportive but structured environment so they could continue to create great products but also finally be successful in the marketplace.

I stayed there less than two years. During that time, we grew LucasArts to the market share leader in PC entertainment. It was also highly profitable, with the highest gross margins in the business.

I left because George and I didn't share the same vision for the company. George was content to see it as an extension of his extremely successful entertainment company; I believed it was much more significant than that and deserved the opportunity to do more original work and to expand into new areas. I also wanted to acquire a couple of companies to build a stronger foundation. There was no denying that, ultimately, it was George's company, so I politely opted out.

And from there I came to Crystal Dynamics.

CHAPTER 19

OBTAINING START-UP FINANCING

An Interview with Brian D. Frenzel,
President and CEO,
Centaur Pharmaceuticals, Inc.

Centaur Pharmaceuticals is in the business of discovering new drugs to treat major diseases. But this noble goal is only half of its mission; the other half is to make a large bundle of money. And a number of firms and individuals, by putting up very sizable chunks of investment, have bet that the company can succeed.

There's nothing easy about this process, and Brian Frenzel knows that better than most: he's been through the start-up process several times.

Centaur was incorporated in 1992 but did not have a facility for more than a year. The first 18 months of operations were conducted on a "virtual" basis, before the beginning of experiments in a real laboratory of its own.

At the time of this interview in March 1996, the company was completing a third major phase of expansion and had fully completed its metamorphosis from virtual to operating company.

THE VIRTUAL COMPANY

How do you explain the term *virtual company*?

BRIAN FRENZEL:
I would define a virtual company as one that has a skeleton management team but does most of its work—or, in some cases, all of it—through outside

233

contracts; it may not have physical facilities or full-time employees, but it has the other elements of an operating business.

Centaur is an example. The time from the date of incorporation until we commissioned our first facility was about 18 months. Before that, we had no in-house operating capability: We couldn't perform experiments, we couldn't develop drugs with our own hands, but we had everything else—we had the key people of a management team, and we had the ability to draw up contracts, take licenses, file patents, and pay for outside research.

And we spent our first million dollars doing that.

In fact, our strategy was not to have bricks and mortar and not to try to bring in the staff that we would need to support an in-house operation until we had achieved our first important milestone—which was to develop a proprietary pharmaceutical compound. When we started the company, we didn't know if this was feasible, and we spent the first year establishing that we could do it. And, once we had done it, we knew it would be worthwhile to move forward from there.

I'm a proponent of the virtual approach. It has its problems and limitations, but I think it's the most efficient use of resources early on because you're not spending a lot of money on infrastructure before you've demonstrated proof of principle.

Your example, though, is a very special case because there was some research done already that looked as if the research was going in the right direction.

We licensed technology that had been under development for approximately five years and had demonstrated its potential. Researchers at the University of Kentucky and the Oklahoma Medical Research Foundation had been smart enough to file four broad patents on their work. So we licensed these patents, signed up the scientific founders as consultants to the company, and took off from there.

I was operating out of my home office, and John Carney, one of the scientific founders, had his own home office and an office at the University of Kentucky. Bob Floyd, another scientific founder, had a home office and an office at the Oklahoma Medical Research Foundation. Our accounting and administrative functions were handled by Mark Collins at the Glenn Foundation for Medical Research, our founding lead investor.

For the first 15 months or so, we operated at four different locations; none of them was a formal Centaur office.

That's more virtual than I think most people mean when they say "virtual company." That's really strung together with baling wire.

I've done even more "virtual" than that—Centaur wasn't that bad off. We had a financial backer who was with us from day one. Paul Glenn and Mark Collins at the Glenn Foundation for Medical Research were "angels" in both financial and human terms. So we were able to afford to pay for travel, patent attorneys, contract research, and things like that.

LEARNING TO CREATE A START-UP

One of the challenges for people who are trying to get a start-up off the ground is being sophisticated enough to put together the right kind of documentation and ask for the kind of financing package that's appropriate for them. Where does somebody acquire that kind of financial wisdom for a start-up?

I don't think there's anything better than the school of hard knocks—having been there and having worked with people who have been there. Also, a number of books have been written on these topics, and there's merit in reading some of them.

You have to put together a business plan that excites potential investors. And you have to convince them that not only do you have a good plan but you've got the energy, enthusiasm, and tenacity to pull it off.

To some extent, I've played both sides of the venture capital game, having started several companies, having invested in a few, and having worked with venture capitalists to evaluate investment opportunities. In the case of Centaur, I invested both my own money and "sweat equity," putting in time and energy to help found the company. Ultimately, I bet my professional life by joining Centaur as its full-time CEO.

Fundamentally, there has to be a concept that's attractive enough to convince people to invest. You have to recognize that early stage venture investors are people with very high return objectives—in the venture business, they want to make 100% annual return if they can, and certainly at least 30% to 50% annual return on each investment.

Obviously, they'd like to see a lot of upside above 30%, but they have to be fairly comfortable that 30% is readily achievable in order to invest. You have to come up with a formula, a plan, an idea, a concept, a technology, that has the potential to yield those kinds of returns.

And, usually, that means it has to be a fairly big opportunity. It can't be just a mom and pop operation. I've come across many good business concepts, some of which I've personally found interesting, that weren't large enough to attract a significant amount of venture capital investment. Some of these were good small-business opportunities, ones that could make good money for an owner-entrepreneur but are just not large enough to attract venture investors.

HOW BIG IS BIG ENOUGH TO GET FINANCING?

That's an interesting point. How big an opportunity does a company have to present before venture capitalists will be interested?

Generally speaking, the business needs to have the potential to be worth $100 million within a few years. And, really, it comes down to value because, when you're starting a company and looking to fund with venture capital, you're in the value-creation business. You're taking something that doesn't have value or has a small amount of value and turning it into something that has a large amount of value.

Centaur is in that process. We come to work every day looking to make a lot of money for our investors, and we've gone from zero to the high double-digit millions of dollars in value in four years. We did that by starting with a few good ideas and some technology that we licensed from academia and the desire and commitment to make something out of it.

THE POTENTIAL TO BE VERY SUCCESSFUL

When does the payback come for the investors—if the company is successful, at what point do they get their riches out?

They get their money when the company goes public or gets bought out. Very early on, the founders should start thinking about the "exit strategy"[i.e., when the investors will be able to draw a cash return on their investment—get a very large amount wire-transferred to their account or sell their stock on the open market]—because the investors they're talking to are going to ask: "How do we get our money out, and how soon is that going to happen?" Sooner is obviously better in their view.

If it's possible to give a general answer to this, how quickly do you have to be able to reach $100 million, or whatever the number happens to be, to be able to attract investors?

You can compute the numbers on your calculator, using a minimum of a 30% annual return. In the past, the rule of thumb has been something like a fourfold return within five years, at the least.

The standard by which you're judged today is an even faster exit than that, or else a larger return multiple. Investors need to have a few big winners to compensate for the losers, so they will look more favorably on those investments that have a chance for a 10-fold or a 50-fold return.

Obviously, you can get more sophisticated in your analysis by running models that have a certain amount of investment on day one and more money later—the concept being that you need to raise money every couple of years until some sort of exit opportunity materializes.

Companies that are in high tech or software tend to move much faster in terms of time to market but may not be faster in terms of time to exit than, say, a pharmaceutical or a biomedical company.

GETTING THE FIRST INVESTOR

I suppose it's frequently true that somebody who's worked in a particular field long enough has formed some contacts who are in a position to help find financing or who know people that are interested in investing in that area.

When we founded Centaur, the initial investors were willing to invest a small amount of money at a reasonable valuation so they'd have a foot in the door for the next round.

Invariably, the most difficult investor to get is the first one. That's true when you first start a company, and it's true at every subsequent round. If you can get a lead investor and set the value, it's much easier to bring followers.

That was a very attractive route to go. What was the fairy dust you sprinkled that made them willing to give you those favorable terms?

It was the potential of the technology, and it was the accomplishments that the scientific founders had made before the company was founded. And it was the founder's willingness to invest sweat equity. I participated as an investor as well as a member of the management team, and so, to some extent, I played both roles.

I think there are a lot of people out there like me who have some experience and have some money in the bank and are willing to take a chance.

But you're probably not going to get a $5 or $10 million initial round this way; you have to wait.

If you want the bigger amounts, you have to go to the larger, professionally managed venture funds. But, as an alternative, you can get money from private investors, you can draw on your own family resources or mortgage the house, and government financing is often available. Also, if your technology is attractive enough, you can get money from other companies that are willing to invest through buying stock or licensing product rights.

In the movie business, the independent filmmakers face the problem of spending at least as much time raising money as they do making movies, probably more. Is it the same thing in a start–up business?

Yes, that's certainly true. The objective, obviously, is to get out of that mode as soon as possible. But, in the early days, in the prefunding days before a company has raised its first round of financing, you may spend essentially all your time doing that because, without seed capital, you're not able to accomplish much.

I try to minimize the amount of time spent on that because it's a diversion and it takes your eye off the ball—it takes your attention away from creating the value through product and technology development.

BALANCING THE FUNDING SOURCES

Isn't getting money from other companies a very tough route to take? People seem to have great difficulty finding the person in a large company that they should be talking to and, then, if they do find the right person and there's some interest, it seems to take forever to get a corporate decision made and an agreement written and a check actually in the mail.

Starting a company is the hardest thing there is to do in business. It's tough. My advice concerning the various sources of funds is to use them all. If you ride just on venture capital, you end up owning very little at the end. If you ride solely on corporate deals, you end up selling off most of your technology.

So, in a well-managed start-up, you have to put all these together. And Centaur is a good example of this—we have drawn money from each of these sources. We've been in operation for about three years and we have a large corporate relationship, we have government funding through government research grants, we have a number of private investors, and we now have six venture firms that have invested.

Basically, we needed all of these to maximize our chances. It's synergistic—once you have one, it becomes easier to get the others.

HOW TO AVOID GIVING UP CONTROL

It seems that people who have something solid enough to get a hearing from venture capitalists often come away stunned by how large a piece the venture capitalists are asking for. What do you say to people about that?

I usually ask them if they really need venture capital, because venture capital is extremely expensive money. You're typically selling stock very cheaply when you sell it to a venture capitalist.

The first question I would ask is, "Can you somehow create value without having to dig into that till?" I was talking to an entrepreneur today who's putting together a business plan for a genomic services company [a company that provides genetic testing to researchers and physicians]. According to his plan, he needs a $700,000 DNA sequencer. With all the infrastructure around that—a $50,000-a-year person to run it, a maintenance contract, and so on—you're talking about an operation that's probably going to cost $2 or $3 million a year in the first couple of years, even on a relatively small scale, before the first product revenue. For that type of money, you'd probably need a venture capitalist or two behind you.

So I asked him, "Is there some way you can do it on 10 cents on the dollar, do it on $200,000 a year?" because, with those kinds of numbers, there are alternative, boot-strapping methods of financing. In his case, I asked if there was any way to buy time on someone else's DNA sequencer—say, on nights and weekends. It gets back to the virtual company idea: Can you do it with a contractor? Can you buy used equipment? Can you struggle and make it pay off?

If so, then having created a sizable amount of value without giving away 50% or 75% of your company, you can raise money at a much higher value—on much cheaper terms. If you're looking to raise, say, $5 or $10 million dollars on day one before you've got a product, or proof of principle, you're probably going to give up more than 50% of the company to do that.

And venture capitalists would often rather invest a little later, and pay more, after you have reduced the risk profile. In other words, not only do you make out much better in the end but it's ultimately much easier to finance. Of course, you pay the price by taking more risk and working harder earlier on.

Most people who want to start a company don't have much choice about getting money up front. Steve Jobs and Steve Wozniak were youngsters, without families, and both had nine-to-five jobs when they created the Apple computer. The average working person with a great product idea needs some kind of funding to put bread on the table while he or she is trying to get the company started.

Again, there are a lot of different sources of money. One approach is to go to one of the big-name venture firms like Kleiner Perkins. It has a lot of money at its disposal, it invests in big chunks, and it provides support and advice.

On the other hand, if you start with the big venture firms, you give away a lot of the company—you get diluted a lot. You also tend to give up management control very early on. They will want to control the board after the first or second round of investment. They may want you to agree to step aside in favor of a management team they choose—they may have this in mind from the outset whether they tell you or not.

OTHER FUNDING SOURCES

You've mentioned the private investors, the "angels" as they're sometimes called.

Generally speaking, you get less support and less money from them, but they're less price-conscious. And they let you run the show. Centaur was an exception to this rule because we got both seed financing and a tremendous amount of support from the Glenn Foundation.

How does the small start-up guy find these angels?

There are lists of angels just as there are lists of venture capitalists. In the San Francisco area, there is an informal association of private investors—an "angel" club, which meets monthly. Generally speaking, you want to go to somebody who knows something about your industry, who's done it before, who has started or managed the sort of company you are founding. If you're in the electronics business, talk to somebody that was a founder of Sun Microsystems or something like that; if its software, find an ex-software executive.

If you're in biomedical in an application that deals with aging, talk to somebody like Paul Glenn, who's interested in the aging phenomena and sponsors research in that area.

Find a kindred spirit and, ideally, a kindred spirit who has money, experience, and contacts and can help to bring in more money.

VALUING THE COMPANY

I know that the vc firms will arrive at their own decisions on valuations and how much they're willing to invest but, clearly the founders ought to go in knowing their fund-raising objectives. What's the basis for deciding?

There are lots of different ways to look at this. You really should run financial models to analyze several scenarios. If you're a founder/entrepreneur, how much are you going to end up with? What's a moderate success? What's the upside? What are the salvage plans?

The ultimate downside scenario, failure, is that you walk away with a lot of scars and good experience, and that's it.

You have to be prepared to face this outcome before you start. If you can't handle a failure—either financially or psychologically—don't start on this path.

A good way to think about this question is through valuation. What can I do today that's going to create a company worth at least $10 or $20 million in a couple of years? And how much is that going to cost, in terms of money and blood, sweat, and tears.

If it's going to cost $1 million to create a company worth $20 million a year or two hence, that's a pretty favorable scenario because, with that prospect, you can raise the first million on terms that allow you to keep control of the company. You might sell 25% of the company, which yields a post-investment valuation of $4 million.

That's how you figure the valuation—based on how much the investors put up and how much of the company they get for it?

You just divide by the percentage you're giving away to get the post-investment valuation. If you're giving away 25% of the company for $1 million, then the post-money valuation is $4 million. To get the preinvestment valuation—that is, the value of the company not counting the cash invested—subtract the amount invested from the post-investment valuation.

Suppose you come up with a business concept or a technology that requires $1 million to get it going. With $1 million, you're not going to have a big operation—you might have only a virtual company with a small office, a couple of personal computers, voice mail, and a facsimile machine.

You spend that $1 million to increase the value to $20 million in a year or two. Then you can raise another, say, $5 million by giving up another 20% of the company. Or perhaps you can raise $10 million and give up another quarter or a third of the company, implying a value post-investment of $30 to $40 million.

Doing it in this way, instead of having everything you need in the bank account on day one, you have less security, and more risk. But if you raise $3 to $4 million in the first round of financing of the same company, you'll probably give up control. You might end up having a boss you didn't choose.

And then the tendency when you have more money in the bank than you really need is to spend it. So you create value less efficiently than you would have if you had raised less initially. Of course, the other side of the coin is not having the resources to get the job done. So you must be careful how you make this trade-off.

I had lunch with a finance professor at Stanford whose wife is founder in a start-up company and now owns only 1% or 2% of the company. I didn't understand how it came out to be that small.

That happens more often than you think. People oftentimes brag about how much venture capital they've raised. Then the next question you might ask—or, if you're polite, you probably don't ask—is, "It's really impressive that you raised $20 million in venture capital. How much of the company have you retained for the founding team of people that came up with the idea and worked 80 hours a week to make it successful?" And, oftentimes, the numbers are very small.

As small as 1% or 2%?

Sure. Of course, the professor's wife probably had some cofounders. If there were five of them and they end up with 2% each, that's 10% for the founders, which is not bad. It's not unusual to find the initial founders and employees retaining less than 10% after a few years.

But it doesn't have to be so small. In the case of Genelabs Technologies, another company I helped to found, we went public with the founding group and the employees owning approximately half the company. And we had raised, if you count corporate contracts, more than $50 million before we went public. So there's a counterexample in which the founders and early employees did much better.

NET PRESENT VALUE OF A START-UP

How do you measure net present value when you don't even have a product yet?

The financial markets do it every day. There are hundreds of companies that have no significant product revenue but are worth a lot. The important consideration is potential future value. If you have a chance to cure cancer or, as in our case, Alzheimer's disease, and you have a technology that people think might work, they look at the potential future value of an Alzheimer's cure in the year 2005 and extrapolate back.

In the case of Alzheimer's disease, a product that has reasonable acceptance could be worth $5 or $10 billion dollars after it is approved and sales begin to ramp up. That's the future value of the technology, and investors discount that number for the time value of the money, and discount it for the probability of success, and come up with a number that represents the risk-adjusted net present value. Even with heavy discounting, the present value can be hundreds of millions of dollars.

In your industry, what proportion of ideas that sound promising actually prove to be marketable drugs?

I don't know that there's a reliable statistic on that. If you review the literature, you'll see numbers like 1 out of 1000. But a good management team can bring the odds up to 1 in 5 or 1 in 10 pretty quickly. With 1-in-10 odds, and the possibility of pursuing 10 or 20 ideas beyond proof of concept, you're not in such bad shape.

LEARNING HOW TO RUN A START-UP

For somebody who's trying to get going in this process, are there consultants who are good enough to come in and give advice on which of these funding routes make most sense?

There are a lot of people out there who are willing to help. If somebody's actually pursuing a pure start-up with no experience, I would say forget it. You have to get some experience; you've got to work for somebody else.

Work for a company like Centaur and watch us do it. When you're ready, we'll help you get going.

We've nurtured and trained a lot of people here. In my career, I count as a major accomplishment having trained or mentored a number of people who are now successful entrepreneurs. At least a half a dozen are now involved with successful start-ups of their own. That's what happened to me—I obviously learned a lot before I went to my first start-up, and then I learned a lot more trying to actually make it work.

Are there certain financial measures that you find most useful in an environment where you don't yet have a revenue stream?

Well, the most important thing that you are always worried about, particularly in the early days, is cash—whether you have enough to pay the rent, to make payroll, to fund the project even on a "virtual" basis—and how long you can survive before you reach the "cliff"—the point at which you run out of money. And you have to be ruthlessly honest about answering those questions because probably the worst thing is to be so underfunded and so stretched that you don't make it to the starting line. That is very frustrating. I've been there.

It's good to stretch and be parsimonious, do things at a lower cost than the bigger companies can but, if you don't have the minimum resources, then you're probably not going to make it.

So you have to bridge that gap—you have to find a way to fund the difference, or boot-strap in some way. Every six months at Centaur, we go through a strategic review of every project in the company. And one of the questions we ask, which a big company wouldn't ask, is, "How are we going to fund this?" Because a project that gets high marks on fundability can sacrifice something on the other dimensions.

What makes it fundable? What are the measures you look at?

How does it fit into somebody else's portfolio? Can you get it to a certain stage where it'll be attractive to the U.S. Government's Small Business Innovation Research program or other similar grant awards from research foundations? Can you get it to a point where it'll be attractive to a potential corporate partner whom you may have already contacted but who's waiting for certain benchmarks?

You've had experience through founding several companies. Are there one or two things that you wish you had known earlier that would have made a difference?

If I'd known how hard it was going to be, I probably wouldn't have jumped in on the first one!

Look at the fun you would have missed.

Right. There were a number of times, during the first six months of my first start-up, where I wondered if I'd made a horrible mistake, because it turned out to be much harder than I thought it was going to be.

What made it so much harder? What were the things you hadn't anticipated?

I guess the fund-raising challenge was the biggest one in that case. We looked at other companies that had been funded in the past year and felt we had as good or better a story. We didn't anticipate a trough in the venture capital cycle. Venture capital cycles tend to follow the stock market but are more severe. My start-up experience begins in 1984, and I can tell you when every crash has happened since then, particularly in biomedical. It seemed as though I was always raising money when there was a crash going on.

Also, Murphy's law is fully operational in a start-up company. There are always unanticipated delays, the "unknown unknowns" that can have a huge impact when you are running without much reserve capacity.

Does the fund-raising get tougher only when the market as a whole is crashing, or does it also have to do with what industry groups are in favor at the moment?

I think it's both of those. I operate in the biotech/biomedical arena. Here the cycle of availability of investment is driven by general market conditions and factors specific to our industry. For example, in medical devices, there was a significant decline in venture capital interest a couple of years ago when the FDA became much more demanding and began looking for the same sort of clinical studies that they required for drugs.

The stock market, particularly the IPO market, has a significant influence because one of the exits people are looking at as venture investors is how easy it's going to be to go public—and sometimes it's very difficult. And that tends to flow down through the various stages of venture capital financing. And, conversely, if the stock market is very bullish, it becomes much easier to raise money.

A CONTRARIAN VIEW OF THE BUSINESS PLAN

You were talking about things that you wish you had known earlier. Besides how hard it is, what else would you list?

There are a lot of things. Conventional wisdom suggests that you need a good business plan in order to raise money. In reality, the people making investment decisions often don't pay much attention to the detail in the business plan. What they're looking for is the business concept, the thing that you can express in a few words or a few sentences. If they can conceptualize—for example, "This is a gene therapy company, and it's got a chance to win big because it's got the prominent Dr. So-and-so working on a breakthrough,"—then you've given them something they can grasp quickly.

They don't usually look much at the formal details of the plan or the numbers. Sometimes, people preparing business plans spend many hours refining those numbers; I've certainly done this. But what the investors are looking for is the concept, the vision—so that's something that you want to be able to get across quickly. If you're calling people on the telephone, you usually have only one or two minutes to get their attention and, if you get their interest in that one or two minutes, then you might get to the next step, which would be a formal meeting.

PLAYING THE VENTURE CAPITAL GAME

In the movie business, especially in terms of television "movies of the week," that short description you're talking about is sometimes referred to as the "log line": how is *TV Guide* going to describe this movie? If you can describe it in few enough words to fit into those couple of lines of description in *TV Guide,* and the description is a grabber, then it's a story the producer or network executive will be interested in listening to.

Exactly. It's very important to have this sort of conceptual description handy at all times. I suggest having a 30-second, a 3-minute, a 20-minute, and a 1-hour presentation ready to go before you start making serious calls on potential investors. You'll learn as you make contacts, so you may want to hold some of your best prospects back and practice on those who you think are long shots.

Also, you want to be diversified not only across different groups of venture capitalists but across different sources of funding. That's one reason it's desirable to have private investors and other sources of money—so that you're not dependent on a single person's decision.

If possible, you should go in with references—people you know or who you've at least talked to and who would say you have a good idea. Ideally, these are people they know, prominent people.

Another approach is to get a referral from someone they know so that you can say, "So and so said I should talk to you before I talk to anybody else."

The venture capital lists tend to be very conservative. They like to do as much as they can to minimize risk. Also, it's more than money they're investing. Their egos and reputations are on the line. They don't want to risk being associated with a bad deal, a deal that blows up.

In television and films, the studios don't share information with each other—producers don't call each other and say, "What did you think of this idea?" It's very competitive. Is that pretty much true in the venture capital world as well?

No, not really. Early on, I didn't realize how information flows in the venture community. You need to have competition in order to get a deal done—in other words, more than one bidder coming in to try to control the deal or set the price. But the first thing venture capitalists will ask you is, "Who else are you talking to." And, in the past, I have very naively answered that question, "We're talking to so and so, and so and so." And now I know what happens when that question is answered: they call those people up and say, "What'd you think about Brian and his new company?"

So you have to assume that potential venture capital investors, most of whom know each other, are going to talk about you and compare notes—and any one negative thing that they can come up with may kill your prospects. They may say, "There's this problem or that problem I'm concerned about." And the person you might have had as a potential lead may respond, "Yeah, you're probably right."

There are many venture capitalists on Sand Hill Road in Menlo Park, California. If you talk to more than one of them, you should assume they're talking to each other. So, if you're talking to Sand Hill Road investors, you need some other group of potential investors that you're pursuing as well—as many as you have time to manage.

The hardest thing, of course, is getting the first one to commit. When the first one commits, then you can tell the others, "The deal is now going down—it's going to happen—are you in or out?"

Any other advice to people who are in start-ups or would like to be?

Keep at it. It takes a tremendous amount of tenacity, and you'll probably suffer many frustrations and disappointments before you actually get one off the ground.

Somehow or other, you've had a good enough experience in start-ups that you're still willing to do it.

I love it. It's tremendously exciting. The wealth creation opportunities are great. You can make a major contribution to society through developing new technology and creating jobs. You work long hours, but you're in control of your own destiny. You can reach for the stars!

I think if you have the right temperament, a high energy level, and a strong desire to build something, it's the only thing to do.

BRIAN FRENZEL

Personal Perspectives

How did you get into your first start-up?

Through a guy that had worked for me at Booz-Allen & Hamilton. I got a call from a group that was interested in starting a company, which ultimately became Genelabs Technologies. He was with a venture firm interested in investing in this company, and he said to the founders, "You ought to get some management help—I know a guy who's in the pharmaceutical business."

My first response when they called me was, "I'm not interested in a start-up company." But I was involved with a group at Syntex that invested in small companies and was interested in technology acquisition, doing corporate deals with biotech companies, that sort of thing. So I thought, "Why don't we get together and talk about the potential interest Syntex might have in your company?" One thing led to another and I ended up leaving Syntex to join Genelabs, and later Syntex invested in the company.

How many start-ups have you been through at this point?

I've been heavily involved in six. Not all of them have been successful.

What was your background before you began starting companies or being part of start-ups?

I began as a physicist and spent about four years teaching in the Navy's Nuclear Power Program. I decided, instead of going to graduate school and pursuing a career in research, to attend business school and get more into the commercial side of things. Then I spent about five years doing a variety of consulting jobs, mostly for large multinational companies.

Consulting in what areas?

Soup to nuts—from Barbie dolls to transcontinental aircraft, forest products to beer distribution. It was quite an eclectic range of projects and quite interesting, a great postgraduate education in business.

You did some work for Mattel?

I helped to optimize their worldwide manufacturing and distribution system. That's a very interesting side of the business. They're one of the largest clothing manufacturers in the world, both in terms of dollars and in terms of square yards of clothing material.

Square yards? It seems like a curious measure—especially for the doll business.

Yes, all in doll clothing! It may be an old data point but, at least, that was true in the early '80s.

We both made career leaps—my original degree is in electrical engineering and I've been a freelance writer all my working life. But your leap from physics to business seems a fairly profound change.

Yours was an even a bigger switch, I think. It's fairly common for people like me to move from science or engineering to management, which is a route you're encouraged to pursue if you're good academically in school.

A lot of scientists and engineers realize, at some point, that that's not exactly what they're made to be, and that was my process. I was in an environment where I had the luxury of thinking about it for a while because I was fulfilling a military obligation. For those not interested in a military career, there seemed to be two paths out of the Navy Nuclear Power Program. Everybody had come in from top academic programs. And out of it, people went either to business or law school or back to graduate programs in their primary scientific discipline.

Gil Amelio, who's now running Apple Computer, is a Ph.D. physicist with several patents who became a manager by chance. He had an idea he was working on that was really a research idea but with the potential for having products built around it. He was hired by Fairchild, which said, "That group of 70 engineers over there—take them and see if you can make a product out of what you're doing." And that's how he happened to become a manager.

I think I'm "hardwired" to be a manager, but that's more or less how I got into the pharmaceutical business. I really had no time to think of changing jobs or even going to a job interview, but this guy wanted to buy me lunch, and I figured I might as well walk down the street and talk to him. And that turned out to be my first job in the pharmaceutical business, managing the corporate planning department at Syntex.

One of those unexpected moments that changes your whole life.

Indeed.

CHAPTER 20

THE WORLD OF THE VIRTUAL CORPORATION

An Interview with Geoffrey Darby, Vice President, Finance, and CFO, Visioneer, Inc.

Geoff Darby has lived and worked in Germany, France, Sweden, South Africa, Brazil, and the United States, as well as his homeland, the United Kingdom. Like so many top executives in today's technology-based companies, he has degrees in both engineering and business. He was educated in England, and is a Chartered Accountant (the British equivalent of a C.P.A.). Before joining Visioneer, Darby worked for IBM, Rockwell, and Compaq, and was CFO and VP of finance for Megatest, a company that he helped restore in only four years from virtual insolvency to sufficient strength to go public.

Visioneer is a start-up company that Darby helped steer through a management transition, a mezzanine financing, and a highly successful public offering. The company's best-known product is a small, convenient desktop scanner.

THE START-UP AS A VIRTUAL CORPORATION

We hear a lot today about what's come to be called the virtual corporation. But, for a small company just starting out, there doesn't seem to be much choice—you have neither the need nor the resources to build a legal department, HR, creative services or, in most cases, a factory.

GEOFF DARBY:

I think that's exactly right. Taking our example at Visioneer, or even my previous company, Megatest, there's normally an idea, driven by a marketing requirement, or there's a technological find—an engineer who's come up with a project, and wants to develop it and market it. What you have to do is assemble a small team of people who will work together, and the company just grows from there.

The venture capital firms—such as Mayfield Fund, Kleiner Perkins, TVI, and so forth—take a company into initial embryo stage. That's normally done with a very small group of people, maybe five or ten. Obviously they have to focus totally on the technology and develop it.

As the company expands, it's like adding rooms to a house: You need somebody to mind the cash and the books, so you bring in an accounting person—another room; you need a sales person and a marketing person to start thinking about how you'll get the product into the marketplace—more rooms.

At Visioneer, we chose people who not only knew their disciplines very, very well but could also help to access and establish virtual services, such as a manufacturing capacity, or who, as in my case, had knowledge of banks, knowledge of the whole investment community, who were the best people for patents, who were the best people for corporate counsel.

What companies are doing today is tapping into people who have all those contacts, all that knowledge. That permits them then to expand very quickly, without hiring people, building laboratories or manufacturing plants, and so on. And that's what we mean by the "virtual corporation"—where you're hiring services and contracting for capabilities on the outside instead of spending the much greater amounts that would be required to do all those things in-house.

But you didn't know all that in your first start-up.

Absolutely not, and it makes a very big difference. This is where I'm pushing back on the venture capitalists: They should collectively document a lot of this information—which I think they're now beginning to do. Because, today, in 1996, companies, to be successful, have to move so much faster than they did just four or five years ago that they're going to have to behave much more like a virtual company in terms of bringing in some core people who can very quickly know exactly how to contact all these resources on the outside.

WHO'S FIRST ON BOARD?

Most companies of the kind we're talking about, of course, form around one or two or three people who conceive of a new product or technology and who have the expertise to create it or lead the

creation because of their background or knowledge in the field—they're the technologists or inventors or whatever. But beyond those initial people—as soon as the company has some money from whatever source—what outside expertise would you say is needed at the very beginning to get the company going?

For a small company, a corporate counsel, in my mind, is number one—before you hire a Big Six accounting firm. Because that corporate person can be a mentor to the board, can be a mentor to the management team, can be a great bridge between the management team and the investors, and can command tremendous expertise on how to structure contracts and deals and everything else.

And then, make sure that you have a very good audit partner, who will again be a mentor, helping the CFO or the controller—advising on accounting issues, on software, and so forth.

Those two players also help look for venture capital funding and for people they know who might blend in with the team.

It all comes back to having the best possible core team, with the best outside advice—so that, if the business takes off, everybody is capable of riding it to a very significant level. You don't want to have to keep changing people because your current team can go only to a certain level.

In my mind, you can go from zero to about $100 million with the same team. But it's not often done—companies stay with one team until they go public and then make some changes and hope the new team can take them straight on up.

If you chose the team really well just before doing the IPO, you can stay with that team all the way.

It's interesting that I asked you a question in financial terms, and you gave me an answer mostly in personnel terms—about the makeup and importance of the team.

To me, the pure financial side of business is easy—it's all secondary to the product team and the execution. If you've got a brilliant idea, there's money out there. You say to an investment bank like Morgan Stanley, "If you like this idea and if you believe in this team . . .," and the money will be committed. Tonight. That's not a problem.

A bigger problem may be how to invest it until you need to spend it. So, sometimes, it's, "Morgan Stanley, here's the $10 million you just gave me; now, invest it for me until I need it."

But then, as this core team makes progress, as they get the product ready, how do they decide the order in which they need to start bringing people into the company—real instead of "virtual" people?

One of the key ingredients in making something work is not just the technology, not just the product, but the team's ability to function as a team. Are we all on the same team?

I'm not fond of sports analogies but, even so, you've got to choose early on who the quarterback is going to be—and whether the quarterback is really going to make the calls on the field or is going to rely to some degree on the coach, who may be off the field. That's got to be established.

The CEO has got to have the ability to pull a very intelligent group of people together, to have the charisma eventually to go outside to raise funds, and then to get the market to agree that this is what it should be investing its money in.

I've seen a lot of cases, especially raw start-ups, where one person gets the seed money and gets the ball rolling, and then the venture capitalists come in and say, "Some of this technology is working out—it's looking good—and we want to put the next round of financing in." To the technologist who started it all, they say, "You're brilliant at technology, but you're not the material it takes to actually run a company."

So the first person in after the initial group is a CEO.

The guy who started the company doesn't get to run it? I suppose it's unusual to find one person who's a whiz at the technology and also a great business leader. I suppose your point is that if the goal is to get the company up and running, the technologist should stick to creating the product and let somebody else create the company.

Indeed.

Okay, so the man or woman or group who had the idea is focused on turning it into a product, and now there's a CEO doing the driving. It would differ in each situation, of course, but who would you expect to see come in next?

You've got to start to make some money; you've got to sell this wonderful invention that you're developing. For a company that has a consumer-based product like ours, you've got to have good marketing and sales. Not everyone makes the necessary distinction between those two—marketing develops what we call the "pull-through," the way people want to pull boxes off shelves; sales normally looks at distribution channels and gets the boxes *on* the shelves.

So, early on, you've got to get the sales and marketing functions up and running.

If you're going to be manufacturing, you'll need an operations person. We have a very slim operations group, yet we brought in a VP of operations quite early.

If the product is technological, out of the team of initial people who started the company, someone will probably step forward to become VP of engineering; that's, of course, not always a good assumption—the founders may be a group of engineers who are very good in the garage but, when it comes to managing a team of 50 engineers, they don't want to do it or don't excel in it. They've never done this before: Do they know how to network in terms of getting other companies to provide them with the computer chips or the other hot component that's at the heart of the product; and can they find a design that's already available instead of reinventing the wheel?

SHARE PRICE AND P/E FOR A START-UP

Share price at IPO often seems more than a little arbitrary. In the case of Visioneer, how was it set?

When we originally considered going public, the analysts were saying, "You're possibly grouped with other companies that have P/Es in the high teens but, because of the potential of your market, we'll try 25"—which is a key approach they use to establish a fair price. That gave us a stock price of $7 to $9, based on forward earnings. So it was our turn to take a deep breath, and we did, and then we said, "Okay—yes, we'll be happy to go."

We went out priced at $12 and, immediately, our stock opened at $20. That pushed the P/E to 50! Three months later, in February [1996], it was still up in the $40-plus range. So you look at us, and you draw a graph, and we're sitting waaaaay up there on our own, nobody near us. And we're selling hardware as well as software—it's not as if we're just a software company.

You could say, *that's* increasing shareholder value in the short term. People are prepared to buy and sell shares at a very high P/E. I think, ultimately though, it's the total package—it's the total story. I think you've got to look at a company in years, not in quarters.

The primary metric in terms of what is going to attract an investor is the potential price/earnings ratio.

THE NEED TO MOVE QUICKLY

For a start-up today, it seems as if there isn't much room for trial and error or looking for a marketplace. Is the pressure to succeed quickly as great as it seems?

I saw Compaq being founded back in Houston in the 1980s. At the time, there was really only one kid on the block, and that was IBM, which was very much a dinosaur getting into the PC market. There was no established disk-drive industry as such; there was no infrastructure. IBM didn't have a clue as to how to sell the PC. And, therefore, at that time, a company *could* come up with a good idea and could wander around trying this and that, and could go international over a period of five years.

That's history. Since then, the BusinessLand stores were born and died. IBM stores came and went. In came the disk-drive manufacturers, and in came all the infrastructure. A lot of people went belly up. Companies learned by making a lot of mistakes, and the marketplace itself became much more sophisticated.

So, if today you come in and think, "Well, okay, I'll spend a couple of years setting up my international distribution," that won't do it. If you've got a hot product, you're going to get steamrollered by the herds of very large multinational companies coming right over the top of you before you know what's happening. So you can't afford not to have people who know how to move within months.

Netscape is a good example: It brought in a core team of people who knew how to move very quickly.

THE UNIVERSAL NEED FOR BEING NIMBLE

So there's a need for start-ups to move very fast because they have to scrap to find a place in the sun. Are there lessons here as well for midsize and larger companies?

The speed of innovation and the speed at which you have to conduct business are just going to keep increasing. I think the small technology companies are way, way ahead of anything that the rest of the world understands.

I've worked in seven different countries on four continents and, from what I've seen, if you want to be competitive in *any* industry, you're soon going to have to be used to working at the same pressures, the same speeds, and the same efficiencies that are common in the small high-tech companies today.

Take as an example the financial planning process—big companies are going to have to go through what we go through, and as quickly, and will have to make decisions as quickly. If their products are in any way related to what we're doing, they can't be taking six months to decide on a new product because the product cycles themselves are down to six months.

You've got to come up with an idea and put it on the shelves within six months—period. And that'll become *five* months next year. It's come down from about 18 months just in the last few years. Incredible!

DECIDING WHERE THE DOLLARS GET SPENT

From the financial perspective, what's the greatest challenge for a start-up like Visioneer?

Right now, we're facing the problem of how to open up the market, which becomes a question of how many dollars in this P&L model we'll be able to spare, after engineering, to put into marketing and sales. And then, if there are any crumbs coming off the table, we'll drop them into corporate and into finance and administration. But, right now, the total focus for us is spreading the word about the product.

The problem is that it's not very easy following the example of other companies because you're looking at points in time, not only in the life of that company but at the industry, which might not be relevant to what you're doing today. So dividing up the pie becomes a very, very difficult question.

ON SELECTING THE PROJECTS TO FUND

Looking at the internal perspective, how do you decide whether *this* investment will be better for increasing shareholder value than *that* one?

That's a very, very good question, and also a very, very difficult question to answer because it goes to the core of a small company.

A lot of the feeling is that, in the early stages, you should put money into R&D because it's bound to reap projects that give you additional sales in the future. True enough—but go down inside an engineering function and use a measure like ROI—this is something I've been through so many times in various companies. At the end of the day, when you're looking at the analysis prepared by the project team, they've got a beautiful spreadsheet, but behind it there's a person flipping a coin to say how many units of this widget they're going to sell and at what price.

258

And, tomorrow, you get the presentation from another team that's competing for those dollars, and there's another person flipping a coin on the project.

So a lot of it does come down to intuition and crossing-the-fingers guesswork.

You hope it's more experience-based intuition than guesswork.

THE CFO AS AN HR MANAGER!?

In this new company that's getting started with so few executives and administrators on board, what happens to functions like human resources—do they just drop through the cracks?

The CEO in a small company doesn't have the time to worry about the mechanics of an HR function, about questions like: Are we getting the best salary grids? Do we have job descriptions? How do we handle the hiring process? So I've usually managed human resources myself in other companies. The terminology we use is "finance and administration."

These are very important functions that need face-to-face time between the manager and the person who's handling that function. In a smaller company, you'll normally find someone who's been a manager of HR in another company, wants to be a director in your company, and needs mentoring. The CEO doesn't have time to properly mentor that individual in a small company. If you have a CFO who's got the right personality and likes people, then it's a very good fit for the HR director to report to the CFO—albeit, absolutely, 100%, there has to be a very solid dotted line to the CEO because, obviously, that HR person has to negotiate with the CEO on the bonus programs and compensation programs of the VPs and the CEO, too and, ultimately, has to be able to go to the board.

But somebody has to take the day-to-day management of the HR function, and I've found it's very efficient to have the CFO do it. A lot of people are surprised; they say, "It's such a sensitive function, it should go directly to the CEO." But at the end of the day, the CFO knows everything about everybody. Whether it's through the medical program because finance pays the medical bills, or salary, bonus, commission programs—whatever it is, it all comes through the CFO, one way or another.

When contracts are put together, you see the compliance issues; you have stock programs; you've got to make sure that offer letters don't say the wrong thing and get the company into trouble.

What kind of trouble, for example?

Down the road, at a time of merger or acquisition, there may be some pooling problems because the CEO got overly enthusiastic and agreed, when hiring a senior executive, "Sure, we'll put in your contract that, at a change of control, all your options are vested."

Oops! That can become a sticking point in the next round of financing or if you have to replace the executive.

It's the CFO who's in the best position to stay on top of all the iterations and the cross-linking of all this information.

Now I'm almost afraid to ask about facilities; the CFO gets saddled with that, too?

I have had facilities under me, also security, and the telephone system. This is all mundane. The simple stuff is sometimes left off the map; people just don't want to be bothered with it. But the telephone, for example, is the front line of communications with the company.

For a start-up company, finding a good CFO is tough enough to begin with; how do they find somebody who's also willing to be responsible for the telephone system?

Who's going to do it—the VP of technology? The marketing VP? In a small company, there's nobody around to oversee travel or a leak in the ceiling or problems with the computers. That's why I say, "Chief cook and bottle washer." In terms of the expertise needed to make that company come to life, the CFO needs to wear many hats.

As the company gets larger, it can afford other people to do these things. At the same time, the CFO's role is becoming much more important; as a public company, the CFO is a mouthpiece to the public and to the investors second only to the president.

But, initially, in a small start-up, there isn't anybody else around to do these things. Besides, the CFO is going to be very cost-conscious.

But to attract somebody who already has those credentials, a company needs to be very well focused on a 12-months-to-IPO horizon.

If the CFO is wearing all those other hats, is there time to be an effective CFO?

If somebody doesn't focus on the mundane things, the company will not succeed.

At what point does the CFO become more financially oriented rather than doing all those other things?

It's a difficult question, and one that's dear to my heart right now: I've recently been asked to advise a couple of companies on how to address this particular problem. I think you have to address each situation individually.

WORKING RELATIONSHIPS

What's the greatest danger—from the perspective of finance? Where is the start-up most likely to fail?

The all-important thing here is the chemistry of the team, the chemistry between the CEO and CFO—that's the number one thing. If the chemistry is not there, it won't work—end of discussion.

I've seen a lot of cases where a company's leaders have taken what they thought were pretty good people, at the 18-month stage [i.e., 18 months from the inception of the company], and it hasn't worked out. They've had to change just before doing an IPO.

It happens a lot!

And that happens because the people with a full set of qualifications weren't attracted to the position because the company was too far from an IPO?

People like that don't need to take the risk. They will say, "I'm looking for an equity kicker [*company stock*]." This is the thing that really fuels this Valley— the Holy Grail. The individual is going to be looking for a good equity stake.

How much of an equity position does it take to attract a qualified person?

Right now I'm told it's 1% of a company. By itself that doesn't mean anything. Will they have to do another mezzanine round [a subsequent round of financing, which dilutes the value of the stock already in the hands of founders and

261

executives]? I'm just using as a ballpark that a CFO would want to see the ability to make half a million dollars a year for four years as a minimum target—and a fairly achievable one. (Laughing) Now, obviously, I have friends in the Valley who have recently made $5 to $15 million in four years. And, of course, everybody would like to do that.

Rocky Pimentel, who went into LSI; Ken Levy, who went into Pixar with Steve Jobs—both of those men took a significant stake in their respective companies. Obviously, both of them have done extremely well. People will look at that and say, "That's what I'd like to do."

And the potential is there.

TEAM PLAYER BUT STILL A COP

In larger companies, people in finance still have the problem of being seen as cops; in many companies, the attitude hasn't changed much, and maybe it can't. Is that true as well in the small company and the start-up?

I'm the bad guy. You ask any of the VPs around this company. A lot of them don't like the fact that finance is constantly on their backs. That's just a cross the CFO has to bear, and it's no different in a start-up.

And, if anything, maybe worse?

Maybe worse. It's a balancing act, because you've got to work the issue constantly. You're walking a fine line. You're looking after the shareholders and the investors.

And the CFO's own reputation is on the line—especially when you take a company out [i.e., go public], it's not just the reputation of the CEO, it's that of the CFO as well. The investors say, "Oh, I invested with you last time; I know how you behaved. I know what your track record is."

THE MAJOR ROLE OF VENTURE CAPITALISTS

You've put a lot of emphasis on the role of venture capital as more than just providing money.

A start-up company would do well to expect the venture capitalists not just to pick the CEO but to help find the people who have the various kinds of expertise the CEO will need.

It's something they've done, but I think it's something they need to become much more aware of. It's a key to the success of the companies.

The vc's nurture the company and are in the best position to help choose the team. Somebody else supplies the seeds—the ideas—the vc's supply the rainwater and the soil.

GEOFF DARBY

Personal Perspectives

RUNNING FINANCE IN A START-UP

I'm sure the role of a finance department in a start-up is very different from what most people are familiar with. What are some of the most significant differences?

Historically, what companies have done is, initially, to look for a person to handle the controllership function. And, of course, that's very important—you've got to have someone who can operate in a small environment, who is *very* hands-on, knows how to close books, and how to do the payables, the payroll, the receivables, and the general ledger—all this must be an absolute slam-dunk. And this is someone you need as soon as you have any money to spend.

It's difficult to attract the right caliber of individual who has the experience—not just a young Turk out of accounting—to a situation where there's no guarantee the company will be successful. So, for the first couple of years—especially if you're a year or two away from being able to go public—the vc's and the management team have difficulty getting the right caliber of individual.

Sometimes the attorney who organized the company has steered it to one of the Big Six accounting firms. When the client company needs a controller, the firm perhaps has this senior who they think is great but who they know, for whatever reason, will not become a partner. So they decide he would be ideal for the position. And if this person is attracted to the company's prospects, he gets nominated for the job.

I've chosen a different route in terms of how I've structured finances at Visioneer. I can buy C.P.A. talent very easily; what I can't buy is financial planning talent. As a company starts to grow, the financial planning control becomes very important—the quarterly planning, which needs to be done in a lot of detail.

You need a person, then, who can not only handle the detail associated with controllership but also has some imagination and can converse with and deal with and manage *people* across all the facets of the company.

So what I chose to do was to appoint my manager of financial planning, who's never been a controller of a product company, to be our controller—as a cross-training for him, as a development for him.

What I would do if I were ever in another start-up is look for a C.P.A. who maybe had moved into financial planning and give her or him the whole ball of wax. Now, whether that individual is able to rise to the position of CFO as the company grows—especially as it approaches going public—is entirely up to him or her. You don't necessarily need somebody who's been there, done that—even though everybody will tell you that you do. Companies prefer going that route because the individual knows the ropes.

But, if a person is properly networked, has access to other CFOs or controllers, and has good mentors, and if the company has a good corporate law firm—very important—it's not necessary that the CFO has done a public offer.

Obviously, I'd like to see people move up the ranks like this. Younger people who have a lot of fire in their belly, very detailed, C.P.A.-trained, show promise of understanding the importance of financial planning. I love to see people like that come up through the ranks and make it.

In a lot of cases, though, you find that people who are very numbers-oriented—especially if they've been schooled in a culture that places emphasis on detail—very often find it difficult to talk and converse and negotiate with people. They're brilliant at dealing with number forms, with computers and machines, but dealing with real people, with real problems, across departmental lines, understanding the politics of a company—it's very difficult for people to cross that line.

QUALIFICATIONS FOR RUNNING FINANCES IN A START-UP

What warning flags alert you that someone you thought had the qualifications you were looking for to run the finances in a start-up might not really be the right person?

The first warning sign is, typically, that they become introverted and go back into their detail and are not seen to be members of the team. They don't attend team meetings, and the rest of the team may say, "Oh, they're fine; they do payrolls and all, but they can't handle this or that—we don't really want to use their advice." And you'll see it in a company where the accounting becomes a purely mechanical function and is not seen as a resource.

It's not easy—the best of individuals can be put into very difficult situations; this happens a lot because, obviously, a CFO has a fiduciary responsibility, and it's easy to get to the point of seeing that as diametrically opposed to what people want to do.

I have this example right now. We raised $52 million in our IPO and, believe it or not—and I still don't believe it—half the company looks at me as though I'm brain-dead when I say, "You can't spend money on that because it will impact the P&L." People just don't quite get it, that a company has to make money. They don't really understand the mechanics of making money.

So a CFO can be put in this very difficult situation, and some people respond by just crawling back into a space that is warm and fuzzy and comfortable and nonantagonistic. Nobody is beating them up; they're just doing their job. But they're not standing up and having that stature within a team that makes their views clearly heard.

AFTERWORD

BUILDING BUSINESSES FOR
THE 21ST CENTURY

SHAPING YOUR CAREER

WHAT MAKES A GREAT CFO

AFTERWORD

BUILDING BUSINESSES FOR THE 21ST CENTURY
Dennis Dammerman, General Electric:

DEVELOPING TOMORROW'S EXECUTIVES

I find that the largest single block of time I spend is on people issues—not necessarily sitting across a table because somebody has a problem, but addressing the broad-term issues, such as working with our business CFOs and our human resources people to name, understand, and identify the people in the pipeline and decide what kind of development needs they have—so that, over two, three, four, or five years, they can get the experiences they need.

I want to keep very close tabs on where they're going, what the succession plans are, what the development needs are, and what kinds of education I need to provide. What are the routes they can take through the ranks, and do I need to provide other routes so that I will have more sources of talent?

I have a wonderful source in something we call the Corporate Audit Staff, which is the fastest track for people in this company, early in their careers, to move up very rapidly, whether they're engineers or accountants.

The Audit staff is a fast track not for finance alone—about half of the people that go through this experience don't go into finance; they go into other functions. So I need other sources of finance talent, and I have to figure out some way to identify other "hot" people and move them along with the learning, training, and experience that will prepare them.

That means that you spend an incredible amount of time making sure that, when you sit in a room, a reasonable percentage of the time the person on your right and the person on your left are as good at doing what they do as anybody in the world. That's one of the wonderful things about working at General Electric. That's my belief. And we work very hard to make sure it stays that way.

I do, and Jack [Welch, the GE CEO] does; he's getting ready right now to spend almost the entire month of May visiting the businesses, doing what we call Session C—which is a review of organization, staffing, succession plans, development plans, who the good people are, where they need to go, and what kinds of experiences they are getting.

We really spend a lot of time on this. Sometimes you feel, "My God, I just don't have time for it!" But if you don't do it, you don't have time to do anything. If you had 30 incompetent people working for you, nothing would get done. There wouldn't be enough hours in the day to do your job.

And this is certainly one of the areas that we're most frequently asked about when people want to do benchmarking. When we call some company and say, "We hear you're good at thus and so—can we come see you? And what do you want for quid pro quo?" probably 75% of the time, they want to come in and talk about how we do development.

In a lot of areas, and in finance as well, GE people have a wonderful reputation. Even people who get to a stage where they're probably not going to progress further in GE can go out and have a wonderful career for themselves in some other terrific company.

So I would say that we're lucky that we have been able to spend a lot of time and focus on people. And I do think we're leading-edge in terms of our development of people.

I have to say, though, that a part of it is a long culture in the company, in terms of willingness to accept the bad along with the good part of our approach to people development. This sometimes means that, say, we need a new CFO in aircraft engines, and we move somebody from medical systems. It's hard to relate those two, but our culture is that when you reach into those top jobs, such as the chief financial officer of a division, the breadth of experience is very valuable—even though it may mean that you don't have the depth in that particular business. But the belief is that, if you're smart and you're good and you've got the business experience, you can quickly learn the depth.

People usually stay on the Audit staff for three or four years. If you do it well, it will probably replicate what it would take you somewhere between 10 and 15 years to do otherwise!

The Audit staff began somewhere back around 1919, but it has evolved dramatically. It's the most wonderful group of people. Jack sees them once or twice a year, and always comes back floating because they're so terrific. They spend 50% or 60% of their time doing financial audits, but the rest of the time they're working on manufacturing and pricing, quality, and all kinds of other things.

There's a shared experience here, because most of us who have moved to a high level in finance within the company went through the Audit staff. So there's almost this boot camp sense of shared experience.

The group today, though, is much better than we ever were, by orders of magnitude. And the experience is much better than we ever had because we've changed the mold and the leadership profile of the organization.

But the key is that there are managers out there in the GE businesses who are willing to hire those people and give them the jobs that allow them to make the rapid progression. Obviously, the job someone gets when he leaves the Audit staff says how much that person has progressed.

WHICH COUNTS MORE: DEPTH OR BREADTH?

As part of the culture of our company, there are executives willing to give those people highly responsible jobs. And that's the ingredient that's sometimes hard for other organizations to grasp—whether small, medium-sized, or other larger companies—because many companies, when they look for a CFO, value depth over breadth of experience.

When you're on the Audit staff for three or four years, you're experiencing 15 or 16 different, very real business situations, worrying about all the businesses of our company, domestically and overseas. You may end up moving into a finance job or a manufacturing or marketing job.

But all those experiences, the leadership skills it gives you, the confidence it builds—because you're sent into a business and you know you've got three or four months to have an impact—these are real confidence builders. You learn how to appraise a situation quickly and focus on the things that are wrong, not the things that are right. And all those skills are very highly valued in our company.

I've seen other companies where you move into finance and not only don't you move among businesses but, if you come into finance as a cost accountant, you may spend your whole career as a cost accountant—not moving even among the subfunctions of finance.

So the Audit staff works because of the mind-set that we have, because of our vision of the CFO as a broad business person and the right hand of the leader of the business. In our view, these are very natural roles for finance leaders to play because of their ability to look all across the functions. We don't expect them to have comments on financial issues alone.

SHAPING YOUR CAREER
Cheryl Francis, R.R. Donnelley

For people who would like to see an executive position in their future, do you have some recommendations for preparing themselves?

Get as broadly based as you can; do as many things as you can. I think spending time in a policy or strategy role is very important. Also, I think that I would be a stronger CFO if I had operations experience; I haven't picked that up along the way, but it's something that people respect and that adds credibility and valuable knowledge.

In my case, breadth of exposure included planning, treasury, control, and investor relations—interestingly, this last is a linchpin because you have to really understand how investors think and how the company needs to be positioned as you go forward. It really keeps you focused on creating shareholder value.

Any other advice for people about shaping their own careers?

My career has been fairly nontraditional, like the two and a half years out in the middle, teaching at the University of Chicago.

It's all come together but not according to any plan. I think the thing that's been most beneficial is having very early acceptance at FMC [*her first company*] as a credible person who really understood finance and as a young person relied on by top management, from the chairman on down, to help them think through a lot of thorny issues strategically about positioning the company. On-the-job training is the best thing there is.

I would say also that something I've always found very beneficial was the grounding I got in the M.B.A. program at the University of Chicago, which is a strong economics program. I think one of the risks you run in this business is a lot of smoke and mirrors—people are hawking ideas and trying to convince you of a better way. You've got to be able to be very well grounded in the solid economics of what really works and what doesn't, what really creates value at the end of the day.

Smoke & Mirrors

Tom Zusi, AlliedSignal Aerospace

For people who are interested in moving up to executive positions, how would you recommend they prepare themselves for advancement?

I think they need to always be inquisitive; they always have to think in terms of what's new that the company isn't doing now. They've always got to be a paradigm buster. The ones that will ultimately be successful, I think, will be leaders who can create vision and passion for the organization—both in financial areas and nonfinancial. That to me is what makes a successful executive.

Vision

I think that what makes a great employee, a great executive, or a great

CFO is the passion for doing things differently and the willingness to venture down a different path.

Bill Raduchel, Sun Microsystems

You've indicated that you believe the things a CFO or other corporate leader needs to be able to do are very different from what the same person needed earlier in his or her career. What preparation do you recommend for these top positions?

That's a good question. When we go out and look and run searches for executives, it's not easy.

It's hard to find CIOs today, and it's hard to find VPs, as well as CFOs, because the skills you need to be a top corporate staff officer are very different from the skills you need to be even one level lower in an organization.

The world's best corporate controller can be one of the world's worst CFOs. The world's best director of compensation could be the world's worst VP of human resources. The world's best director of network services could be the world's worst chief information officer.

What is that chasm? What's the skill or whatever that it takes to bridge that gulf?

Good question. We don't know.

But you know it when you see it?

You know it when you see it, but it's hard to say. Certainly, it's a willingness to accept accountability. It's an instinctive focus on outcomes rather than inputs. It's a focus on a bottom line and an understanding that only certain things matter. It's an ability to set priorities. It's the ability to be a very strong influence manager.

Most of your value as a CFO, for example, is not running the finance organization. That isn't what you're paid for. As a controller, you're paid to run the corporate controller's organization, add up the numbers and get it together, or you run disbursements or whatever. As CFO, running your organization is almost irrelevant.

As a CFO, your job is to help the company deliver on its financial results. As vice president of human resources, your job is to recruit talent. What you do is very different from what any of your people do.

And yet, if you don't have that knowledge of what they do, you can't manage them. So, it is a chasm. It's a chasm that lots of companies face. That's why positions go unfilled for enormous periods of time, and there are very few people who make it across the chasm. Most companies do very little to train people to jump across it.

It's basically a survival of the fittest. Okay, you've made it to here—now, can you jump from here to there? No? Okay, you're at the end of the line!

Dennis Dammerman, GE

"A CAREER IS A JOURNEY"

I think a career is a journey, not a destination. People always talk about these young people who say, "I want to be CEO of GE, and here's how I'm going to get there." Those young people may be around, but they're very few and far between. I haven't met a lot of them in my 29-year career here.

But I think of some of the right decisions I've made. I took two *lateral* moves in my career. They weren't promotions but they moved me into another area where I thought I needed experience and thought I would get it to prepare me to move forward. In my view, those moves—if not the two best—were certainly two of the best moves that I made. Yet some people didn't understand why I was doing that.

It's your career. Nobody's necessarily going to come and tell you, "This lateral move is the right thing to do." You're always making those judgments, but you've got to be there pushing and, in some cases, being a bit of a squeaky wheel. If you're good doing what you're doing, your boss isn't going to be excited about letting you go, but you've got to make sure you get the base that you think you need.

MODELING YOURSELF ON GOOD LEADERS

Here's one of the things I urge on all the people in our company who are going through the development process: Identify all those you think are good leaders, and understand why you think they are better leaders than the other people around them. Make that a subject of your intellectual curiosity. Because what that does is to build your leadership skills, and it tells you what you have to be focusing on.

It's interesting that it's an experience you can have from the very first day you're on the job. Start that process of understanding what leadership is all about by comparing people that you work around or work for. "I think Mary is a great leader because _____." Think about what makes her great. And "Mary is a better leader than Bill because _____."

Then, go talk to Mary about it; people love that—when you go in and say, "Mary, I think you're a terrific leader, and I really want to learn from you; here's what I've observed. What do you think about it?" Mary would be ecstatic if you did that.

I think this is an untapped resource, and I strongly encourage our people to do that. And they're doing it more and more.

WHAT MAKES A GREAT CFO

Bill Raduchel, Sun Microsystems

I think somebody can be a great CFO for one CEO, in one situation, in one culture, at one point in time, and be a disaster for another CEO, in another company, at another time. A lot depends on the situation you're in.

Certainly, I've had my critics in this company who may have thought that I was the world's best CFO from 1989 to 1990 but, once the company started doing better, they would have graded me a lot lower from 1990 to 1991 because they thought I was too controlling. That may be true. It's hard.

If you ask me what's the number one trait, it's flexibility. Some days, you've got to be worrying about dotted *i*'s, crossed *t*'s, and commas, down in the depths of what's going on; other days, you've got to delegate and almost completely, totally forget. And yet, what you pay attention to changes day to day, week to week, month to month, quarter to quarter. I think that's what causes people to lose sight of what's important.

Don Macleod, National Semiconductor

I think the conventional wisdom of today is that a great CFO is someone who is a business partner to the executive management team of the company and brings the financial dimension to that role. There are many examples of that today in corporate America.

What am I trying to do here with the rest of the management team? My role is to look at how our business behavior correlates with the creation of shareholder value. And at the end of the day, my role is to ensure that we're focusing on the things that do really create shareholder value for the long term.

It's the challenge of making the right choices. And, when you look at making those choices, you have to be equipped to understand the company's options, the company's products, the company's markets, so you can be a part of those choices rather than just passively looking at the results of the decisions that are made by the management team and reporting or interpreting them.

At the business-unit level, our finance business partners are helping the management teams of the divisions achieve their objectives. But, when it comes to the portfolio corporate approach, you have to understand what the company is trying to do in terms of its overall strategy and what that means in terms of shareholder value—creating it and the investment/cash flow trade-offs that get you there.

And the other part, of course, is convincing the outside world that the strategies the company is adopting and implementing really do have correlation with shareholder value. *Everyone* today says their focus is on creating shareholder value. They *say* it; but we would ask them, "What are you doing in your management process and behaviors to make that a meaningful statement?"

My role in this company is to make sure we have credibility when we make those statements—and, then, when we make our decisions, that they reflect, as much as possible, the value-driving behaviors that create shareholder value.

I think that, if you look in the press, the CFOs that are getting all the kudos are the guys who really can demonstrate that the company they're working for has clearly created shareholder value—not because they've got a great finance organization or because they're really efficient or because they're really up with their reporting practices or even because they're good at raising capital. It's because they can stand up and say, "In the time I was the CFO, the value of this company went from *X* billion to *Y* billion, and we made the following key economic choices that made this happen."

You're trying to get people to buy into the story as early as possible. You're trying to get people to believe your company's efforts will result in shareholder value. That's the hard part.

Ideally, of course, you don't have to wait until the results have been fully discounted by the whole spectrum of investors; you want to presell the likely impact of your chosen strategy or economic choices. If you can articulate the value of your new investments in terms of their cash flow potential—and you have acceptable correlation vehicles—then, ideally, you can presell the opportunity. *That's* the hard part!

GLOSSARY

Above the line On a profit and loss statement, the gross margin is considered to be a pivotal item. Entries on the statement that appear above the gross margin line are referred to as above the line; those below, as below the line.

Asset turns or asset turnover Revenues divided by total assets—a crude measure of how well the investment in assets is being managed relative to the sales volume it supports.

Below the line See "Above the line."

Cash flow analysis A statement showing when revenues are received and payments made, usually as a projection into the future, on a quarterly, monthly, or weekly basis; the principal value is to forecast the company's cash position.

Cash flow on cash invested ("cash on cash") Cash flow compared to the total cumulative cash invested.

Debt to capitalization ratio (D/C) The ratio of a company's debt to its capital; the higher the ratio, the greater the risk of investing in the company.

Discounted cash flow What the cash flow will be in the future, discounted back to the present, to account for the time value of money. This provides a method of estimating an investment's current value based on projected future revenues and costs. However, the results are only as accurate as the estimates used.

EBIT Earnings before interest and taxes.

Economic value added (EVA) The profit that remains after the opportunity cost of all capital employed is subtracted. A measure that encourages managers to return income to investors greater than that they could have obtained from another similar risk venture.

Electronic data interchange (EDI) The computer-to-computer exchange of data, such as invoices and purchase orders. Major organizations such as Sears and GM and, increasingly, the federal government, now require companies doing business with them to use EDI.

First in, first out (FIFO) An accounting method that assumes materials used from inventory were the items first purchased ("first in"), as opposed to LIFO (q.v.). In periods of inflation, goods purchased earlier were less expensive than goods purchased more recently. LIFO more closely represents replacement costs, and is a more conservative approach.

Free cash flow   The cash over and above what is required to finance the day-to-day operating cash needs of the company.

G&A   General and administrative expenses.

Gross margin   The difference between the revenues from sale of products and the cost of producing those products. Gross margin is considered to be the most important item on the P&L statement.

Hurdle rate   The minimum acceptable rate of return that a project must be able to achieve in order to be approved and funded.

Internal rate of return (IRR)   A measure of the rate of profitability of a project or investment. IRR is the discount rate that makes the present value of cash flows equal to the initial investment. The calculation yields a result that can be judged against the cost of capital to determine whether the project is justified.

Inventory turns or inventory turnover   The cost of goods sold divided by the inventory. This provides a measure of how rapidly the inventory is being sold; a low number usually indicates poor performance.

Last in, first out (LIFO)   An accounting method that assumes materials used from inventory were the items most recently purchased ("last in"). See "First in, first out."

Market value added (MVA)   The difference between market value and the economic book value of a company.

Net present value   The present value of a project's future cash flow less the initial investment in the project. A measure of how successful the project will be in producing cash.

Receivable days   The total amount owed by customers, divided by the sales for the preceding month or quarter and normalized for days. A high DSO indicates that customers are not paying promptly.

Return on assets (ROA)   Profit before interest and taxes, divided by average total assets less cash.

Return on equity (ROE)   Net income divided by stockholders' equity. ROE is considered by many to be the single best measure of the performance of a company or business unit.

Return on investment (ROI)   A measure of the net income that management is able to earn with the total assets invested. Return on investment is calculated by dividing total assets into net profits after taxes.

Return on net assets (RONA)   Similar to ROA, except that the denominator is net assets (total assets less accumulated depreciation).

Return on noncash assets before interest and taxes (RONCABIT)   A return-on-assets measurement, RONCABIT is profit before interest and taxes—or operating profit—divided by average total assets less cash. By removing cash, the measure provides a look at the efficiency of the noncash assets and the kind of return being obtained.

SG&A Sales, general and administrative expenses.

Total shareholder return (TSR) TSR reflects the extent to which a business unit of a company is contributing to the capital gains and dividend yield to investors of the overall company.

NOTES

[1]Under balanced metrics, National Semiconductor has redefined the original "Critical Business Issues" (CBIs) as follows:

CUSTOMER DELIGHT

National strives to manage customer value—to provide quality and services that customers can see. Customer delight is a leading indicator of market share, financial performance, and ultimately, shareholder value.

STRATEGIC POSITIONING

National is going to win in its chosen markets by exploiting the core competencies and strengths of our company to provide consistently superior customer value. To win, we use the forums and tools of strategic process and engage tactical experience to focus issues and leverage operating heritage. Key to the success of the company is the focus on strategic, high-growth markets and supporting core capabilities. These elements, combined with continually finding new sources of customer value to add to our products and services, will provide us with significant competitive advantage.

ORGANIZATIONAL EXCELLENCE

National recognizes a need to create a highly flexible, agile, organization that exhibits continuous productivity gains. In knowledge-based organizations, the people are the most important asset. The organization will provide customer delight while pursuing the needs and changes of its current markets, in addition to entering new markets that will drive profitable growth.

OPERATIONAL EXCELLENCE

National will exceed customer expectations for delivering value-added products by excelling in all elements of process management, including design, management of day-to-day production and delivery, improvement of quality and operational performance, and business assessment.

R&D ROI

The R&D return on investment metric is how National measures how effective we are at directing our R&D dollars.

FINANCIAL PERFORMANCE

National strives to return upper quartile shareholder value. National recognizes that portfolio management of each business/product line is important and that the performance goals will be different for each type of business.

LEADERSHIP

Leadership is a subset of organizational excellence. National recognizes that the behavior, actions, and decisions of its senior management are the key driver enabling us to address our critical business issues and strategic imperatives. National's senior management personally leads in creating and delivering quality and service that customers can see.

[2]This is the first version of National Semiconductor's Success Model, as presented in *Profit from Experience:*

NSC FINANCIAL OBJECTIVES

Gross profit	40%
Profit before tax	13%
Break-even sales	75%
R&D	11%
Return on Net Assets (RONA) (pretax)	33%
ROE	20%

[3]MGM has undergone many name changes—Metro-Goldwyn-Mayer, Inc., MGM/UA Entertainment Co., MGM/UA Communications Co., Inc., etc. For purposes of simplicity, the company is referred to in this chapter as MGM/UA.

INDEX